# BEFRIEND

## AND

# BETRAY

# BEFRIEND

# AND BETRAY

## Infiltrating the Hells Angels,

## Bandidos and Other

## Criminal Brotherhoods

## ALEX CAINE

THOMAS DUNNE BOOKS
ST. MARTIN'S PRESS
NEW YORK

THOMAS DUNNE BOOKS.
An imprint of St. Martin's Press.

BEFRIEND AND BETRAY. Copyright © 2008 by Alex Caine and Aranteli Productions.
All rights reserved. Printed in the United States of America. For information,
address St. Martin's Press, 175 Fifth Avenue, New York, N.Y. 10010.

www.thomasdunnebooks.com
www.stmartins.com

Library of Congress Cataloging-in-Publication Data

Caine, Alex.
    Befriend and betray : infiltrating the Hells Angels, Bandidos and other criminal
brotherhoods / Alex Caine.
        p.   cm.
    Includes index.
    ISBN-13: 978-0-312-53719-7
    ISBN-10: 0-312-53719-0
    1. Caine, Alex.   2. Police—Biography.   3. Undercover operations.
4. Organized crime.   I. Title.
    HV7911.C354A3   2009
    363.2092—dc22
    [B]                                                          2008029888

First published in Canada by Random House Canada, a division
of Random House of Canada Limited

First U. S. Edition: February 2009

10   9   8   7   6   5   4   3   2   1

*Dedicated to my children
who suffered through my career and came through it still loving me*

# CONTENTS

———

# P R O L O G U E

————

*Interstate 8, heading east from San Diego, early May 2002*
Ever since I'd started working the Dago Hells Angels, people I trusted had been counseling me to pack my bags and get out of southern California. Things could only end ugly, they'd said. Now, two years later, I was finally taking their advice. And fast.

I hadn't even bothered to pack up my things. I'd just thrown a few clothes, some papers, my computer and some music for the road into my Nissan pickup, called for my dog, Dog, and headed east into the desert.

Goodbyes with my police handlers had been cursory. They'd wanted me to spend one last night in the San Diego area, give us time for a goodbye dinner. I let them book me a room at a local motel. But once I got in my truck and started driving, I wasn't about to stop.

My adieus to my biker buddies had been even ruder: I'd left them in a squeal of tires and a cloud of burned rubber after Bobby Perez, the most volatile and vicious member of the San Diego—or Dago—Hells Angels, made it clear that things were, indeed, about to end ugly.

A few days earlier, he'd asked me to carry a handgun, a little Bersa .380, back from Laughlin, Nevada, to El Cajon, California, after a shoot-up in a casino had left three bikers dead. I didn't know whether the .380 had been used in the gunplay or whether Bobby just didn't want to carry it across state lines himself. He was, after all, on parole and not even supposed to be outside of California, let alone in the company of criminals. Whatever the case, his asking me to drive the gun back to the Dago Hells Angels' home turf in El Cajon was a major vote of confidence. So when my handlers seized the gun, saying they couldn't possibly allow me to return it to a known felon, they were blowing a chance for me to work my way even further into the inner sanctum of the gang. "Tell Bobby you had to ditch it," they'd said. "Or that you lost it. Or whatever. Come up with something."

It was the stupidest of decisions, all the stupider if they had any idea how important the little gun was to Bobby. When he asked for it back during a late night meeting in an El Cajon parking lot, I put him off, telling him I'd hidden it deep in the engine of my truck and hadn't yet had a chance to retrieve it.

That won me a venomous glare and an order: "Bring it tomorrow to the bar. Ten o'clock!" he spat at me.

A memorial ride was taking place the next morning, for another biker killed in the previous days. Christian Tate, a member of the Dago Hells Angels, had been shot off his bike from behind as he headed back to California from Laughlin about an hour before the nastiness broke out in the casino. Bobby, it seemed, wanted the .380 for the ride.

After the scene in the parking lot, I contemplated cashing in the Dago case. It had been going south for a while, from even before the botched—and highly secret—police ambush of a Hells Angels drug run through the California desert had left who knows how many dead. I'd witnessed at least four bikers and two cops bite it before I was dragged out of that particular mess.

The case had never had a clear objective to begin with. It had begun in 1999 as an investigation into a Quebecer who was suspected of running coke from Colombia to California and then up into Canada with the help of the Dago Hells Angels. But the guy had disappeared into thin air the day before I arrived in California. So the case had turned into a basic intel probe of the Dago Angels—accumulating information without a particular goal of making any arrests and putting bad guys in prison. To get close to the gang I opened a photo studio specializing in strippers' "media kits" and bike porn—shots of chromed-up Harleys against a setting sun and that kind of thing. Eventually gang members and associates began inviting me to parties and gatherings to document their fun for posterity (in an uncompromising way, of course—I knew better than to shoot a member with his nose in a big pile of coke).

After several months I began buying moderate quantities of coke and crystal meth—half a pound, a pound—from criminals affiliated with the gang, along with stolen cars and restricted weapons:

fully automatic machine pistols, M-16s, converted SKS carbines, hand grenades and the like. I made myself out to be a criminal middleman interested in pretty much anything that could make me money. Those buys elevated our little intel probe to "operational" status—our sights set on arrests and convictions.

Still, the case had no real focus and my handlers tended to proceed in a dangerously ad hoc way. Over two years I gathered dirt on crooked members of the U.S. military selling government-issue guns, Mexican border runners smuggling arms and humans (both of the very dangerous variety), and Russian mobsters—along with my work on the Hells Angels and their friends. And that created a problem: with so many investigative fronts, we never identified an exit strategy, a predetermined point at which we could say, "Okay, we've got the goods. Time to wind things up."

To make matters worse, I had a vague suspicion from early on that Operation Five Star—the multi-squad task force I was reporting to, comprising the DEA, the ATF and the San Diego Sheriff's Department, along with the municipal police departments of San Diego and El Cajon—wasn't an entirely tight ship. It seemed to me that information was leaking out and finding its way to the wrong people. Initially it was really just a gut feeling with nothing tangible to back it up. But in the fall of 2001, I got a call from an FBI supervisor in San Francisco with a storied career busting bikers asking me to visit him for a chat. It turned out he had the same suspicions.

Along with the shoot-up in the desert, all of this should, perhaps, have been enough to convince me to bail from the case long before Bobby Perez ordered me to give him back the .380. But I like to finish what I start, and there had never been any sustained or substantial threat to my safety on this case, and the money was good: US$5,000 plus all expenses per month, enough to buy a new house back in Canada for my second wife and daughter.

The encounter in the parking lot, however, had finally convinced me that the case was almost certainly done for, at least as far as I was concerned. Still, for whatever reason, I thought I might be able to forestall the inevitable with Bobby for at least a day or two. So, the next day at 10:00 a.m. sharp, I drove to the stretch of El Cajon Boulevard that effectively belonged to the Hells Angels: it was home to their club-house, Dumont's—better known simply as "the bar"—and Stett's motorcycle shop.

When I pulled up, there were already about a hundred bikers hanging around on the sidewalk in front of Dumont's. Right in the middle stood Bobby. I parked in front of a hydrant and left the motor running.

As I approached, I could see that Bobby was in a particularly unpleasant mood.

"Did you bring it?" he demanded.

"I can't find it," I replied. "It must have fell out on the road on the drive back."

Bobby started to vibrate. "You follow me to the back of the bar," he said. I knew what often happened behind Dumont's, and it wasn't a place I was going to visit.

"Sure," I said, turning away. "But let me park properly and turn off the truck. I'll be right there." I got in the Nissan and threw it in gear.

Bobby turned and yelled to an underling to stop me. The guy lunged for the passenger door, but thankfully it was locked. I floored it and he let go. I wheeled around the corner, raced to my studio for a few essentials and was gone.

At this point, a bad novel might describe a wave of relief washing over me as I headed into the pure, clean desert, away from the danger and treachery of the past two years. Yeah, right. Whatever relief I felt was more like a trickle than a wave. Sure, leaving El Cajon and the San Diego area felt good, as did the fact that it was me, and me alone, who was now in control; I no longer had handlers or Hells Angels telling me what to do. But all the turf between San Diego and Phoenix, Arizona, three hundred miles to the east, is Hells Angels country. There was a distinct possibility that before jumping on his Harley for Christian Tate's funeral ride, Bobby had picked up the phone and sent word to the Hells Angels chapters east and north of San Diego to be on the lookout for me. But the last ride for a member—any member, even a relatively unremarkable one like Tate—is mandatory for all

Hells Angels in the region, and strongly recommended for all affiliated clubs. I had to hope that everyone who might have a mind to get in my way was already behind me.

The fact that no one had shown up at my studio as I packed had been a good sign. But if that had quelled my sense of unease somewhat, the desert exacerbated it. While in the San Diego area I'd spent many a Sunday in the desert, walking and exploring, with Dog or alone, the peace and quiet the best therapy available. Now, however, the desert wasn't offering serenity: I just felt exposed.

Still, the farther I drove, the farther the mess was behind me and the better I felt. For the first day or two I caught catnaps in rest areas and truck stops and drove all night, trying to put some distance between me and my problems. Later, once into the Midwest and farther east, I slowed down and made regular stops, to see the sights, have a meal or spend the night in a motel.

All the while I was thinking about the operation that had just ended so unceremoniously and about my whole career as a hired-gun infiltrator.

For almost twenty-five years, almost half my life, I'd been working for an alphabet soup of police forces—the RCMP, the FBI, the DEA, the ATF, the RHKP, the RNC—insinuating myself into criminal groups from around the world and then helping police bring them down. Along with outlaw bikers, I'd gone after Asian Triads and Russian mobsters, Pakistani heroin smugglers and garden-variety drug lords, crooked cops and military types. Even the KKK. It had been lucrative, it had been exciting, it had been a job. I may have been doing the work of good, but what had it left me with? Or, more exactly, what had it left of me? Each job required that I create a new persona and inhabit him fully for anywhere from a few months to several years. Sometimes I'd pretend I was all criminal, a border runner, a hit man or a drug dealer. Other times my cover was more complex: a life insurance underwriter also into investment scams and money laundering; an importer who also brought in drugs and sex trade workers and shipped out stolen luxury cars; a concert promoter who was interested in anything that might make a buck.

I made myself into these people, and any number of other

characters, and became them completely, putting the real me on the shelf. Always I thought, when the game was over, I'd be able to take that real person down and become him again. But as time went by, it was clear that whoever the real me was was withering away for lack of sunlight, drying up for lack of nourishment, atrophying for lack of exercise.

Even between jobs—a period usually lasting several months—I increasingly resisted becoming myself again. If the operation had ended in a major bust, that time would sometimes be taken up with court preparations; other times it was just pure R & R. In either case, resurrecting the real me became a hassle. It would just get in the way of my next assignment.

I'd thought about retirement on a few occasions during my career. Indeed, until the mid-1980s and my tangle with the KKK, I'd never thought of what I was doing as an actual career, just a series of jobs I'd accidentally fallen into, and which I'd just as suddenly and unwittingly fall out of. But no job had been as unsatisfying as San Diego. None had come up so short of what we could have accomplished. None had left me with such a bitter taste in my mouth.

And so, never had I contemplated calling it quits as seriously as I did on that highway-hopping drive across the south-central states and then up the eastern seaboard to Maine. There, crossing into New Brunswick and heading home to my family in eastern Canada, the allure of retirement grew. Not only had the game changed from when I first started—and not for the better—but I was becoming too old for it, or at least worn out by it. All that put me in a mind to finally do what cops I'd worked with over the years had constantly urged me to do: sit down and tell my story.

# CHAPTER ONE

# Far from the Tree

——

Lots of people don't grow up into the life that's expected of them. Farmers raise children who end up as artists. Factory workers have kids who become research scientists and university professors. Thugs and criminals have grown up in the silver-spoon homes of diplomats, lawyers and doctors. Still, there probably aren't many apples that fall as far from the tree as I did. I might as well have landed in a completely different orchard.

I was born into a working-class family in Hull, Quebec, virtually in the shadow of Canada's Parliament—high on a cliff across the Ottawa River, looking down at us—but a world away. It was a French-speaking lumber- and paper-mill town where the Catholic Church continued to call most of the shots but the brothel and tavern still had their places.

My dad didn't work at the mills but at the municipal plant that did double duty as Hull's water filtration works and a generating station for electricity. He'd got the job a year or two after coming home from World War II and shortly before I was born. Prior to the war, music had been his life, and he'd got by playing banjo and guitar at countless weddings and parties. But he came home from the war with my mother—whom he had met in Halifax, his naval base on his way to and from Europe—and he needed real work. He got the gig thanks to a connection made by his brother Alfred, whom we always knew as *mon'onc Fred.*

My family seemed to be set with all the makings for a life of postwar prosperity and happiness—steady employment, family, peace. Except there was one problem, or maybe three: my mother was half Irish, half Indian, and she didn't speak a word of French.

In the Québécois world of my father's family, almost nothing was worse than being English. The English were Protestant conquerors, occupiers and carpetbaggers all rolled into one. They were the bosses, and thus the people who dictated that the French made less money and didn't get the management or foreman jobs.

But being Irish or Native—or a combination of the two—was worse than being English. The Irish were seen as bottom-feeders, willing to work for nothing and steal French jobs. The fact that the Irish were Catholic helped a little perhaps, but their church was over in Ottawa—more evidence that they were stooges of the English. Indians, meanwhile, were looked down on by everyone, for whatever reason was handy. They were drunks, or poor or didn't speak French. And even if many of them were Catholic too, well, they were really still heathens at heart.

Maybe his eyes had been opened by his time overseas in the navy, because my father was able to see beyond these prejudices. Otherwise he would never have married Mary O'Connor and brought her home. Especially considering she already had a child, James, by a Swedish sailor who had passed through Halifax and shipped out before he knew she was pregnant. *Mon'onc* Fred, along with his wife, Émilienne, who for us were the very embodiment of class and dignity, also remained above such pettiness.

But not so my father's mother and his sisters Cécile, Irène and Laurette. They had all the time in the world and all the room in their hearts for Mary's half-Swedish son, but none for Mary herself. She was isolated and ostracized, ridiculed and marginalized by the very people whom, in that sort of community, she needed most to look out for her.

For the first six years of my life, however, this was largely invisible to me. We lived in a little house in a part of town called Wrightville but which the locals knew as Ragville because of the rag recycling factory that employed many local women. In socio-economic terms, it was the wrong side of the tracks, definitely, but in terms of community it was a perfectly fine place for my parents to set about having five kids of their own. I was the third, born on a December evening in 1948 after a snowstorm had buried Hull under a foot of snow.

By necessity, we spent much of our childhoods outside—the walls of the tiny house were too close together to contain us all except when we were sleeping. There, among other kids, our being half English wasn't an issue because we spoke French as well as any of them and because there were enough of us and we were tough enough. But since at home we all spoke English with my mother, my dad included, she never learned much French. Not speaking French (and being Irish and Indian) meant she didn't make any friends. And even if my aunt Cécile spoke good enough English to be employed across the river as a civilian employee of the Royal Canadian Navy, she made no effort to include my mother in the wider family life.

Cécile lived in the house in which my father had grown up, along with her sisters Irène and Laurette, my father's youngest brother Laurent and my grandmother. The house was in downtown Hull, and remained the family gathering place. Every Sunday, after Mass and a quick stop at home to change out of our church clothes, we'd head over to the house for a late lunch and a long afternoon of playing. For the first few years of my life my mother dutifully came along, but the tradition must have been not just excruciatingly boring for her but all the more isolating. By the time I was five, she stopped accompanying us on the Sunday outings.

Not long after, she disappeared for a spell, and then another. In the summer of 1955, when I was six and a half, my mother split for good. We were left entirely in the dark about why she had gone, where, or whether she would ever be coming back. It sounds like a bad cliché, but she went to the movies and never came home—or at least that's what the adults told us.

Right from the start we sensed that this time her disappearance might be final. Our aunts started coming over, managing the household and telling us and anyone else who cared to listen *"bon débarras"*—"good riddance to bad rubbish." There was no blame placed on my father, even if at the very least he had been blind to my mother's unhappiness and deaf to her desires to move back east. Instead, my aunts just made it clear to everyone that they were now going to clear up his mess.

Within a week, all the arrangements had been made. Our house would be sold. My two brothers, Jim and Pete, then aged eleven and nine, would move with my dad into the family home. My two younger sisters, Norma and Pauline, four and three respectively, would go live with a family my dad knew in a small town a few miles away. The middle kids, my sister Louise and I (aged six and seven), would be sent to St. Joseph's Orphanage in Ottawa.

I wasn't told of the arrangements until the morning of the day we were to be shipped off, so I had no time to plan an escape. After my dad took me into the kitchen to tell me what was happening, I just bolted. I headed to a secret hiding place my brother and I had in some nearby woods. I figured I'd wait awhile then sneak back into the house and live there by myself till my mom came to get me. But soon enough my two brothers came and dragged me back home. The orphanage had sent a car to pick up Louise and me. Just before we were driven off, my oldest brother, Jim, gave me his golf ball. I kept it for years.

Louise and I were just being warehoused at the orphanage; my dad had told the nuns he fully expected to be in a position to take us back in a matter of months. He'd bring us toys on occasion, but most importantly he brought us hope that we'd soon be getting out. In mid-September of our second year, after a week or so of school, my father came and retrieved us—but not to take me home. There still wasn't room.

Instead I was sent to live with a colleague of my father's, Doyle Parent, his wife and their countless kids. Their house had no room for another child—all the boys slept in one room, all the girls in another—but Doyle and his wife were big-hearted and generous. Life there was a chaotic but pleasant adventure after the orphanage.

The proximity to the rest of my family was also a big relief. I was just a couple of street corners away from the family home. Still, I wasn't a regular visitor for reasons that would be considered bizarre today: my family's house was actually in St. Bernadette parish while the Parents' house was in St. Rédempteur parish. In those years, the parish where you lived dictated more than just what church you went to. For the women, it determined which grocery store they shopped at. For the men, it made the difference between taverns. And for kids, it determined who your friends were, what pool hall you frequented, what girls you could pursue, even what streets you could walk without fear of being harassed and chased back to safe territory.

So, even if we all went to the same school, as soon as the bell rang at the end of the day we kept within our little tribe.

Still, if necessary, you could change parishes without much hassle. And the younger you were, the easier it was. So after about a year at the Parents' I gave up membership in St. Rédempteur parish and joined St. Bernadette.

Space opened up for me at the Charbonneaus'. They were good friends of the family. They also had a mess of children, but they were older by then and beginning to move out. Which meant that I could move in, as I did in the late summer of 1957, just before I was to enter grade three.

Once at the Charbonneaus' I might just as well have been back in the family home, I was there so often. And indeed I did move back in permanently the next summer when my uncle Laurent died.

I didn't have any illusions that everything would be splendid once I moved back to the family home. I knew my aunts well enough for that. There were upsides, especially living under the same roof as my brothers and having their friendship and support on the street. But tensions between me and my aunts didn't take long to grow more pronounced.

They constantly put down my mother. Any time we did something they didn't approve of, they would say in a disgusted voice, *"Mary tout chié"*—meaning more or less "You're shit just like your mother."

It was during one tirade that I learned belatedly that my mother was half Irish and half Native. The news had a different effect on me than my aunt intended. All of a sudden I felt special, not English or French but something different.

We'd got our first television when we were living on Rouville Street. Back then channels used to broadcast an Indian-head test pattern when they had nothing else to air. I was intrigued. I started imitating the stoic look of the TV Indian and would practice my version of it on the grown-ups. Whenever they would come down on me for whatever reason, I would glare at them. *"R'garde-moi pas avec tes yeux tueurs!"* my aunt would yell. "Don't look at me with those killer eyes!" And then my dad would order me: *"Pis change ta face!"*

My imitation of the Indian head—and the impact it seemed to have on people—got me interested in facial expressions and body language and what effective and subtle ways they were to communicate. This likely had a lot to do with the fact that I had always been short and slight and knew that, if I was going to be noticed, let alone impress people, I would have to do it in a way that didn't involve puffing out my chest and standing tall. So I began to work on developing my own non-verbal ways of sending a precise message, whether through an almost imperceptible tilt of the head or a small hand gesture. I also started to study everyone I met to read what they were saying through their movements. I wasn't necessarily seeing things that other people didn't see, or even picking up non-verbal messages that they were missing, but I was indexing these sorts of subtle cues. Facial expressions and the like became, in that sense, a third language for me, one that everyone spoke but didn't necessarily understand, one in which very few people could tell a lie, but I certainly could.

It didn't, however, help relations with my aunts. I wasn't any more rebellious or up-to-no-good than Jimmy or Pete, but I was more defiant. Jimmy, when confronted with a misdeed, would fold and apologize profusely; Pete would deny everything. I, on the other hand, wouldn't speak and just took my licks. After one Friday night blowout Aunt Cécile declared that on the following Monday she would report me to the local priest. Given the weight that the Church swung in Quebec until the late 1960s, the priest was more than just a confessor and sermonizer; he was also an adjudicator and dispenser of community justice. As such, he was only called upon in very serious circumstances. So I knew what Cécile's threat meant—and it scared me half to death. As an "incorrigible" I would likely be sent to a reform school such as the notorious Mont St-Antoine in Montreal. The Mont was run by "the brothers" and the physical and sexual abuse going on there was legendary, even back then. A friend had spent six months there. When he came back, he showed us the scars on his back from being whipped by a motorized contraption the brothers had rigged up to carry out their punishments for them.

So, the next morning, Saturday, I got up early, went into Cécile's purse, took forty dollars and left. A friend put me up in his house that night and the next, but on Monday morning his mom forced me to leave. I didn't have my books and wasn't in the frame of mind to attend school anyway. So I faked my father's signature on a note claiming I was sick, met up with Pete on the way to class and had him deliver it. If I hadn't done that, the truancy cops would have been looking for me and that would have meant the Mont for sure.

It was February and very cold. My dad had an old car in the backyard that he cannibalized for parts, and after a day of lying low I spent most of the night in there. My father and aunts had to know I was in the car—it was just outside the kitchen window and the kitchen was the busiest room of the house. But they let me sleep there anyway, thinking, I suppose, that it would teach me a lesson. I never forgave them for that.

The second night, I found two blankets on the back seat. Pete had left them there. The next day we met up and he told me of a rooming house across from the local arena that would rent to anyone. The rooms were furnished and cost ten dollars a week. With some of the money from Cécile's purse I paid for two weeks and settled in.

The other tenants were hookers, a couple of old winos and maybe a crook or two. I was the only child. For my first few days there I continued lying low and keeping to myself, venturing out occasionally but spending most of the time in my little room alone. Pete brought me my books and some more clothes, so I was able to get back to school. And after a week or so a friend brought me a bike. He said he'd found it but didn't really expect me to believe him. Wherever the bike came from, riding it around was better than walking, even in the snow.

By that time I had got to know many of my neighbors in the boarding house, especially the working girls. They'd leave their doors ajar and go from room to room to socialize. It was a couple of days before I talked to any of them. Then an older woman with puffy, bleached blond hair and far too much makeup knocked on my door. She was tall and very solid—not fat, just solid—and, standing there at the door wearing a floor-length pink bathrobe, she struck me as something between forbidding and outright scary. She held a plate of food in one hand.

"Have you eaten?" she asked. I said no and she handed me the plate. "My name is Lorraine. I'm in room seven," she said, and left.

I cleaned the plate and returned it to Lorraine. On her turf she took the opportunity to ask me some questions and I spilled the beans. It felt good to open up to someone, and we talked for what seemed like hours. Beneath her tough, all-business exterior, Lorraine was still tough and no-nonsense. It was clear she'd had a hard life full of betrayal, disappointment and probably violence. But she took me under her wing without expecting a thing in return, and looked out for me as well as any of my various mother figures had up to that point.

After that first meal she always made sure I was getting enough to eat. Most of the girls, coming home after a long night working, would bring home food. On Lorraine's instruction—she definitely called the shots, to the extent that in retrospect I think she was more of a madam than a hooker herself—they always brought extra for me. Breakfast was often roast chicken and french fries instead of cereal and toast, but that was fine by me.

Lorraine also had the girls check in with me before doing laundry, to see if I had any that needed washing. There were jobs that she didn't delegate, though, in particular ensuring I was up in time for school and had my homework done. She also made sure that none of the other girls—who were all younger and more vivacious and sillier—got too friendly with me. I was, after all, still only eleven or twelve.

When my two weeks were almost up, I began to get anxious about where my rent would come from. I was enjoying life and the last thing I was going to do was head back home. My father and aunts knew where I was—I was seeing Pete every day—but seemed content to have me out of their hair. I was too proud and defiant to go back to them. I talked the situation over with a friend and he told me how I could steal fifty dollars easily. He worked after school and on weekends as a grease monkey at a garage, and he knew that at the end of each day the boss hid the next day's float in an empty oil filter box on a shelf behind the cash. I could just smash a window with a rock and help myself. I was prepared to do it, but only as a last resort: it would almost certainly cost my friend his job.

I told Lorraine of my predicament. She told me not to do the garage job. "Something will turn up. Don't worry."

Within a day or so, the girls were giving me odd jobs. The first was as a timekeeper. Some of the girls would bring their more regular tricks to their room. I would note when they arrived and after forty-five minutes I would go rap on the door and say "Time's up." Each time I did that was worth a dollar or so. I also would make runs to the store for them to buy cigarettes and the like. One girl bought her tobacco by the tin and liked her cigarettes hand-rolled; rolling them for her became another source of spare change.

Sometimes my errand running took me farther afield. If condoms weren't exactly illegal in Quebec in 1960, they might as well have been. Certainly the girls weren't able to get their hands on them easily. So instead, they would have me bike across the bridge, through downtown Ottawa and to the red-brick house of a greasy old man who ran a surreptitious porn, sex toy and condom business out of his home. I would knock on the side door and the old man would open it a crack. I would tell him which girl had sent me and he would hand me a box. Then I would get on my bike and head back to Hull. No money changed hands; the girls got him his cash—or whatever else they may have paid him in—some other way. A run like that earned me anywhere from two to five dollars, depending on the girl and how rich she was feeling.

One way or another, these odd jobs made paying my $10-per-week rent very doable, and I was perfectly happy living there. Pete was a regular visitor, as were most of the rest of our little gang. Even if their parents wouldn't have been caught dead in that part of town— and would have been appalled to know their children were spending time there—my friends would run the risk of serious punishment for the thrill of seeing the girls and the fun of hanging around chatting with them.

After about four months came the end-of-year school assembly and kids' show. Parents were invited, but I certainly hadn't told any of my relatives about it; I hadn't even seen my father or aunts since I'd run away that Saturday morning in February. I had, however, told Lorraine and some of the girls. My class didn't put on an ambitious act: we just sang two or three songs. Still, when our turn was up, the applause was loud and boisterous—most of it emanating from the second row, where Lorraine sat along with three of the other girls. They hooted and clapped and whistled, and I, oblivious to the dirty looks and scandalized gasps, waved at them.

In those days, hookers really looked like hookers—big hair, bright red lipstick, thick makeup, long eyelashes, bright, tight and gaudy clothes, the whole bit. And even if Lorraine and the girls knew they were going to a respectable community event, attended by the priest, principal and teachers as well as the parents of all the other kids, they had made no effort to dress down. On the contrary.

A day or two later, Pete came over to tell me that my father and Aunt Cécile wanted to talk to me. I went home and they came straight to the point: if I promised to behave, I could return to live at the house; if not, they would send me to reform school and have Lorraine and the others charged for contributing to the delinquency of a minor.

So back home I went. Or rather, back home I stayed: part of the deal was that I never went back to the rooming house, not even to get my things. Instead, my dad went and retrieved them.

I'd been dragooned back into the family home after getting a taste of freedom, so it was, I suppose, inevitable that things were rocky between me and my aunts from the moment I returned. But soon enough an uneasy peace was hammered out, a modus vivendi that kept conflict to a minimum.

Within the house my aunts had absolute authority; their word was the law. But their jurisdiction extended no farther than the front door—as long, that is, as my brothers or I didn't do anything that embarrassed my aunts in front of their neighbors and peers. Our marks at school weren't important so long as we passed; after all, failing a grade would amount to a public shaming. So our routine became simple: after school we'd rush home, do our homework, have supper and go out until bedtime—out of sight and out of mind.

Sunday lunch with the whole family, however, was an obligation and the place where an important Québécois ritual occurred: the induction into manhood of twelve- or thirteen-year-old boys. Pete

had gone through it while I was out of the house and I had the pleasure several months after my return.

After the meal that particular Sunday was over, my father, following tradition, pulled back from the table, reached for a cigarette
and lit it up. Then he offered me one. It was the signal that from then
on I could smoke in the house, in public, wherever. Needless to say, we
were all smoking on the sly by the time the big day came, so we can't
really blame this ritual for creating generations of smokers, but it certainly helped.

In this regard, adults were our role models. But their influence
didn't extend much beyond that. The people we really looked up to
were the older gangs of teenagers—more often than not our older
brothers—and the most rigid and unforgiving rules in our lives were
the rules of the street. These dictated where you could safely venture,
what you could say, what you wore, whom you consorted with, and
any number of other small and large questions of our lives.

Transgressions of these rules were usually met with swift and
painful punishments. Sometimes they were worse than painful. When
I was no more than fourteen, my good friend who had done a stint at
the Mont reform school was murdered for ripping off some Montreal
guys. He had unwisely helped himself to a set of lock picks that
weren't his, so he was taken to a warehouse, tied to a chair and beaten
to death with shovels. The Montrealers were making a bid to take over
Hull's organized crime scene and this was their way of saying they
weren't to be messed with.

Happily, the rest of us generally got—or gave—nothing worse
than a good beating from time to time. Most of our conflicts were
with other French gangs on the Quebec side of the river, and over the
usual adolescent stuff: turf and girls. Occasionally, and almost invariably in summertime, we'd get adventurous and cross the river. Then
we'd run into English or Italian gangs, with whom any conflicts
tended to revolve around the same subjects.

One hot, humid evening in July or August, a friend and I were
faced with a problem. We had been to a party in Ottawa and now the
guy who had brought us there was dead. He had been playing Russian
roulette with a real gun. We were in the apartment's kitchen getting

some pop. Just as we re-entered the living room, he pulled the trigger for a second time. We looked on with amazement as blood and brain spattered the couch and wall behind him. The girl sitting next to him started to scream and just wouldn't stop. The guy who lived there told everyone to leave and called the cops.

We were out of there and standing in the street before we could think. We didn't want to be there when the cops arrived. What if they took us to jail? It was a notoriously bad place to find yourself if you were French. It was not much of a hike to Hull, but the Italians ran the area between us and the bridge.

Approaching Somerset, our last major hurdle, we saw them: half a dozen teenagers hanging out in front of the grocery store. They saw us at the same time and quit horsing around and just stood in place. We might have wanted to run or slip into a shadow, but it was too late. As we got closer, my knees began to give on me.

Then one of the teens turned out to be a friend of my older brother. He stepped forward and asked, "What are you two punks up to?"

We told him the story of the dead guy and that cops might be looking for us. Dead guy. Gun. Cops. All of a sudden we were cool. My brother's friend and one of his friends offered to walk with us to the bridge. We accepted.

We were, like so many others in every town and city across North America, perfectly typical young hoodlums and punks, breaking the law regularly but rarely in a serious way, more for the thrill of it than out of any real necessity. Some of us died through one mishap or another; almost all of the rest ended up going straight and leading pretty conventional lives. None went anywhere in school—that was something that just wasn't expected and wasn't done.

Pete was the first of my siblings to leave home permanently. He had a big fight with Aunt Cécile and was gone. If he hadn't dropped out by then, he did shortly thereafter. He certainly wasn't in school long beyond his sixteenth birthday.

Like my father, Pete had the music gene, and as soon as he left home that's how he earned his keep. He lived with a bunch of guys his age or a bit older, played any gig he and his band could get, stayed out until all hours and had his pick of all the pretty girls. Of course, I spent as much time as possible in Pete's company—and within a year or so followed his example and moved out, and in with him.

I was fifteen and still in school. I stuck it out for a term or two and then, having turned sixteen, just never went back after the Christmas holidays. It was the beginning of 1965.

There were classes I kept attending, however. I had developed an interest in karate, and I started studying it in earnest with André Langelier, the only instructor in Hull and the grown-up brother of a friend of Pete's. Because of the family connection—and the fact that I had no money—he let me join his courses for free. I took full advantage of his generosity, often doing four or more group classes a week. Occasionally I would help him out with odd jobs such as cleaning up the dojo, and I recruited a few paying students, but not nearly enough to pay for all the lessons I took.

Even if I didn't need to pay for my karate classes, I needed a source of income after moving out. My first stable revenue stream came thanks to a bunch of friends who broke into a local department store. They pretty much emptied the clothes department, lugging out boxes and boxes, carting them blocks away to a safe basement. My job was to find a buyer for all the merchandise.

For as long as I'd lived at home, a door-to-door salesman specializing in kid's clothes had come by several times a year. He endeared himself to customers by providing credit, as well as reasonable prices. He could do this because he turned a blind eye to the source of his stock. For months I sold him the clothes, making a tidy little profit on every shirt or pair of pants.

Over the next few years I occasionally took part in the illegal acquisition end of the operation, doing break-and-enters of stores, but, largely thanks to my imagination, what I excelled in was the middling: selling whatever needed to be sold and taking a good cut for my services.

I got by middling and doing other jobs that came my way thanks to membership in Hull's criminal community. There was no violent crime involved, and it was always pretty hand-to-mouth, but no one went hungry. There was usually a dollar or two to be made somehow. If someone didn't make their buck one day, someone else in the gang who might have made ten bucks, say by turning a trick, shoplifting or what have you, would cover them. The solidarity that has always been a strong characteristic of Québécois society manifested itself among the girls and guys in our gang, however lowlife we might have been considered.

As we got older, however, things began to change. The sense of family that had been second nature for us all began to dissipate as relationships got more serious and conflicts arose over girls, as people got greedier, more ambitious and less generous, as misdemeanors turned into more serious crimes and the police came down harder on us and turned one against the other. Things just slowly became less fun. At the same time, Hull itself began to feel ever smaller and more suffocating. Some people headed across the bridge for the moderately brighter lights of Ottawa. Others had bigger plans and went to Montreal.

As 1967 drew to an end, my friend Andy and I were increasingly intrigued by the reports that had been coming out of the West for a year or so. We might have missed the Summer of Love, but the other side of the continent still seemed like the place to be. So, on December 5, Andy and I hit the road with barely twenty dollars between us, headed for Vancouver.

By then everyone had abandoned the greaser look. We didn't become hippies—that was more of a middle-class thing; instead, we were happy to be called *heads*, decked out in ripped jeans and army jackets. The term today suggests a regular drug user, but for us at the time it really just referred to a long-haired, open-minded person. True, hash had arrived in Hull in the preceding year or so and almost everyone had tried it, but I was at best an occasional smoker, rarely more than a couple of times a week.

Still, it was a lot more often than my drinking of coffee or booze, both of which I've never touched. The mere smell of coffee put me off; never has a drop crossed my lips. Meanwhile, it was a film that had convinced me to swear off alcohol. After seeing *Days of Wine and Roses* with Jack Lemmon and Lee Remick when I was thirteen or fourteen, I was convinced never to go near the stuff. It wasn't that I was sure it would ruin me; I just knew it could, and that was enough.

As time went by, my abstemiousness became a defining characteristic, and it probably saved my life over and over again. It kept me in control of my faculties in risky situations. Many a loose word has been traded for a cold piece of ground beside a railway track or in a ditch. It also probably worked in my favor when bad guys were trying to evaluate whether I was really one of them or perhaps working for the police. Going into a biker bar and ordering a Pepsi tends to make a person stand out. And the police, the bad guys might have reasoned, would never send someone as conspicuous as a 130-pound teetotaler to infiltrate their organization.

But that was all later. Back in the late 1960s it was the sweet smell of hash and pot smoke that were in the air, not the reek of stale beer.

Andy and I hung around a couple of months in Vancouver. We both did a lot of work—unpaid—for Cool Aid, a non-profit support network for young travelers and homeless people. I organized sleeping arrangements for them at the various "digger" houses—free flophouses, generally subsidized by pot dealers.

Andy helped the travelers make a little money, since they were almost all broke. He also worked on increasing his own revenue by beginning to sell drugs. It wasn't beyond me to steer customers in Andy's direction in return for a kickback—my middling reflex—but I never sold directly myself. It was the beginning of a lucrative career for Andy; his dealing grew in scope steadily, and the last I heard he was one of Quebec's cocaine kingpins.

After a couple of months under the gray and rainy Vancouver skies, Andy and I headed south to San Francisco for several weeks to visit the ground zero of the peace and love movement. After that it was back to Vancouver for a while before venturing farther south in California and elsewhere in the U.S. for some of the summer festivals and concerts. We caught Jimi Hendrix in Phoenix, Canned Heat in Tempe, Janis Joplin at the Shrine in L.A., the Grateful Dead, also at the Shrine, and many others I've forgotten. There was a lot of just wandering.

I came back to Hull in March or April 1969, with no particular plans. One of the few things I was sure of was that I didn't want to go back out west or stay in Quebec. I kicked around for the summer, but I was just killing time and I knew it. I also knew I needed something totally different. So, in October, once any trace of summer had disappeared and winter was beginning to whisper, I cut off all my hair, hitchhiked to Montreal and then south to the U.S. border, and signed up to fight in Vietnam.

There are several reasons why I willingly did what so many Americans desperately avoided doing.

The first was the shallowest: pure, simple adventure.

The second developed out of my year or so hanging out with hippies. They were overwhelmingly and reflexively antiwar, often without any understanding of geopolitics, human nature or history. They seemed to be demonstrating everywhere, all the time, and I quickly realized that most of them really didn't have convictions—at least not informed convictions—and that their demonstrations were often just mob action and trying to be cool. I was especially bothered by the way they treated the soldiers, both those who had returned from Vietnam and those who had yet to go—the spitting, the heckling, the chants of "Baby killer! Baby killer!" The worst, however, were the phone calls made to the families of soldiers who had been killed in Vietnam, saying their sons, brothers and husbands had got what they'd deserved.

Almost all the demonstrators and hippies were middle-class, and I wasn't one of them. I had a lot more in common with the poor grunts who'd been drafted, had been given the choice of prison or Nam after being convicted of something or other, or who simply saw the army as their one chance of escaping the ghetto, the backwoods or the farm. After all, if they survived a single tour of duty, the GI bill and other benefits from Veterans' Affairs would open up the world to them, with their opportunities for education and housing.

I had met any number of draft dodgers back in Canada, and even if some of them were cool, they invariably pissed me off. I admired people like Muhammad Ali. He refused to join up and went to jail for it. He didn't run. The draft dodgers just struck me as cowards, usually spoiled, bourgeois cowards.

The final reason I signed up had to do with my father and the war stories he had filled my head with as I was growing up. How he and my uncle had had not one but three ships blown out from under them as they patrolled the North Atlantic, protecting the convoys. The D-Day landing, during which my father piloted a landing craft attached to the HMCS *Prince Henry* at Juno Beach and watched the water turn pink around him. The camaraderie, the thrill and sometimes the sheer pleasure of life at sea during a war. In retrospect, I understood that many of my father's anecdotes were shined up by nostalgia, and edited so as not to give me nightmares. But at the time and for years afterward the stories inspired me.

My dad also never let us forget that World War II was the good war, and he was a strong believer in the adage that the best way for evil to thrive is for good men to do nothing. And just as my father taught me about the horrors of fascism, I'd become a strong anti-Communist. I learned enough about Stalin's purges and the Cultural Revolution in China to feel that, as in World War II, the U.S. was again doing the right thing by lining up beside the South Vietnamese government. Fighting the good fight.

That's why I signed up.

Where I signed up was Plattsburgh, New York.

"You here on business?" the customs officer at the U.S. border asked.

"Kinda," I replied before giving him the details. Up to that point I hadn't told anyone of my plans. As far as my friends and family were concerned, I'd just taken off to bum around the continent some more. The customs man happily let me in and pointed me in the direction of a recruitment center about a mile down the road in Champlain. After I filled out a form there, an army car took me to Plattsburgh, where I filled in a raft of other forms, underwent a preliminary medical assessment and got put up in a motel. There were about twenty other Canadian boys there, two to a room, with the same plan as I had.

The next day we did another physical and more paperwork, including writing out our wills and doing the MMPI test. The test—requiring yes or no answers to such questions as "Do you still have sexual desires for your mother?" and "Have you found the person responsible for all your problems?"—had us all cracking up. By the time we finished up, the bus was waiting to take us south to Parris Island, South Carolina.

For eight weeks we were drilled and indoctrinated, all the while being scrutinized and assessed some more. Thanks to my martial arts background (I'd got my black belt in both karate and tae kwon do) the physical side of basic training wasn't much of a challenge. Fairly early on the SFSA (Special Forces Selection and Assessment) team took notice of me and certain other recent arrivals and began streaming us toward something other than regular grunt duty. They never told us what we were being groomed for and of course we never asked—lesson number one in the Marines is keep your questions to yourself.

We got special instruction in interrogation (both withstanding and administering), escape and evasion, and radio, as well as a lot of hand-to-hand combat training. We didn't have to do the extended runs with heavy packs, the latrines and all the menial tasks; those were for the guys going through regular boot camp, the ones the Marines had decided needed to be utterly exhausted physically and mentally to mold to the Corps's specifications. Those of us who had caught the eye of the SFSA seemed to have something worth cultivating.

The regular recruits were allowed letters and phone calls, but we weren't. And when basic was done, the rank and file were given a plane ticket from Jacksonville to San Francisco and ten days before they had to report to the transport terminal there. We, on the other hand, were put on a special chartered plane (a bright pink Braniff Airlines 707) and flown direct to Fort Lewis, Washington, our transport terminal and the last bit of North America we'd see for a while, perhaps ever. There was no leave for us.

Along with a bunch of SFSA selections from other boots, I was in-country ten days or so before Christmas 1969. First stop in Vietnam, as it was for all U.S. soldiers, captain on down, was KP duty in a camp. Serving food, doing dishes, cleaning latrines, what have you. It was a way to acclimatize new arrivals—to the heat, the smells, the rhythm, the long periods of inactivity—at a safe distance from enemy shells or bullets.

For most people this gradual integration period lasted five days, but we were pulled out after two and a half and driven to Camp Bearcat, a sprawling base set up on a rubber plantation not far from Saigon. There we spent about two weeks undergoing more training and more assessment to determine our MOS, our "military occupational specialty."

I was classified 18A—my specialty having been boiled down essentially to extracting information from and killing people. After five days or so I was assigned to shadow another 18A. He was supposed to be my mentor, the experienced soldier helping me do the job and stay alive, but for the week or so we were at Bearcat together I could hardly find him—it was R & R as far as he and his buddies were concerned. Shadows tended to be hated by those they were shadowing. We were know-nothing newbies and, worse, liabilities. We were the ones who might walk around with a half-empty canteen, sloshing away for the enemy to hear. The ones who might fall asleep or light up a cigarette while on watch. The ones who might plant the Claymore mines facing the wrong direction, actually activate the safety on our M-16s or bother to peel the leeches off our bodies, thereby concentrating on something other than killing the enemy.

The shadows, part of a larger fraternity known as FNGs— fucking new guys—stuck together (the other guys I just called "fuckers," though not to their faces). At Bearcat we were divided into small squads of a dozen or so men, each squad half FNGs, half in-country veterans. My squad's first assignment was to head north about five hundred miles and keep a section of Highway 9 clear. It bisected Vietnam near its skinniest point, not much north of Hue, running from near the coast at Dong Ha west through hills to the Khe Sanh base near the Laotian border and thus the Ho Chi Minh Trail.

It was grunt patrol work, trudging back and forth along our nine miles of highway, which happily was in the flatlands closer to the coast. Sometimes we'd escort refugees or drag out evacuees (the former were willingly relocated, the latter unwillingly). Occasionally we'd have to clear a mine planted during the night; more often we just kept our eyes open for them. It was more feet-wetting, as it were, this time wielding an automatic rifle rather than a dishcloth.

After that, the real work began. For the next twelve months our squad was an efficient and deadly unit of Operation Phoenix, a secret CIA program designed to erode the Viet Cong infrastructure in South Vietnam. Its methods were simple: capturing, interrogating (usually accompanied by torture) and assassinating Communist operatives and sympathizers—anyone, really, who helped the National Liberation Front and the parallel government it had in place in much of South Vietnam.

A lot has been written about Phoenix and its role in the war, but there is little consensus on what its activities were, even who ran it. Some accept the official line that the CIA handed it over to the South Vietnamese military to run in 1968 or 1969, leaving just a few American "advisers" in place. Others maintain American forces played an integral role in all of Phoenix's activities, including its most brutal and bloody. Some say that its targets were almost exclusively military—active NLF operatives, even if they weren't necessarily wearing a uniform—while conceding there may have been some civilian collateral kills. Others insist Phoenix went after anybody—farmers, teachers, doctors, the more respected and influential the better—in a vicious, evil and heavy-handed attempt to convince the South Vietnamese people that collaboration with the VC was suicidal.

I can hardly remember hearing the terms "Operation Phoenix," "Phoenix Program" or "Phung Hoang" (its Vietnamese name) while over there, and never from an official source. We were certainly not told we were part of it or what its goal was. But I know what Operation Phoenix was all about, at least my squad's participation in it.

We were stationed out of a series of firebases, perhaps fifteen to twenty, some large (as many as 1,300 men), some small (perhaps 100 troops), some barely more than clearings in the forest that served as makeshift LZs (landing zones). We had no real division designation, although at Bearcat we were told we were part of the Third Brigade of the Eighty-second Airborne, even if the Eighty-second had been pulled out of Vietnam once and for all in December 1969. Still, we had clout. If we needed to get somewhere, they got us there fast, whether by chopper or truck, bumping whoever was ahead of us in line.

Never were we directly told to kill anyone; we didn't need to be. The base commander would give our squad leader a file folder containing perhaps a map, a photograph, name and aliases of the target and close associates, and whatever other pertinent information was available. Usually the file was pretty thin, but always there was a piece of green or red tape attached to the file tab. If it was a green cell job, as we called it, it was an instruction to bring the target back for interrogation. If it was a red cell, the message was "don't bother." During the eleven months I was with the squad, we saw a lot more red tape than green.

It didn't take long for us to fit one stereotype that has emerged of American soldiers in Vietnam: crazed potheads with guns. And we fit it better than most, insofar as we were as close as American troops got to being irregulars and thus were largely left to our own devices, both in camp and out. No one got on our back to shave or cut our hair, we weren't required to take part in the morning parade and raising-of-the-flag crap, our tents weren't subject to inspection.

Sometimes we went out on an almost daily basis; sometimes we just had three or four outs, as we called them, over a two- or three-week period. We'd lose a guy, on average, every week or two. Sometimes he was KIA—killed in action—sometimes wounded in action; occasionally he was killed or injured by some sort of booby trap. These might be explosives attached to caches of arms or food or—a favorite—placed under wounded Vietnamese we'd be tempted to help. Or poison placed on the sharp-tipped leaves of a plant that often lined the trails. We lost a guy to another common booby trap: sharpened bamboo spikes attached to a sprung branch triggered by a trip wire. It was one of the more gruesome ways to go and did more than its share of ramming home the point: everything in that fucking place wanted to hurt or kill you—the weather, the plants, the people. That led to both depression and cold-bloodedness: if they were after you, it justified you getting them first, if only to stay alive.

So while our squad may have lost twenty or thirty men during my time with it, it took out a whole lot more, perhaps ten for every one we lost. Of these, about 70 percent were red cell jobs.

It's not as if the killing was ever easy, let alone pleasurable. But as time passed, it became less personal, just a job to get over with. And it certainly became unexceptional very quickly: when death and killing are all around you all the time, death and killing become mundane in no time flat. The banality of evil and all that, I guess.

It helped, of course, if you had a strong belief that you were doing the right thing—something I did have, at least to begin with. Most of the squad felt likewise and that kept us relatively on the level. No one ever went out with a self-inflicted injury or a section eight—psychological reasons. And we never committed what could be termed an atrocity—not against the enemy, at least.

On one out, our squad was assigned a target in a particular ville. Entering it, we found the place utterly empty and eerily quiet. Fires burning, food in the midst of being prepared, but no one anywhere. It took us a few minutes to find the villagers. They were all laid face up in an open pit, stacked like cordwood. The lime spread over them looked like pancake makeup. All dead. Mostly old, mostly women and small children. Our arrival had probably surprised the killers—we just assumed it must have been a VC action—because they hadn't stuck around to cover the bodies with earth. So we went after them. It didn't take long for our tracker to catch up to them, but it came with a surprise: the killers—there were a dozen of them—were fellow Marines.

That kind of action confirmed something that was already clear: by the time I got to Vietnam, the character of the average American soldier had changed. The best had been either killed or rotated back to the world. Many of those left were the bottom of the barrel.

After about three months, I ended up one of the squad's leaders. The guy I had been assigned to shadow had been transferred, leaving me the senior 18A. At twenty-one, I was one of the oldest as well. My seniority meant that I was the guy who was usually handed the file with the red or green tape on it, but not a whole lot more; all of the older guys were responsible for training the FNGs and making sure they didn't do anything that might get us killed.

But there was also the imperative to set an example. Not necessarily a good example—I smoked as much reefer as the next guy. (Though not in camp. No matter how little oversight we enjoyed, no one with half a brain smoked in camp. We never knew when some brass might roll in for a photo op, and no one wanted to be the un-lucky goof walking around with a joint in his mouth.) But we older guys had to keep our shit together and not lose it. No combat "me-mentos" such as ears, no risky heroics or excess, no letting the deaths of squad members get to us.

The shorter I got—the sooner my tour of duty was due to end—the more obsessed I became with making it out alive. Since I didn't drink and have never been one for whoring or partying, I didn't take leave; the downtime between assignments was enough R & R for me. There was lots of card playing and reading—I went through more Reader's Digest condensed books than I could count. Leave was also just more unnecessary exposure. The VC knew perfectly well that our nasty little squads existed, and their networks in the bars and fleshpots of Saigon and other towns were on the lookout for our kind in particular.

In December 1970, I turned twenty-two and everything looked to be winding up as planned. I'd been in Vietnam for a year, and tours of duty lasted between twelve and fourteen months. As squad leader, I had stopped checking in on a daily basis with the CO of whatever camp we were in to see if we had an assignment. If we didn't but I was standing in front of him, it was human nature for the CO to find us something to do. So we stayed in our tents, out of sight, out of mind, meaning another day or two or three of inactivity. Which, with the clock ticking ever closer to discharge day, was a big deal.

Then came Christmas Day. I woke up early, around seven, and made it to the mess before the good stuff was gone. We'd been convened to a meeting set for nine. Such meetings invariably meant a red cell job involving a significant target. Instead of just being handed a file, there was a full briefing. Usually a CIA or military intelligence agent would be present, having been flown in by chopper, as well as maybe a scout, the translator we would be taking along (if interrogation was required) and perhaps another veteran or two from the squad.

On this occasion there were six of us in total, including two spooks and a demolition specialist from our squad. We were ordered to a ville that was harboring VC and keeping stashes of food and

weapons for them. We were to take out the village headman as an example, find the weapons cache and blow it up. (Most of the VC
weaponry was of no value to us; the guns were mostly Russian, Polish
and Hungarian and often modified for field use. If there was one
thing we were never short of, it was hardware.) Finally, we were to
burn the village to the ground.

We were trucked a couple of hours into the hills, and then got
out and walked maybe half a mile. When we were just across a stream
from the ville, we could see a lot of activity on the other side. One of
our guys saw a villager tear up the hill away from the ville. I figured
the villager was going to pass the word to VC in the area, so I grabbed
my guy's bolt-action M1—with its greater range, it was better for
sniping than the automatic M-16 I was carrying—and fired off three
shots in quick succession. I saw the target tumble and then lie still.
While the FNGs searched the place, we went up to see the rabbit.

As I approached, I started to get a bad feeling: the runner wasn't
getting any bigger. It turned out to be a young girl, perhaps twelve years
old. She wasn't quite dead, but close. I turned her around and she never
said a word, just stared at me with a look of incomprehension.

My first reaction was anger. I grabbed the headman.

"Why did she fucking run? Why?" I shouted at him through the
translator. "She shouldn't have fucking run! It's your fault! Why the
fuck did she fucking run?"

It wasn't rational—I wanted someone to blame, someone other
than myself. The headman just told me the girl was his granddaugh-
ter and he didn't want her to get raped.

A moment later my second came up to me and asked for instructions. They had found the food stash and some weapons. I said,
"Burn it, burn it all!"

He then asked me about the old guy, the headman. I told him to
bring him to base camp. Those were not our instructions, and my second's face reflected his concern. "Just do it!" I shouted.

Merry fucking Christmas.

To say I stumbled through the rest of my time there would be generous. The brass had seen burnout before and didn't take disciplinary

action. Instead, my state may just have hurried up my DD214, my separation papers. They came in two or three weeks into 1971, and a few days after that I was making my way south from the Dong Hoi area to Saigon. There I had my bowl of cornflakes and did the duffel bag drag, as they used to say.

From Saigon I was on a military flight to San Francisco. As suggested by the military, I got off the plane in civilian clothes—jeans and shirt. My hair wasn't military short, either, but that didn't make any difference—the protesters were there to heckle us. I didn't stick around. After a day or two in San Francisco I caught a plane to Vancouver.

I'd left the Marines with slightly more than six hundred dollars—my per diems for traveling home and the money I'd saved by taking a plane ticket from San Francisco to Vancouver rather than all the way back to my point of enlistment, Plattsburgh. I'd decided after my return never to touch the military pay that, during my service, had been deposited directly into a Bank of America account. There was probably eight or ten thousand dollars in there, but it now looked to me like blood money. I'd had no problem dipping into it for cigarettes or pop when in-country, but once back in North America, I wanted to close the book on Vietnam fully and completely.

Still, doing so meant that I was as good as broke. I went back to Hull and took up small-time hustling again. While that may have paid my rent and club-sandwich bills, it wasn't going to earn me any real money. So when Paul Richer approached me one day to see if I was interested in helping him out in a drug deal he was putting together, I couldn't say no.

Paul was right-hand man to Arnold Boutin, an older guy who came from a different neighborhood in Hull. Boutin had become the big dealer in town, but neither he nor Paul spoke English, and Arnold wanted to make a connection in Vancouver's drug underground. In Canada in the late sixties and early seventies, Vancouver was the place for quality, supply and price, especially for LSD and other chemicals. Arnold and Paul came to me because they were aware that I knew my way around Vancouver and spoke English well. Their offer was generous: if I accompanied Paul out west and connected him, they would give me a pound of pot plus five hundred dollars. It all made for a good payday. I agreed on the condition that they'd pay my way and my expenses once out there.

So in mid-May 1971 we flew off to B.C. After checking into a room at a hotel we got right down to business. I made a few shopping-around calls, inquiring about price and availability, and we eventually decided to do all our business with a friend, Spooner, who lived in the hippie part of town. He could get whatever was necessary. Arnold was in the market for acid and mescaline, both in substantial quantities. I wanted to make the buy all from the same person to minimize risk and avoid attracting attention.

Spooner provided everything Paul wanted, including my pound of pot. But someone Spooner had sourced his supply from ended up being a police informant. The cops had thus started watching Spooner and, after we paid our visit to him, they tailed us back to our hotel. Still, they didn't have any idea who we were or what we were doing. For all they knew, the packet we carried out of Spooner's might just as well have contained beads or meditation manuals.

Our next stop was the bus station, from which we were planning to send the drugs home via Greyhound. It was just a short walk from our hotel but the police managed to lose us along the way. Had we headed straight to the airport after we'd unloaded the drugs, my life would have been entirely different. But after leaving the station, I realized I'd forgotten my carry-on bag in our hotel room and so we stopped there on the way. The cops were back on us. As our taxi pulled up to the airport departure terminal, they busted us and hauled us into an interrogation room. I was calm—after all, we had got rid of the stuff. But it turned out Paul had kept the receipt from the bus station. They quickly traced the box and found the drugs.

I pleaded guilty and was sentenced to five years' federal time. Paul, who also pleaded guilty, got a very different sentence for some reason I've never figured out: two years less a day definite and two less a day indefinite, all of it to be served in a provincial jail.

The New Westminster penitentiary was a nineteenth-century institution, built for punishment not rehabilitation. The tall gray walls and towers were intimidating, exuding authority and severity. Rats over-ran the place.

Any prisoner sentenced to federal time in British Columbia was sent there first for classification, so we arrived by the busload—everyone from small-time dealers like me to multiple murderers. After a shower, clean clothes and a haircut we were all taken to a special cellblock for new fish. There, over a three-week period, we were assessed by corrections officials for assignment to the appropriate federal facility. Those pegged as maximum-security prisoners would stay in New West.

It may have been the fact that I was French. Or maybe I just rubbed someone the wrong way. Whatever the case, I wasn't going anywhere. I was assigned to the morning shift in the New West kitchen and moved to the appropriate wing. Getting up at five wasn't easy at first, but it meant I'd be off at two and free to play tennis or poker or whatever turned my crank. But wherever I was, whatever I was doing, I had to watch my step: violence and death came suddenly and without warning in there. I had spent enough time on the street to know that this place had to have its own rules. Until I knew them, my best bet was to shut up and watch. I picked a couple of friends, also kitchen guys, and minded my own business.

The first serious violence I saw was in the weight pit, three months or so after my arrival. A kitchen guy, Jack, who was doing life without parole for murder, had for a while been trying to punk out—force into sexual slavery, prison-style—a Chinese guy who was no bigger than me. At the end of a workout it was customary to do some reps with as much weight as you could manage. Jack could lift a lot. He was lying on the bench and had just hoisted the bar above his chest when the Chinese guy came up with a tennis racket and forehanded him in the face. Hundreds of pounds of steel came slamming down, crushing Jack's throat. He died almost instantly.

In many respects, prison was a lot like boot camp—boot that kept going on and on. The purpose of the two was much the same: to break you down and then rebuild you. Fortunately, I was well suited to survive in an all-male, tough-guy environment. I knew how to mind my own business, avoid troublemakers and do what was expected of me without standing out. I didn't suck up, but I didn't take any shit.

The only time I screwed up was by saying yes to a friend, another French guy who also worked in the kitchen. One day he was called for a visit and, being an IV drug user, he asked me to take his works—an eyedropper with a needle at the end of it—back to G unit with me when I went. It was serious contraband, but I still said yes. On the way out of the kitchen, the guards did a spot search and found the homemade syringe. I was charged for contraband and appeared in front of the disciplinary board. The norm for such an offense was fifteen days in the hole on reduced rations. It was obvious that I wasn't a junkie and I'd never had any previous trouble, so the board wanted to know whom I was covering for. I wouldn't say and they sentenced me to thirty days on reduced rations.

If the purpose of prison is to break your spirit, the purpose of the hole is to crush it completely. Not once in thirty days did they let me out of the windowless cell; not once did they turn off the light. The only indication of what time it was, whether it was even day or night, was the delivery of the meals and of the blanket and book that were given to me at about four o'clock every afternoon and taken away every morning.

Even keeping track of time by the meals was confusing: reduced rations meant seven slices of bread for breakfast, lunch and supper, and one real meal every second day. I used some of my bread as a calendar, putting a large crumb in the corner once a day. The surplus bread served another purpose: we were allowed a towel, so I would wrap uneaten slices in it to make a pillow. It was the only comfort available; there was no mattress to sleep on, just a raised cement slab.

From a psychological standpoint, the hole—which wasn't in the basement but rather on the fifth and top tier of G unit—served as a test that people responded to in very different ways. Time spent in there offered two basic activities: exercise and daydreaming—and you can only do so much exercise. So daydreaming took on a whole new significance. I avoided dwelling on memories, especially of Vietnam; that could have led to trouble. Instead, like many others in the hole, I just created fantasy lives for myself, peopling them with whomever I wanted and directing the action as I saw fit. But I kept my imagination under control and tried not to get too carried away, erring on the side of exercise and then more exercise. Not like some people I'd heard of in the hole: they hadn't wanted to leave when their time was up. They'd become more interested in the lives in their mind than the one behind bars.

Everyone in the prison knew how much time I'd been given in the hole, and they were counting off the days almost as assiduously as I was. Their motives were different, however: they wanted to see if I buckled. It was prison practice that once half your time in the hole was done, you would receive a slip of paper every second day. It arrived on days when you didn't get a real meal. Written in the first person, it said that you realized you had made a mistake and asked the warden to release you early with a promise to behave. All you had to do was sign it and you would be out. It was very tempting, of course, but I knew that I wouldn't get the same respect from the rest of the prisoners if I signed it. So I didn't. Instead, I just did more exercise— sit-ups and push-ups were measured in sets of a hundred at a time— and also invented games for myself.

As luck would have it, my thirty days were up on a Sunday, which meant that I had to wait until the next day to get out. Still, they did give me my tobacco and regular meals for the day. When I finally did leave the hole and went into the yard again, many people who had ignored or barely tolerated me before now stepped up to chat or just say hi. I had risen several ranks up the prison's social register. One guy in particular, doing two life sentences plus eighteen, became a good friend. My elevated status relieved a lot of the regular prison stress since I didn't have to spend so much time watching my back.

While I was inside, a government program geared toward modernizing incarceration policy recalculated the sentences of all federal prisoners according to a new set of criteria. It meant most had a year or so taken off their time, including me. As a result, a bit less than a year and a half into my sentence I faced the parole board. I answered all their questions and, sure enough, it seemed pot had gone down a few notches in the serious crime department. Two weeks after my hearing, I got a letter from the parole board setting a release date of just a few days later.

I was given $120, a new suit with sleeves of different lengths, a small suitcase with my old clothes in it and a bus ticket to downtown Vancouver. It was October 20, 1972.

"I'll keep your cell open, asshole," said the guard who opened the last prison door for me. There was no malice in his voice.

"Fuck you," I said, smiling.

We were both just playing our roles.

# CHAPTER TWO

# Hobo and the Triad

———

If you wear a disguise long enough, it eventually becomes part of you, another skin, so much so that not only do others define you by it but you don't know how to be yourself without it.

I'd been playing the tough guy for as long as I could remember. Growing up with no real family to speak of; signing up for the Marines and heading out to Vietnam; surviving in New West. Still, I wondered whether the tough guy was the real me or just layers and layers of scar tissue. Upon leaving prison, I was determined to find out, to discover whether there was a different person lurking under the streetwise, suspicious, standoffish and much too serious hood I saw reflected in every mirror and window.

A good way to give myself time to figure this out: go to university. While in prison I had taken a few correspondence courses, history and psychology mostly, and not only enjoyed them but passed. So, soon after finding a place to live in East Vancouver, I enrolled at Simon Fraser University. My parole officer was only too happy to assist me in applying for student loans and grants, and they proved sufficiently generous to survive on quite well.

Everything was in place for me to remodel or at least reimagine myself, which I set about doing—but only to a certain degree. I made a few new friends at university and started chasing a different, straighter kind of girl. Still, I kept one foot on the street. I studied Hung Gar kung fu at one school and taught full-contact Kempo at another. Rubbing shoulders with no-goodniks is pretty inevitable at these places. I also spent hours at a pool hall, sometimes making a few bucks but usually just hanging out. Occasionally I'd get in on a poker game in the back of the place. More often, though, I'd play poker at a social club, Ukrainian or Russian I think. I'd always played poker—as a kid, as a Marine, as a prisoner—and I'd got pretty good at it. If I won, I tended to take home a hundred or two; if I lost, it usually wasn't more than twenty-five or forty dollars. So, along with government loans and grants, poker and pool helped subsidize my life as a student. As did the odd middling job.

One time an acquaintance needed a storage facility for a bunch of fur coats he'd stolen from a store in a local mall. He'd hidden in a neighboring business at closing time and then just smashed through the Gyproc wall during the night. The place he'd stashed them at first was damp, and he was worried the high-end coats would suffer. I let him use my cupboard for a couple of weeks; when he came to retrieve them, he left me one for my services. I turned around and sold it for $2,500.

In general, though, I kept my nose clean. After all, I was still on parole and had no interest in finding myself back inside. During my third undergraduate year, one of my friends from university introduced me to his girlfriend. They were having a tumultuous relationship. Ray was a wannabe tough guy and Liz was a young campus feminist, flush with the fervor of the times. The worse their relationship got, the better friends Liz and I became. When they finally went their separate ways, she and I got together.

By then Liz's family had taken me in as a stray. I had a linguistic connection with Louise, her mother. She came from a francophone family. But my real bond was with Liz's stepfather, Frank, a tough Irish guy who had been a semi-pro boxer before settling down. He was the first person I ever told about my time in Vietnam and what I'd done there. Part of our bond may have stemmed from a shared difficulty with Christmas—me, because of what happened in that ville on Christmas morning, 1970; him, because when he was a young teenager he and his siblings had found their father dead in an armchair when they went down to open their presents.

After Christmas 1976, I cashed my grant check but stopped going to classes. I was about a semester short of graduating but had never really been in it for the diploma. I had been specializing in criminal psychology, meaning my classmates were destined to become the social workers and parole and classification officers of to-morrow. Having recently finished my parole, I'd certainly had my fill of corrections system functionaries.

A few weeks after my release from prison, I dropped in on a mixed martial arts club recently taken over by an acquaintance of mine. As I watched a class train, I struck up a conversation with another specta-tor, who turned out to be named Joseph Jack "Hobo" Mah. In the months that followed, our paths crossed regularly at different clubs, tournaments and the like. Occasionally we'd go for coffee; sometimes we'd work out and spar casually together. He became something of a friend, if not a particularly close one.

In many ways we couldn't have been more different. Even if we were about the same height, he was built like a fire hydrant and had about seventy pounds on me—he probably weighed almost two hun-dred. And Hobo was all about bringing attention to himself, whether it was the long ponytail he wore down his back, his expensive clothes and fancy car, his fifty-dollar tips to waitresses or his outgoing, back-slapping persona.

Initially we never discussed any involvement in crime, past or present. Still, it had become evident to me after a certain amount of hanging out with him that Hobo was a crook of some sort—he just had too much swagger, too much money and no obvious source of in-come. But the subject was never broached until early 1976, after I had begun practicing Choy Li Fut kung fu. Throughout these years I was studying tae kwon do—I loved all its flashy jumping and kicking—eventually reaching sixth-degree black belt. But I had switched kung fu disciplines, dropping Hung Gar, which is well suited for taller people with a longer reach, for Choy Li Fut, a much more explosive style good for a person my size.

Hobo had been doing Choy Li Fut since he was a child, so it was only natural that when I took up the discipline we began spending more time together. He never explicitly stated his criminal business; rather, he just began acknowledging it in offhand comments.

"How're things going?" I'd ask.

"Not bad," he might answer. "Except there's this asshole who bought an ounce off me two weeks ago and still hasn't paid. I'm having to chase him all over for my money."

Eventually I realized he was a heroin trafficker. And gradually Hobo began making overtures to me to partner up with him. At first he only proposed a marginal involvement—backing him up, say, on a collection he was doing or laying a beating on an errant debtor. I always passed, saying I wasn't interested in finding myself back in the can. The more I declined, however, the harder Hobo came at me, proposing ever greater involvement, ever more directly. This meant an invitation, first, to get in on particular heroin deals and, later, to be involved in all his operations as a full partner.

Hobo was a member of an international Triad, the Sun Yee On, and had been assigned—or had simply taken up—the task of enlarging its eastern Canadian distribution operations. He needed someone who knew the East, ideally spoke English and French (for the rich Montreal market), and had criminal contacts. Hobo was aware I had done jail time, so in his eyes I fit the bill—all the more so because he trusted me and we shared a common interest. The fact that I had declined his overtures so often and over such a long period—a couple of years passed between his first proposal to do a bit of business together and his suggestion that we become partners—just made him sweeten the offer.

By mid-1977, every time we got together he would tell me more about his business problems. He'd complain about a shipment that needed to get to L.A., a collection that had to be made or a big buy for which he required backup. Invariably these laments ended with a variation on the same theme: "I could really use the help of a full-time partner on this . . ."

We were at a bar one evening when the ultimatum came.

"You'll have to decide," he told me. "Either you're in or you're out."

"Well, if that's the case," I answered, "I guess I'm out."

"That puts me in an awkward position," Hobo replied in an uncharacteristically cold voice. "What am I supposed to do now? You know way too much."

"Deal with it," I said, closing the book on the subject for the evening.

I knew, however, that Hobo wouldn't leave it at that for long. I had learned that his easy smile and jovial facade were just packaging for a ruthless businessman who didn't let anyone get in his way. He could turn serious in a heartbeat, and although he was heavyset, his reflexes were lightning fast. He was in your face at the drop of a hat, the smile only a fading impression. Hobo, I understood, would soon push his case again. And if I refused him once more, I would be courting serious danger.

By the time Hobo gave me the ultimatum, Liz and I had moved in together. At first we lived in an apartment not far from downtown. Then, in the summer of 1977, an apartment her parents rented in their house came open and we moved in. The move brought me even deeper into Liz's family and made me feel that a straight, regular life was not only possible for me but what I really wanted. In this way, Hobo's ultimatum was a direct threat. The night after he leveled it, I discussed things with Liz.

"What would a regular guy do in this situation?" I eventually asked her. I already knew the answer but wanted to hear it anyway.

"He would call the cops!" Liz said immediately.

Still, it was an agonizing decision. I saw snitches and stool pigeons as the lowest of the low, selling out their own to get themselves off the hook or make a few dollars. I lay in bed awake all night thinking. Liz had gently worked the argument, knowing she couldn't push too hard. Nonetheless, by nine the next morning I was reaching for the phone.

But whom to call? I didn't know any narcs, so I just dialed the general number of the RCMP and asked to be connected to the drug squad.

"Gary Kilgore," said the voice. "Can I help you?"

I told him the story over the phone, Kilgore methodically questioning me on every detail. When I finally hung up, I thought it was done. The police, I imagined, would launch an investigation and soon bust Hobo. I went to work and lay low for the next couple of days, avoiding Hobo's calls. Then, on the third day, Kilgore called back. He came straight to the point.

"We'd like to sit down with you and discuss your story some more," he said.

Within a day or two I was in a hotel room rented for the occasion by the RCMP, facing four Mounties in bad suits and full of false bonhomie. Kilgore was the one who stood out, largely thanks to his red hair and height. He told me that when they had run Hobo's name through the system, the bells had gone off.

We went over all the same questions again, and then another time. I realized that I knew more than I thought. Names and locations took on new meaning. They'd ask me if I had met such-and-such a person and I would be able to answer, "Yes, he's Hobo's cousin," or "Yes, he owns a grocery store on Hastings." The whole conversation was taped.

As our meeting was wrapping up, they asked me what I expected as a reward for this information. I was taken by surprise, and a bit insulted: I felt bad enough about snitching on Hobo; being paid would only make me feel sleazier. I told the Mounties that I made a decent living and I didn't want anything.

Maybe they could do me a favor then, they asked. Did I have charges pending?

No, I told them, I did not. "I discussed the situation with my girlfriend and we decided this was the right thing to do," I said, not for the first time.

They finally seemed to get the message. They thanked me, there were handshakes all around and I went home. Still, I was left with the feeling that at least two of the cops didn't believe my motivation. I didn't give a shit, though. Again I thought it was over and done with.

Frank had got a good contract to renovate an old house, so I was busy and didn't see much of Hobo. On the few occasions we did get together, he was cool and relaxed, not pressuring me in any way. I, on the other hand, had had my interest piqued. Even if I had no expectation of seeing Kilgore and the Mounties again, I found myself asking questions I'd normally have kept to myself. Hobo took my curiosity the wrong way; thinking he had finally convinced me to get involved in his criminal ventures, he happily answered all the questions.

Two or three weeks later, Kilgore called again. He was a lot friendlier and asked if I could meet once more at the same hotel. Sure, I said.

We went over the basics again, though this time I supplemented them with information I had gleaned over the past two or three weeks. Then Kilgore came to the point: the Mounties couldn't find a way to break into the gang and they needed my help.

"If you could take a few weeks off work, we'll cover your lost wages," he said. "Nothing more—we won't be paying you to rat out your friend."

I agreed then and there to give it a shot. Liz was less than thrilled about the new gig, but she knew she had helped get me into it so she had no choice but to support me.

The investigation had no specific direction at first. I kept working with Frank for the most part, hanging around afterward with Hobo, meeting other Triad members and crooks. My reports helped the Mounties develop a portrait of the Triad's organization and activities. In this way I met Tommy Fong, one of the most senior members of the Sun Yee On in Canada and the godfather of the Red Eagles, a street gang then responsible for extracting "tribute" to the Triad from as many Chinese store owners as possible in Vancouver.

With me on board now, Hobo began setting up a major deal that would provide us with enough heroin to expand into new markets eastward, and even into the U.S. beyond just L.A. He had always been in the middle of the food chain, buying his heroin from an importer who had brought it into Canada. Now he was eager to buy it where it was cheaper—directly from Hong Kong—and have it brought in by mule.

In mid-1978, Hobo finalized the details and laid them out to me. It was clear he was going to teach me to swim by throwing me straight into the deep end. Since he was on probation, I would be the one going to Hong Kong to complete the purchase of a first, sample shipment. If things went smoothly, we would make a bigger buy and then do regular business for as long as everyone was happy. Ultimately, he planned to buy ten pounds per month.

My assignment from Hobo excited the Mounties—the case would go international and could put feathers in a lot of caps. But soon a major kink developed. Gary Kilgore and I had become reasonably good friends and we worked well together. Then one day, without any notice, he was gone, put back in uniform and instructed not to talk to me. Another handler, Sergeant Scott Paterson, was brought in, and the transition was less than smooth.

Paterson was inclined to give orders, and I suppose I was inclined to question them. When I did, he didn't want to discuss my point of view. "From now on, you'll do things my way!" he announced one day.

My response was simple. "If that's how it is, goodbye," I said, and went home. The trip to Hong Kong was about a week away. But that was the Mounties' problem. I've always had a stubborn streak, and now I was prepared to show it to the RCMP.

I was prepared to be just as hardheaded with Paterson.

The phone rang pretty much as soon as I got home. I told Liz to tell whoever it was that I wasn't in. After two or three days the Mounties got the message: I wasn't bluffing. So they ordered Kilgore to phone me and change my mind. He didn't tell me why he'd been so abruptly yanked. Instead, he pulled out the predictable speech: "The case is more important than personalities . . . We've put so much work into it . . . Don't blow it just because of some asshole." That kind of thing. Still, I went back. After all, I'd been contemplating my options and they weren't encouraging. I would have had one seriously grumpy Hobo had I backed out of the Hong Kong trip.

I was utterly out of my element in Hong Kong, and loved it. I'd get up early in the morning and make my way to the only McDonald's in the city, a trip that involved a ferry ride across Victoria Harbor and a long walk through streets crowded with hawkers and market stalls and merchants opening up their stores for another long day. The noise and smells and bustle and strangeness were so far removed from Hull that I had the urge to call someone in Quebec—anyone, perhaps Pete—just to say "Hi, I'm in Hong Kong!" I didn't.

Just as well—officially, my brother was here with me. The Mounties had brought me in a partner as a backup, Corporal Jean-Yves Pineault. We didn't look anything alike; he had almost a foot on me and was balding. I also only met him two days before leaving for Hong Kong. Still, the Mounties thought it best that we pretend to be brothers. At the time I didn't think it was a bad idea. It would allow me to credibly justify why he was there if he made any screw-ups. I also thought his size might come in handy.

Pineault and I were the undercover contingent. Backing us up were sixteen—count 'em, *sixteen*—other Mounties for security, support, surveillance, what have you. Many of them treated it like a taxpayer-funded junket (they brought their wives over or met them in Hawaii once the trip wrapped up). After all, what good is a Canadian surveillance squad going to be in the strange, twisting streets of Hong Kong? And since this was now a joint case with the Royal Hong Kong Police, there was more than enough backup to begin with.

The RHKP was a truly colonial affair. The inspectors—the RHKP equivalent of staff sergeants—were all white Brits. The Chinese, meanwhile, were relegated to rank-and-file positions and were not much trusted by their bosses. Of course, the Mounties were being entertained by the Brits, whose prejudices manifested themselves again when they were told I wasn't a cop. They pretty much ignored me afterward. That was fine.

After acclimatizing to Hong Kong for a couple of days, we got down to business. Hobo had arranged for me to negotiate a deal with his fellow—but much more senior—Sun Yee On Triad member, Rocky Chiu. Rocky spoke no English, so we made contact through Davey Mah (no relation to Hobo), a lower-level, English-speaking gangster who had lived in Canada for several years before being deported.

When I called him, Davey acted as if we were old friends and I got the distinct feeling he was talking for someone else's benefit. He would come to the hotel that afternoon, he told me. At two o'clock there was a knock on my door. The two Chinese men standing in the hall when I opened it couldn't have been more different, but at least they weren't pretending to be brothers. The tall younger man—Davey—had a huge smile on his face and immediately entered and gave me a big hug. Rocky, short, well fed and unsmiling, just stood there. I feared another hug, so I tried to pre-empt it by sticking out my hand. I didn't need to worry. Rocky wasn't the hugging type.

After introductions—Davey still pretending that he and I went way back—we sat down with Pineault and the discussions began. Rocky didn't want any incriminating words uttered, so we used a pad and pen to write down figures, and words such as *heroin* or *kilogram*. After reaching a tentative deal on weight and price, we arranged to continue discussions about the delivery and scheduled another meeting for the next day. Further talks, Rocky said, would take place outside the hotel. Before our guests left, Pineault and I pretended to flush all the notes down the toilet. Thanks to a little sleight of hand, however, we saved them for the RHKP, who filed them away for court.

Rocky and Davey came by at ten o'clock the next morning to pick us up. The team was in place to follow us and, as if he knew he was being tailed, Rocky was soon driving wildly, turning here, doubling back there, until he came to a garage. He opened it by remote and, inside, parked next to a second car. He and Davey got out of the one car and straight into the other. Pineault and I followed. We were immediately off again.

Rocky drove us up and up a winding road, the houses farther and farther apart, until we were in open country—the New Territories, I later learned. Finally, Rocky pulled off to the side of the road and we all got out of the car. I had been certain for a while that the surveillance team had lost us and we were now on our own, but I didn't anticipate the reaction from my partner. After Rocky and Davey started walking up a dirt trail, Pineault said to me in frantic French, "We have to make a run for it now!"

Even if I'd agreed, it was too late. By then two other Chinese had appeared out of nowhere and fallen in behind us.

"Do something and I'll shoot you myself," I answered in a voice that was a lot more calm than I felt. "If they wanted us dead, we'd be dead already."

The narrow trail turned and twisted its way through scrubby forest up the hill. Finally, we rounded a corner and came into an open area where four more Chinese men leaned on shovels near a VW van. At their feet were two freshly dug holes that looked a lot like graves.

The urge to fight or flee seized me. I started to plan a move. We could take Rocky and Davey out and maybe two of the shovel guys. I wondered if Pineault would run or stand and fight. Although he was inexperienced, he was still a Mountie, so I had to give him the benefit of the doubt. But it was useless—my legs started to wobble as we approached. Still, the men did nothing. No words were exchanged. Rocky and Davey just kept walking past the diggers and we followed. Soon the whole line of us had filed by. A little bit farther along the path, Rocky picked a place on the crest of the hill and sat down. The two fellows in the rear dropped out of sight.

Our discussions from the day before resumed. Needless to say, we worked things out. Pineault and I didn't drive too hard a bargain and we soon had a deal. On the return trip down the hill, we passed the clearing and the van was gone, the holes filled in. The empty graves had been a warning or a bluff. Nothing was ever mentioned, but it had had its effect.

Pineault and I would buy one pound of high-grade heroin as a sample on this trip and arrange its shipment back to Vancouver. If everything went well with the sample, we'd return to Hong Kong for the first of Hobo's recurring monthly orders. This would be delivered to Canada by Vietnamese boat people Rocky said he "owned." They'd be provided with false passports and serve as disposable mules.

Back at the hotel room, I gave Rocky $7,500, half the money for the sample. The rest was to be handed over on delivery, which Davey told us would happen on Friday, three days later. But on Wednesday there was a knock on my door. A young Asian girl, who couldn't have been more than sixteen or seventeen, was standing out in the hall, looking terrified. She handed me a manila envelope and ran toward the elevator. When she was gone, I called the adjacent room and the team came in through a door that connected their room with mine. Scott opened the envelope and, sure enough, it contained a plastic bag of heroin.

The phone rang. It was Davey, saying he'd be by tomorrow for the rest of the money. Early the next morning, before ten, he came and collected the other $7,500. He asked me if I wanted to take in some sights that day and then enjoy some of the nightlife before going home. Having spent so much time in Vancouver, I think he missed the Western ways and speaking English. I knew that the cops had a reception to go to, given by the Royal Hong Kong Police. I passed on the sightseeing but told Davey I'd meet him at nine o'clock and let him be my guide through the underbelly of Hong Kong.

He certainly knew his way around. I don't think I've had an evening of such concentrated sleaze since; I'd definitely never had one before. From one tiny and smoky back alley bar to another—gambling, live sex shows, full-contact fighting. I loved it, but needed a very long shower afterward.

We returned to Vancouver a day or two later, at least those of us who didn't stop off for a Hawaiian vacation. One of the first things I did after unpacking was to phone Hobo's parents. I knew from the cops that during my time away he had been picked up and was back in prison. The police cited a parole violation for the arrest, but the real reason had to do with the pound of heroin we were bringing back. The RCMP couldn't let him have it—and move it—but if he was free, we couldn't keep it from him without blowing the operation. He'd given me his parents' number to call if he didn't answer his own phone, and sure enough they told me that he was in prison.

A day or two later I was talking to Hobo through a thick glass barrier. He'd taken his seat with his usual bounce and swagger, and he looked healthy and fit. His hair was done in a long braid down his back and he wore pressed prison greens; clearly he wasn't at the bottom of the jailhouse ladder. He gave me a big smile and said he believed the breach-of-probation charge was just harassment.

"My lawyer'll have me out soon," he said confidently.

In oblique language, without mentioning any incriminating

words or details, I told him about the results of the trip. He was happy to hear the deal had gone well. Hobo indicated that he had never met Rocky Chiu but had spoken to him by phone on several occasions. He added that Rocky's main areas of expertise were money lending and gold and people smuggling; heroin was a relatively new product for him.

Then Hobo put his palm against the glass. On it was written the name Al Lim and a phone number. With his other hand he pointed to me and then put his hand to his ear, indicating that I should call Al. Clearly, he had decided it was Al who would move his heroin for him. I quickly memorized the number. The proceeds, Hobo added, should be given to his sister, Lucy, though he wanted some deposited in his prison account if his lawyer didn't get him out as quickly as he expected.

After fifteen minutes or so, I excused myself and left. I couldn't wait to breathe the outside air.

My understanding of entrapment was pretty old-school: to cause or facilitate a crime and then arrest someone else for it. To me, for a crime to be a crime, it would have to have happened with or without my involvement. So if I were to phone Al Lim and sell him the heroin and then police were to bust him with it, would it be entrapment? I was mulling that over when I stopped at the nearest pay phone and called Scott Paterson, my main handler. Relations with Scott had much improved. He'd learned not to treat me as he might a criminal informant; I'd learned that he, like many cops, tended to see things in a rigid, hierarchical way.

I reported the details of my visit with Hobo. Scott said he would call me after he checked out Al Lim, but his first move was to call the prison and flag Al's name so he would not be allowed to see Hobo or be contacted by anyone inside the prison.

Nothing came up on Lim in the system and none of the cops working Chinatown knew anything about him. So, not knowing what to expect, Scott ordered "close surveillance" when Pineault and I got together with Al a day or two later at the rundown Knight & Day restaurant on the southern edge of Chinatown.

He had to be the most unassuming drug dealer I had ever met. Tallish and thin, he was in his late twenties but still looked like a high-school geek with his black-rimmed glasses, his hair parted on the side and a blue nylon jacket. This, I thought, is the guy who can move a major quantity of heroin? I'd have had him pegged for a waiter or a clerk in an electronics store.

Al's skittishness reinforced my impression. So I did my best to put him at ease, asking him if he came to the restaurant often and that kind of thing. Eventually I told him I'd seen Hobo in prison and that he was anxious to get out. Al didn't seem to be into small talk, and if he knew about the sample pound of heroin that Hobo wanted me to give him he made no mention of it. Instead, he surprised me by declaring that Hobo was out of the picture and launched into the Triad's new plans for eastward expansion, and Pineault's and my involvement in it.

Both he and Hobo worked directly for Tommy Fong, the godfather of the Red Eagles gang, Al said. Tommy had decided that dealing with Hobo was too dangerous for everybody, at least while he was in jail. We had nothing to worry about, he continued, provided that from now on Pineault and I dealt with them directly and stayed away from Hobo. There was no choice in the matter. He did assure us that they would "take care of Hobo's interests," but I didn't believe a word of it. Still, it was clearly an opportunity to expand the investigation, maybe even target someone as high up the Triad ladder as Tommy Fong.

Pineault was generally a silent sidekick, though I was always afraid he'd put his foot in it. I told him in French to play along but not to badmouth Hobo or commit to anything in case it was a test.

Al then said that we were to go back to Hong Kong to do business with a man named Phillip Yu. But, he added, if we wanted to meet Yu first, we could: he happened to be in Vancouver at the moment. It wasn't at all clear how Al's new plan was supposed to work. Was Yu going to be our supplier or a partner? Did he live in Canada or Hong Kong? Would we still be dealing with Rocky and Davey? The only thing crystal clear was that Hobo was out. I told Al, yes, I would like to meet Yu, and we agreed to get together two days later back at the Knight & Day.

Later that evening, at the debrief in a hotel room with Scott and a contingent of other Mounties, Pineault and I wrote our notes and the debate started. Should we forget about going to Hong Kong and take down Lim and company on conspiracy charges as soon as possible? Should we go to Hong Kong and open up a whole new front to the investigation? Everyone had a different opinion. Finally I told them that I was going home and to phone me with instructions. By the next morning the only thing they'd managed to agree on was that Pineault and I should go ahead with meeting Yu.

So Friday evening found us back in the restaurant, in the same booth, waiting for Al and our new playmate. I watched them come in, assessing Phil as he walked toward us. Now here was a gangster! Mid-length leather benny, black silk shirt, dress pants and well-polished boots. Shortish hair slicked right back. Not big—he and I weren't far apart in height and weight—but he sure acted big. It all made for a menacing look. As he came toward our table, his eyes surveyed the room, checking all the booths and looking at everyone but us.

Paterson had run Yu through the system; he was, as they say, "well known to police." But it was all suspicions, no convictions. Smart and dangerous, I thought—this should be interesting. I tried to mirror Yu's attitude, and any warmth disappeared from my face. He stared at me, I stared back, and we let Al and Pineault do the talking. My input amounted to a simple yes or no when required. Yu said even less, just nodding when absolutely necessary.

Phil was going to either supply us with heroin directly or be a conduit to another supplier—but the deal would only happen in Hong Kong. Pineault finally came out with the $64,000 question: "How do we know you can produce?" Al looked at Phil and Phil nodded. Al took a package from his pocket and passed it under the table to Pineault, who put it away. It turned out to be an ounce of number-three heroin—coarse and tan-colored, almost like rice. It was the same-quality product as the pound I'd bought from Rocky. The Chinese, at that time, sold it that way, not bothering with the last step in the refining process, which would have bleached it to a fine white powder.

Phil then stood up, nodded goodbye with his hands in his pockets and headed out. Al, saying he would phone me to confirm everything, scurried to follow. But the understanding was clear: Phil was leaving for Hong Kong within the next couple of days and we would see him there.

Once the product in the package checked out to be heroin, I thought that was that: we had them cold on conspiracy and more—takedown ahead. So I was surprised when Scott phoned the next day to tell me the trip to Hong Kong was on. His rationale: it would keep Al quiet and thus safeguard the Hobo deal and, more importantly, it might allow us to get Tommy Fong upon our return. We were leaving in four days.

There were fewer Mounties accompanying us to Asia on this trip—perhaps ten or twelve—but there was more of a party atmosphere on the plane over. We already had these bad guys in the bag, we all felt. How could we have known that the Lord Guan Yu, god of the Triads, was looking out for his own?

Our instructions from Al were to check into the Sheraton Hotel, where we'd stayed on our previous visit, and then phone him in Vancouver. He would then make the arrangements for us to meet up with Yu.

Pineault checked us in at the desk while I lounged in the lobby. When he was done, I joined him at the elevators and he handed me my key. While we were unpacking our stuff, Scott went out to change C$20,000 into Hong Kong dollars. Instead of converting the money at the hotel—which offered a rate of HK$4.5 for C$1—he went to a private exchange operation. There he got almost HK$6 for a single Canadian dollar. In his notes, of course, he wrote up the hotel rate. After all, the money would be used up for a drug buy, so who would know? And who would get hurt?

He told us of his financial finagling when he got back to the room and promised to take us all out for an expensive dinner with the proceeds. Then we got down to business. The tape was set up and I made the call to Al in Vancouver. He answered promptly.

"Hey, we're here," I said. "I'm in room 425."

"Tomorrow afternoon at two p.m.," was all he said before hanging up.

The next day, we were all ready by 1:30 p.m., so we sat down to wait. And wait. Two o'clock came and went, 2:10, 2:30, still nothing. I called Al back.

"Hey, what's the deal?" I asked.

"The deal is off," Al announced. "I'll talk to you when you get back." Again he hung up. I called again and he didn't answer.

To say the mood was somber after Al Lim's announcement would be an understatement, especially after everyone's cockiness on the flight over. We had barely arrived and already the trip was a waste. The only thing to do seemed to be to return to Vancouver, seriously chastened—and utterly confused.

Soon enough, however, intel from the local police had tracked down Phillip Yu booking a flight to Taiwan. He was scheduled to stay overnight and head to Vancouver the next day. The Mounties called a meeting. Tens of thousands of dollars had been spent on this trip and there would be no payoff. Clearly, they needed a plan, or at least a good excuse to give the bosses back home for returning empty-handed. My input wasn't solicited. This time I went sightseeing.

Back at the hotel in the evening, I called Scott and was told we were leaving for Taiwan in the morning to chase down our elusive friend. We would meet at 7 A. M. hours to discuss the plan, he said. I arranged for a wake-up call and tried to sleep. Nothing was happening in that department, though, so I called Pineault and he dropped by. I told him that I had misgivings about chasing a guy who didn't want to sell to us. He said that was because I didn't know the plan and that everything would be clear to me in the morning. He watched a movie with me and went back to his room.

There was no meeting the next morning. Instead, Scott simply came to my room shortly before seven and said it was time to go. That didn't clear things up, nor did anything that followed. Four of us— Pineault, Paterson, a Brit who I assumed worked for the RHKP and myself—flew the three hundred miles or so to Taiwan in a small chartered plane. Once in Taipei, we were taken straight to a downtown hotel—the Brit had our passports and we hadn't even had to go through customs. We all went for breakfast, and conversation around the table was just general chitchat. Nobody mentioned what we were doing there.

Dealing with cops, I had learned by then, was not all that different from dealing with criminals or Marine Corps officers. Direct questions were best avoided and most everything was discussed on a need-to-know basis. If they had something they wanted you to know, they'd tell you.

After eating and lounging a little, with no mention of checking in, Scott announced that we had a plane to catch. Back we went to the airport and back to Vancouver. I never heard why we took the useless side trip to Taiwan. Months later, however, when I was testifying at the preliminary inquiry for charges that stemmed from our investigation, I got an indication of what the Mounties' game was.

By then we'd learned why the meeting in Hong Kong had been so abruptly canceled. Criminals are as superstitious as anyone, and Asian criminals much more so, especially when it comes to numerology. My room number—425—was about as bad an omen as possible. Four is what the Chinese call an enhancer. If it's matched with a good number, it makes that number extra lucky; if it's with a bad one, it's that much worse. Meanwhile, Triads use numeric codes to differentiate the ranks and roles played by people within a gang. Few are as bad as a twenty-five, which refers to someone who is a spy within and against the gang. In fact, calling someone "twenty-five" was common slang in Hong Kong, designating the person as a traitor or simply untrustworthy.

Thanks to all my martial arts training and hanging out with Hobo and company, I knew what twenty-five meant. But when Pineault gave me my room key, and for the rest of that trip and afterward, I didn't put it together. Phillip Yu sure did, however.

The police didn't know this was the reason Yu was a no-show at the Sheraton by the time we went to Taiwan. They did, however, know that his blowing us off didn't look good. So, in the official accounting of the case, they alleged that Yu had moved the meeting to Taiwan. And we only went there to create a paper trail to back up this version of events.

I only figured this out when, at the preliminary inquiry, I was asked why we had turned down the Yu deal in Taiwan and put it off to negotiations in Vancouver. I skirted the issue in court, testifying vaguely that I was not the one making the decisions and did not question my instructions.

The day after our return from Taipei, the team reconvened at a hotel in downtown Vancouver. From the room we met in I called Al Lim and pretended to be furious with him. I demanded that he and Phil provide me with an elbow—a pound of heroin—that afternoon. I also told him someone would have to reimburse me for my expenses. Al, to my surprise, agreed to come by my hotel room with Phil.

Twenty minutes after the appointed time, they still hadn't showed. Scott came into the room. "Okay, guys, write your notes. It's over. We took them down on the way here."

In what the cops had pretended to be a routine traffic stop, they'd found a pound of heroin in the trunk of Al and Phil's car. They were promptly charged with a number of things, including the ounce they had given us at the Knight & Day.

"Doesn't that blow our cover?" I asked Scott.

He said that they had sealed the indictment on the ounce while we finished the Hobo operation.

The man in question was still in prison, stewing. I visited him the next day and asked if he had heard from Al. He hadn't. I told Hobo that I had given Al the stuff and still hadn't heard back or got any cash from him.

"Don't worry," he said. "You can trust Al."

Yeah right, I thought.

As it turned out, however, I was almost as deluded about my associates as he was about his. I thought I could trust the Mounties.

With Al and Phil busted, everyone realized that we had to wrap things up, and soon. We already had Hobo several times over—at least for conspiracy—but the RHKP, it seems, wanted more evidence at their end. That meant one more trip to Hong Kong.

Since Hobo was still in prison, I took charge of phoning Davey Mah to make arrangements for our next trip. He was happy to hear from me—clearly the money we'd paid for the sample pound was making him and Rocky pine for more.

Still, no one was eager to get on the next flight. It had been a pretty action-packed and jet-setting couple of weeks, and we all agreed a bit of downtime would do us good without jeopardizing the case.

For a few weeks back in Vancouver I got to know Liz again. She had dealt well with my increasing absorption in the case over the preceding months, but wasn't unhappy that it seemed to be coming to a close.

We arrived in Hong Kong on the morning of Tuesday, September 19. Because it was the takedown trip, the brass went straight into meetings and I was again left to my own devices. I was cautioned against wandering around town; someone might see me and, as far as Davey and Rocky knew, we weren't arriving until tomorrow. I stayed in the tourist area and called it an early night.

On Wednesday morning, I phoned Davey Mah and told him we were ready to go. He immediately said that he and Rocky would pick us up in half an hour. I was a bit surprised by his rush; still, I agreed to meet them in the lobby.

There were no hugs this time, barely a hello. Rocky, who was in the driver's seat, looked straight ahead, saying nothing. We were soon flying down the expressway, then turning and weaving through narrow streets. Davey asked to see our passports. This was getting very unsettling. I showed him mine and demanded an explanation. He said the entry stamp was yesterday. "So?" I challenged him.

Pineault then decided to start chattering. We had taken a day to set up our part of the deal, he explained, transfer the cash, that kind of thing. Before he dug us any deeper, I cut him off.

"It's none of your fucking business when we came," I told Davey. He asked why I had lied.

"I didn't lie," I said. "I told you that we were now ready to see you. You think I'd advertise that we were moving all that cash? What the fuck is the matter with you?"

He explained things to Rocky. It was hard to tell if the boss bought it or not. I looked out the window as if the question was settled. No one spoke until we arrived at a harbor quay. We left the car and got into a small outboard, which took us five or ten minutes across the water to a group of boats tied together with planks running between them. Davey explained that these were the Vietnamese boat people under Rocky's protection. We got off our boat and walked from boat to boat across the planks toward the center. The water was green and murky with garbage and raw sewage floating on the surface. I had no intention of jumping into that swill unless my life depended on it.

The boat in the middle of the floating village was large and wide for a junk. It had car tires tied all around it acting like bumpers. I saw no cabin, just a large open space with walls and a canopy made of split, interwoven bamboo. The floor was covered in red and white tiles—it looked almost like a dance floor, I thought. A table surrounded by four chairs was in the middle of the room. A Chinese man with what looked like an AK-47 in his hands stood in the corner, staring straight ahead. This was no bluff.

After we sat down, Davey looked me straight in the face. "We got word from Canada saying you guys were cops. Are you?"

I took the offensive, standing up, pushing the table toward them, outraged at the accusation. "You say that, we have a right to know who it is!" I roared.

Rocky was looking at Davey, who quickly translated what I had said. After Rocky nodded, Davey said, "My friend Joey Howden."

Uh-oh, I thought. I knew Howden from prison. He was a smooth, handsome and tough-as-nails career criminal. In Vancouver he had joined up with a crew run by another hood called Bobby Johnson; their main business was heroin.

Davey continued: "Howden's crew has a cop on the inside who told them, and Howden told us because he's Hobo's friend!"

I sat down, lifted both my hands and forced a smile.

"Let's see if I got this straight," I said. "A crooked cop told Howden and it got to you?" Davey nodded but seemed confused. I knew I had him. "But he hasn't told Hobo? Who's there in Vancouver and is supposed to be Howden's friend?"

I had to exploit the fact that Hobo hadn't raised any doubt about us himself. I hadn't told Davey and Rocky that Hobo was locked up, and I had to hope they didn't know.

"Why hasn't Hobo got word to you? Have you heard complaints from Hobo? If this is just an excuse 'cause you guys can't produce, then just say it—don't insult us with that garbage."

Davey was speaking rapid Chinese to Rocky. I got up again. Now that I had them confused, I had to keep them on the defensive and make sure their greed for our green overcame their suspicions.

"Fuck this shit," I said. "I thought you guys had it together! As for Howden, I'll take care of that piece of shit when I get home."

Finally Davey said the magic words: he apologized and added that he hoped the deal would go on. I grabbed the life preserver Davey had just tossed us and my tone changed. "I can't really blame you, I'd want to know too if someone calls from across the ocean telling me shit like that."

Pineault never said a word throughout the whole confrontation. He and Rocky had sat like spectators at a play. Eventually, though, Rocky waved his hand and the bodyguard with the AK disappeared behind the bamboo curtain. I had so much adrenaline pumping through me that my hands started to shake. Pineault noticed and took over the negotiations when we finally started talking business. We'd already agreed to buy ten pounds for something like one million Hong Kong dollars, half up front, half upon delivery by Rocky's boat-people couriers to Canada. The discussions that day all revolved around process and the transfer of the first installment of cash. We told them we'd give them the cash once we saw the ten pounds and tested it. Finally, the details were sorted out to everyone's satisfaction. The transaction would go ahead the next day at 1:00 p.m. at the hotel.

We shook hands and headed back to the edge of the floating village, where our boat was waiting to take us ashore. The trip back was silent and strained. Rocky and Davey dropped us off at the hotel. Once in the lobby, Pineault said, "What a couple of maroons." We both laughed a little more than necessary.

I wasn't, however, laughing once we were doing the debrief up in an RCMP suite and Paterson let me know how Davey Mah had got the goods on us.

Howden's boss, Bobby Johnson, was accountable to two groups, it seemed: the Palmer brothers, who supplied him with his product (and who in turn got it from the Dubois mob from Montreal who got it from the Cotronis and the Mafia); and the RCMP. The Palmers supplied the drugs to Johnson's outfit; the Mounties let them sell it. The former, Johnson paid in cash; the latter, in information.

The Mounties had long had visions of Johnson allowing them to work their way to the top—possibly all the way to Montreal—and were in deep with him. By 1978 their nasty and complicated relationship was already several years old. But Bobby Johnson was proving to be more of a liability than anything else. After signing on as an informant, he, Howden and a third member of their crew had spent a year in jail for the torture and murder of another drug dealer. The trio had been released on appeal. Still, the Mounties hadn't cut Johnson loose—maybe he knew too much incriminating information about them. But his participation in the murder meant that he could never testify for the Mounties. So now they wanted Johnson to introduce an operative—an actual RCMP agent, I was led to believe—who could work his way up the ladder and eventually testify.

The scenario the police came up with could have been an elegant piece of infiltration; instead, it almost got us killed. The idea was to have Johnson pretend the operative was a crooked cop who could provide inside information on police investigations. That made for a hitch, however: to prove he was the real deal, the guy would have to deliver the details of a real undercover operation to Johnson's criminal associates, something that, ideally, would soon culminate in a high-profile bust. Guess which one they chose?

The mistake in the RCMP's planning was a big, stupid one. They blithely assumed that just because Johnson's crew got their heroin through Montreal and Europe, they didn't have any dealings with Asian criminals. Obviously, Howden and Davey Mah were good friends and Howden had been aware that two guys had gone to Hong Kong to do a deal with him.

"You win some, you lose some," was all Paterson had to say about our close call. "Anyway, you guys came out okay."

It would be fifteen years before I fully trusted a Mountie handler again.

If Pineault was angry, even somewhat concerned, that the Mounties had almost got him killed, he wasn't showing it. Instead, he was happily in my hotel room reading a newspaper at 12:50 the next day, waiting to finish off what, for me at least, had become a very unpleasant operation.

The plan was simple enough. We were to have the down payment of HK$500,000 in another room somewhere in the hotel. Likewise, Rocky and Davey were to have the ten pounds of heroin in another room. We would give them the key to the money room; they would give us the key to the drugs room. While Davey and Pineault made sure that the other side was good for its word, Rocky and I would sit on either side of a table with a single, loaded handgun between us. One gun, two people—a guaranteed recipe for messiness if either side didn't fulfill its side of the deal.

The RHKP had done its homework and got information that Rocky's crew would have about a dozen people fanned out in the hotel and two getaway vehicles waiting at different exits outside. That was one reason the brass decided not to take them down as they arrived. Another was the building of a solid case beyond simple conspiracy charges. It was almost certain that Rocky and Davey would not arrive with the drugs; those would be brought to the hotel by a third party. But if they were to hand us a key to a room containing the heroin, it should be sufficient to get the pair on possession.

The plan was that ten minutes after Rocky and Davey arrived in our room, Scott and the boys would come through the front door while a British tactical squad working on behalf of the RHKP came through the door connecting our room to the one next door. Those ten minutes would give us enough time to collect some incriminating talk on the wire and allow the dozens of undercover police around the hotel to isolate the members of Rocky's crew.

At 12:58 there was a knock on the door. I looked through the peephole and saw Davey looking back at me. I nodded to Pineault and he hit the timer on his watch. In they came, looking like Mutt and Jeff.

Davey immediately put his finger to his lips and Rocky turned on the TV and cranked up the volume. Pineault gave up his seat for Rocky and sat on the bed.

I leaned against the dresser next to Davey. Each of us was very nervous but doing his best to hide it. When Rocky sat down, the bottom of his shirt opened and I saw the grip of the gun.

I started chattering to Davey about a ring I had bought recently, trying both to cut the tension and to use up time. Suddenly ten minutes seemed like an eternity and, this being my first takedown, I was imagining everything going wrong, especially after the events of the day before. I asked if he thought the ring was real gold. He looked at it and then passed it to Rocky. After some Chinese, Davey gave it back and said it was. Then we got down to business. Rocky took out his key while I took out ours and we exchanged them.

Davey wrote on a pad: *When will you be back and get more?*

I wrote down *Next month,* or something like that, and we exchanged notes back and forth.

At one point Pineault said, *"Une et demi."* There were only ninety seconds left to kill. We moved into position. I made sure Davey was between me and Rocky. Pineault edged over on the bed, in position to hit the floor—as the RCMP instructs its undercovers to do in a takedown—but also in a position where he might jump Rocky if there was a screw-up.

I was shaking hands with Davey when, in a burst of sound and fury, the front door swung violently open. Unfortunately, none of us had noticed that the front door opened to the left while the connecting door opened to the right. The doors were so close it was impossible to fully open both of them at the same time. Scott, to his credit, led the charge, his three-man team close behind him. But before he was fully inside the room, the lead tactical squad guy crashed his door against the front door and Scott was pushed back. The rest of Scott's team couldn't see what was happening and continued to push in from the hallway. That caused Scott to trip and fall into the room. As he hit the floor, his .38 snub went off, the bullet exploding the mirror over the bed. True to his training, Pineault hit the floor. Scott's team thought he had been shot.

In the confusion, I saw Rocky start to get up and reach for his gun. I still had Davey's hand in mine, so I yanked him toward me with my right arm and simultaneously kicked him as hard as I could in the chest area. When the kick landed, I let go of his hand and he flew into Rocky, knocking him down.

It was then my turn to hit the floor, which I did. The precaution was hardly necessary: the guys were in and Scott had regained his composure. Pineault and I were whisked into the other room while Rocky and Davey were being cuffed. The door shut behind us. There was no point protecting our cover. The investigation was over.

# CHAPTER THREE

## Family Comes First . . . Smugglers Second

——

The investigation was over, yes, but the case's second life, the court proceedings and the meting out (or not) of justice and punishment, was just beginning. It was a stage I would get to know well. By the end of my career I had given evidence against 168 bad guys (of whom maybe a dozen were women and maybe another dozen weren't so much bad as just unlucky).

Happily, the court proceedings in the Vancouver cases were short and relatively painless. Hobo pleaded guilty to conspiracy to import heroin at pretty much his earliest opportunity. He got ten years. Al and Phil made a deal and pleaded guilty after their preliminary inquiry, scoring eleven and eight years respectively for trafficking and conspiracy.

Rocky and Davey were the only accused I had any dealings with who put up a fight. Their trial required me to go back to Hong Kong several months after the bust. I was there for about ten days and on the stand for most of three days. I remember being struck by two things in particular. The first was the fact that the accused were brought into the courtroom in a cage that came up through a hole in the floor, and remained handcuffed to their seats the entire time. The second was how lame their lawyers—or barristers—were, despite their powdered wigs and plummy English accents. Not that they had much to work with: we had Rocky and Davey cold. They each got twenty years for conspiracy, and in a Chinese prison. I felt a bit bad for them.

By the time their trial wrapped up, I was back to my old life, with a few modifications. I refused the RCMP's offer of relocation to anywhere in Canada I might want to go. Instead, Liz and I moved out of our apartment below Frank and Louise's place and into a cottage we'd been renting for a few months, forty-five miles up the coast from Vancouver. There was one offer the RCMP made that I did take up: a name change. It wouldn't be the last. That's how I eventually became Alex Caine and discovered that wearing a new name was not all that different from putting on a new set of clothes. Certainly, it didn't lead to any existential crises.

I'd banked a bit of money over the course of the investigation and remained on the Mountie payroll until the trials were all wrapped up, so there was no need to go back to work.

In the back of my mind (and sometimes the front) I was trying to figure out what I would do for a career. I was turning thirty in December 1978, and arriving at that landmark brought some anxiety with it. Liz and I were also talking about getting married and having kids, which would make a steady income more of an imperative. I wasn't much interested in going back into the renovation or construction business, with or without Frank. So I began contemplating buying a club or a bar. Or getting into music promotion and putting on shows. Or both. Or something like that.

Naturally, I assumed jobs such as the Hobo operation were one-shot things, the result of a shady acquaintance, a girlfriend who convinced me to talk to the cops and a police force that needed a helping hand. What I didn't fully appreciate was that, if you were good enough at this kind of work, an in with the target wasn't necessary. Nor did I know that people capable of pulling off an infiltration assignment were in serious short supply. On both sides of the border.

Nineteen seventy-nine wasn't more than a few months old before Scott Paterson called, asking me to talk to the Seattle office of the FBI. I was happy to do so. It had been about six months since the bust in Hong Kong and I was beginning to pine for excitement. I hadn't done anything about my idle plans to become an entertainment entrepreneur. And my anger at almost getting killed thanks to the Mounties had abated. Pineault and I had been sold out, but it hadn't been intentional or personal, just part of the game. Anyway, this wasn't the RCMP wanting to talk—it was the FBI, the big time. Who wouldn't at least make the short trip to Seattle to see what they wanted?

It turned out to be another heroin importing ring. The FBI had information that members of a Thai Airlines flight crew were smuggling small shipments of the drug into the U.S. and establishing contacts for larger suppliers. That was about it—all the FBI had beyond that was the name of the hotel where the flight crew overnighted once a week in Seattle.

I took the gig and it turned into a three- or four-month operation. And a successful one, as far as my work went. I got in with the Thai pilots thanks to some strippers I hired to come and hang out with me in the hotel lounge and to the pilots' taste for female companionship. That led to a phone number that led to a contact who was prepared to provide as much heroin as I might ever require, so long as my cash supply was good and plentiful. I even got a one-pound sample delivered personally by one of the Thai pilots.

For reasons unknown to me, however, the FBI pulled the plug on the operation before we could build a solid case and make any arrests. It left a bitter taste in my mouth, since the one thing that was clear was that politics—whether of the office or geopolitical variety—were very much involved in the case's getting kiboshed. Still, the Thai pilots investigation made me realize that even if this wasn't a career found on any list offered by high school guidance counselors, even if there were no classified ads in the back pages of newspapers announcing "Experienced Infiltrator Wanted," maybe there was a future for me in this game.

But family comes first, as they say, and before I did any more infiltration work I would first get myself a family.

Liz and I were married not long after the Thai pilots case ended, and shortly after that she became pregnant. Life was good. The FBI had been paying me US$4,000 per month, which was big money in those days, so we had some savings. Then I was seized by the ridiculous notion that my baby had to be born back east, and that my family should be part of the child's life. The plan Liz and I came up with was for me to go back to Hull alone, get our new home set up, and then she and her bulging belly would come join me. So in early 1980 I bought a new 38-foot Coachmen trailer, parked it on her mother and stepfather's North Vancouver property and settled Liz in. She would be close to her family but still have her privacy. Then I loaded up my 1965 Ford Econoline, called for Pepper, my Australian blue heeler dog, to join me and drove the 2,772 miles to Hull. Without realizing it, I was resuming my search for ways not to live a straight, sedate life.

Soon after my arrival, I rented an apartment in a high-rise as well as a small street-level commercial space. In the storefront I opened my first martial arts studio. I didn't expect to make any serious money from it. Rather, it was a hobby business, something I hoped would support itself and maybe make me a little extra between infiltration assignments.

I called the studio Dragon's Kung-Fu, School of Martial Arts, and wrote the usual stuff in the window—terms such as "self-defense" and "group or individual classes." Within a week I got a visit from a provincial official telling me I had to redo everything, this time in French. Bill 101, Quebec's hard-line language legislation, had come into effect. Almost all commercial signs in English—or anything other than French—were now forbidden. Or rather, *interdit*. It hadn't taken long for me to start feeling out of place again in my hometown. One unintended laugh came out of the change, though. Le Dragon Kung-Fu, as the business was renamed, was pronounced the same way as *le dragon confus*—"the confused dragon."

Confused might have been a good way to describe my general state back in Hull. Nobody was hostile or cold or unwelcoming; I just didn't meet with any enthusiasm at my return, not from my family or whatever old friends still remained. Maybe I had flitted in and out of their lives once too often. Or maybe they just didn't give a shit. Certainly, it was presumptuous and big-headed of me to expect more—a mixture of respect, affection, admiration and interest that people weren't prepared to hand over so easily. They all seemed indifferent to me now.

But not indifferent to my money. That really interested my siblings—if nothing else about me did—and they set about getting some of it for themselves. I had some cash and didn't hide it, but of course I couldn't tell them where it came from or what I'd been doing for a living. So they just naturally assumed I was a criminal. And if I was a criminal, I must be loaded. So they were constantly hitting me up. It was always a hundred bucks here, forty there. I couldn't refuse—they were family.

Liz's arrival in Hull a month or so before her due date made my life there a lot more pleasant. At the same time, it brought back an old ghost—my mother's unhappiness. In my obsession to see my baby born in the same town I was, I realized I hadn't taken into account something my father had neglected almost thirty-five years earlier: how isolating Hull could be if you don't speak French. It wasn't an issue initially—we had the baby to prepare for—but would inevitably become one if we stuck around.

So, after our daughter Charlotte was born at the same hospital I had been born in, we packed up the van again, left the apartment and the furnishings for my brother, and headed back out west together.

In Vancouver, we settled into the Coachmen as our primary residence, with our cottage as a getaway. Liz, understandably, wanted to be close to her mom and spent most of the day in her parents' house with the baby. That left me with time on my hands. So I picked up the phone and called Scott Paterson to advise him I was back and available for work. He said he'd keep his ears open. It wasn't long before he called.

There was a three-month job with the RCMP in Toronto if I was interested, he said. Again it was heroin. I talked it over with Liz and took the contract.

What concerned the Mounties, and in particular Sergeant Tom Brown and his band of Renowns (as his unit was affectionately called), was an influx into Toronto of what was called "black tar heroin." It was poorly refined but unpredictably potent, which was leading to a spike in the number of overdose deaths.

I got in with the main players through an elaborate *mise en scène*. We had two undercover officers stage a mugging of one of their regular dealers, a guy named Bruce. As the mugging was in progress, I happened along and came to Bruce's rescue. The UCs backed off, saying to me, "Hey man, sorry. We didn't know he was connected to you." The dealer, who didn't know any better, was both grateful for my intervention and impressed by the clout I appeared to carry with the low-life muggers. I made sure the dealer was okay, introduced myself and then split.

A few days later, I entered a McDonald's when we knew Bruce was meeting a supplier named Moe—one of the guys we were really after. This time I let him notice me. When he did, he called me over, telling Moe how cool I was. As of that moment I was in—at least as a friend.

Moe and his partners were a very careful bunch; it took almost two months of stroking their egos before I convinced them to sell to me. Finally, though, we put a deal together. Once again I would be buying a pound of heroin. That led to a meeting in a parking lot one afternoon shortly before Christmas. As the dealers went into their car's trunk to retrieve the drugs, the police pounced. The bust was as smooth as any I've been involved with. The police got a pound of heroin and arrested the four main guys we were after.

But it was all for nothing. On his way back to headquarters the RCMP corporal responsible for bringing in the evidence stopped off at a store to buy a snack. That broke what's called "the continuity of evidence": since the drugs were in an insecure environment and out of the Mountie's sight and control for a minute or two before being taken to the lab and tested, it was possible they had been tampered with. Or even that a package containing, say, popcorn had been taken from the cruiser and replaced with one containing heroin. It sounds absurd, but it's a sound legal principle; the judge thought about it for perhaps five minutes before deciding to throw the case out at the preliminary hearing in early 1981.

By then, of course, I'd gone back out west to be with Liz and Charlotte. I'd also reported back in to Scott Paterson, planning to tell him I was ready and willing to take on a new job. But before I could get that far, he interrupted me.

"Gary Kilgore is looking for you," he said.

"Why? What's up?"

If Paterson knew, he wasn't telling me, so I called Kilgore myself and met him in a coffee shop a few days later. It was always a treat to watch big Gary—he was six-four if an inch and probably weighed 280 pounds—trying to squeeze into one of those fixed, hard plastic seats.

"Why do you always pick these places?" he'd ask unfailingly.

"Because my belly isn't a crime against humanity," was my routine response.

"Everybody's a fucking comedian!"

Kilgore was dressed in jeans and a T-shirt, with his perennial beige nylon Windbreaker and cowboy boots. Tufts of curly red hair stuck out under his ball cap. With his wide, old-fashioned mustache he looked like Yosemite Sam trying to blend in with the locals.

That day he was off-duty, but it wouldn't have made much of a difference: he had returned to plainclothes policing and was back on Asian files. After giving me a present for the baby and an update on his life and the goings-on in Mountie-land, he got down to business. He was being transferred to Bangkok, where he would be attached to the Canadian embassy. His job was to liaise with local law enforcement on drug files. He wanted me there to work some cases with him.

I agreed on the spot. The rapport and working relationship I'd had with Gary back before Paterson replaced him was better than I'd had with any of my subsequent handlers, and if I had a specialty it was Asian crime and criminals. It also sounded like fun. Kilgore told me that I would get some bogus job tied to the embassy—chauffeur, cook, something like that—as a reason to be there. My real work, however, would be to infiltrate drug exporting operations and schemes, especially those shipping, or planning to ship, to Canada.

Kilgore was pleased at my enthusiasm—he was already feeling like a fish out of water, even if he hadn't yet left for Bangkok. His departure was scheduled in a week or so. Getting everything organized for me to join him would take much longer, he warned; I couldn't expect to find myself in Bangkok for at least a couple of months, maybe three. That was fine with me, I said. I wanted time to spend with my family.

When I got home, I called Scott and gave him the scoop.

"Are you sure you want to do that?" he asked a bit cryptically.

"Talk to me, man," I told him. "What are you saying?"

"Well," he fumbled, "you never know what opportunities could pop up closer to home. You have a baby now."

"Good point. Is there anything I should know about?"

"No, no," he said. "I'm just making a point."

I didn't believe him for a second—Paterson never "just" said anything. On the surface he appeared to be a company man through and through, but his relationship with the Mounties was growing strained and complicated. After the Hong Kong caper, he'd been busted for his currency exchange fiddle and was going through a long series of internal disciplinary boards, rulings and appeals. Was he more concerned with my interests than the RCMP's all of a sudden? It was hard to know.

About a month later, Paterson called me up again and invited me for coffee. Scott wasn't as big as Gary, so I let him choose the place. He had another job I might be interested in, he said, this one not so far away—in fact, just the other side of the U.S. border.

"In Blaine, Washington," he said. "A friend of mine is with the DEA there. He'd like to talk to you. His name is Andy Smith."

I was somewhat suspicious as to why Scott would be dangling another opportunity in front of me when he knew that I'd agreed to take the Bangkok job. Still, I was intrigued and flattered, even though I had no idea what the Blaine job was about. I called Smith the next morning and was off to see him that very afternoon.

Blaine was only a half-hour drive from Vancouver and all I expected was a casual chat with Smith. But when I arrived at the DEA (Drug Enforcement Administration) building, I was shown into the office of the top guy, special agent-in-charge Larry Brant, where a welcoming committee of five or six cops was waiting for me. Most were DEA, but also there to meet me was Corky Cochrane from the FBI. With both agencies represented, I knew the meeting was going to be more formal than I'd anticipated.

Smith, who had been recently transferred from New York City, started right in by asking me what I knew of bikers in general and the Bandidos in particular.

"Nothing," I said, adding that I'd never been on, much less driven, a motorcycle. That was only partly true: I had been a passenger on a bike once or twice, but I thought it best to start building a back door.

Smith didn't appear concerned. He outlined their problem and what they wanted to do about it. Members of the Bellingham chapter of the Bandidos, he said, were working with Hells Angels from Canada, and running drugs, guns and other contraband over the border. Whether this business was being done on a chapter-to-chapter basis or was happening simply between a few individual bikers the DEA didn't know, but they sure wanted to. If the smuggling was chapter-to-chapter, the cops could go after the bikers as organized crime using the RICO (Racketeer Influenced and Corrupt Organizations) statutes. Otherwise, it was just garden-variety criminality. This was where I would come in. The DEA wanted me to infiltrate the Bandidos to find out just how organized the smuggling was. They also hoped I would "build a book" for them—establish a comprehensive list of local Bandidos members and associates as well as their addresses and places of employment.

There was a bit of pressure on them, Smith admitted. "The President of the United States," he intoned, apparently expecting me to jump to my feet and salute, "has declared war on the big four outlaw motorcycle gangs: the Hells Angels, the Bandidos, the Outlaws and the Pagans."

The DEA, the FBI, the ATF (the Bureau of Alcohol, Tobacco, Firearms and Explosives)—all the federal agencies—were under pressure to produce results, he suggested. The "war" had been sparked by the suspected involvement of the Bandidos in the assassination of a federal judge, and by the shooting-at of an assistant U.S. attorney in Texas two years previously. Apparently, police in the Pacific Northwest hadn't been doing their bit.

After listening to Smith describe the job, I explained to him about waiting to go to Thailand. "And if you've done your homework, and I assume you have, you know my area is Asians," I added.

The truth was, Ronald Reagan's exhortation notwithstanding, I didn't think I was the right man for the job anyway. I didn't have all that much experience in infiltration, but I had enough to know that the key to survival in that kind of work was to know your limitations.

When it came to bikers, I felt out of my element. Not to mention that, like almost everyone, I was a little intimidated by their image.

Smith was fully aware of my Bangkok commitment, but he pressed his point, saying they could use help in the short term while I was waiting to ship out.

At that point another cop joined us, this one from the Whatcom County Sheriff's Department. Andy explained where we were in the discussion. Acting as if I wasn't there, the deputy had just one thing to ask: "Does that mean he's in or not?"

I didn't like the deputy from jump and felt provoked, as if he was challenging me.

"It means I've agreed to take a look at it for thirty days," I announced.

# CHAPTER FOUR

# The Border Bandidos

——

After the meeting in Blaine, I went back to Vancouver to figure out a plan while the DEA, as the "double A" (anchor agency) on this case, drew up the paperwork for my involvement.

One thing I knew for sure, bluffing my way in as a biker was not even a consideration. So the only real option in my mind was to appear on their turf as a regular crook and border runner.

Still, I figured that a bike would be a good thing to have, insofar as it would at least provide an excuse to make small talk with the Bandidos. There was no way I could handle a Harley—they are just too big and powerful for novices—so Andy had rounded me up a 900cc Norton Commando. It was a good choice. Back then, anything other than an American or European bike was considered "Jap scrap." For example, Mongo, one of the more colorful—and color obsessed— Bandidos I was to meet, had a sticker on his bike that read "Better to have my sister in a whorehouse than my brother on a Honda." Many of the hardcore bikers had started their careers on Nortons, Triumphs and BSAs, so the 900cc Commando would do fine.

Andy also had Scott Paterson register me for a one-day course given by the B.C. Motorcycle Safety Association. It took place at a municipal airport and I learned the basics—shifting, braking and handling—by bombing down a disused runway on a small Honda. I figured I'd learn the rest as I went. (And never told Mongo about the Honda.)

Scott also made arrangements for me to visit the RCMP "barn" in Victoria that week, where a new license was made up in my name, one that had a motorcycle permit added to it. I was almost ready to go.

The last thing to do was to move the Coachmen trailer stateside. Liz's stepfather and a buddy of his from the fishing club took care of that, driving it to a trailer park off Highway 5 between Blaine and Ferndale. Frank wasn't fully up to speed on exactly what I was doing, but he began to figure things out when Andy Smith greeted him at the border crossing and just waved him right through, the customs officers deferring to his DEA badge. It must have been reassuring to see that I was working with the good guys.

For the time being, Liz and Charlotte would move in with her mother and stepfather. I stayed with them for most of the first month and didn't use the trailer across the border more than three or four nights a week. I knew the guaranteed way *not* to get in with a criminal group was to be pushy. If I was always around, they'd start wondering what my game was and question my motives. The best approach was to let them invite me into their world. So I had to get noticed without getting in their faces.

Andy and Co. had told me that the local Bellingham Bandidos chapter held their weekly "church" meetings every Tuesday evening, after which they would repair to the Pioneer Tavern in Ferndale for a round or ten. As far as the cops knew, that was the only routine that, as a group, the Bandidos kept to.

So, at dusk one late summer Monday, I went to the Pioneer to familiarize myself with the bar's layout and say hello. I had brought over my new car, a souped-up Firebird, in an attempt to even the scales on the mechanical end. Bright purple with a red air breather on the hood (a hood, by the way, that was held down by padlocks), it was not a car meant to be subtle. Completing the muscle-car look were rear air shocks, wide tires made for pulling out in a squeal of burned rubber, and a chromed chain steering wheel. When the car idled, it vibrated and sounded like a snarling beast waiting to pounce—that is, if the deafening sound system wasn't drowning out the engine noise.

Driving the Firebird into Ferndale, I felt like a Texas Ranger riding into town to take on the bad guy. Before pulling into the Pioneer's lot, I did a little prowl and growl around town. It was sleepy quiet. The Pioneer wasn't much more happening, which was fine by me. I ordered a Pepsi and hung out for a while, playing pool by myself until another customer came in and challenged me to a game. He was a huge man named Chuck who in due course told me that he owned the local bike repair shop. It was a good start—I figured there was no way he could operate such a business without being on good terms with the main bikers in town. I didn't tell him anything about myself, in such a way that he could only suspect I did something shady.

"So, what's it you do?" he asked at one point.

"The first thing I do is I mind my own business," I said definitively. Then, having slammed a door on him, I opened a window, saying something friendly such as "Nice shot," or "Hey man, it's your turn."

Gradually people started to drift in. Every Monday at the Pioneer they held what they called a Turkey Shoot—a small pool tournament. Chuck's regular partner didn't show, so he and I teamed up. We did okay but eventually were knocked out, at which point I called it a night.

The next evening I was back not long after eight, again drinking Pepsi and playing pool by myself. Toward nine or nine-thirty the Bandidos started to drift in in small groups. By ten o'clock there were almost a dozen members in the bar and me in the back by myself. It was suddenly a very lonely place to be.

When Chuck came in, I was relieved to see him. He said hi to most of the Bandidos but wasn't invited to sit with them. Instead, he came and shot some more pool with me. I made a mental note of his status, or lack thereof.

I half expected one of the bikers to come up and challenge me, sneering, "Who the fuck are you?" So I made myself extra small and even avoided going to the bathroom. That would not be a good place to have to explain what I, a stranger, was doing on their turf. But they seemed to have decided on a wait-and-see approach. If they were really wondering who I was, they could always question Chuck later. They might also have noticed the Canadian plates on the Firebird, which may have made them more cautious; their relationship with Canadian bikers and crooks was their financial lifeline. Still, it didn't make them any friendlier that first evening. If looks could kill, I would have died several times over.

I didn't push my luck and slipped out before any of them got too drunk and decided to have some fun at the stranger's expense. At least

I'd got on their radar. Certainly, Andy was thrilled that I had been in the same place with so many of them and been able to walk out—even though it meant he had lost a friendly bet with one of the other cops that I wouldn't make it through the night.

Over that first month, I'd go to the bar two, maybe three nights a week, and always on the Tuesday. Still, I didn't exchange a single word with any of the Bandidos. I just played pool with Chuck or whoever and played it cool, chatting with the staff and the regulars, sipping my Pepsi in the back. The gang sat around a few tables in the front, ignoring me in their disdainful way.

I also took to visiting Chuck at his bike shop during the day and shooting the shit with him and whoever else was around. Often these were guys who had cordial relations with the Bandidos, so I knew that getting in good with them could help me penetrate the gang. On a couple of occasions I'd invite them back to my trailer for a beer or whatever. Increasingly I would make allusions to my work, which I let on to be smuggling and border running. "I was sneaking across the border a few days ago when this-or-that happened," I would say. But going any further would have been silly—admitting, for instance, that I was moving drugs across in the trunk of my car or illegal immigrants across by foot; no self-respecting crook would have copped to that.

Still, after a month or so I hadn't made any real progress and something had to give. Especially since my regular absences from Ferndale had started to become an issue with Corky. Theoretically, he and all the other cops could appreciate that it would only hurt the infiltration if I was around the whole time. I wouldn't have any mystery, I wouldn't be away on my nebulous business. Still, Corky was a nine-to-fiver and some part of him deep down must have wanted me to be one too, especially since I was getting a salary that likely eclipsed his.

"We've noticed how many times you've crossed the border and how long you stay," he said at one of our meetings. "This isn't a part-time job, you know."

"I can go home right now for good if you want," I shot back at him. I wanted to force him to shut the fuck up. I was all they had, and even if by that point my work still hadn't produced any useful evidence, I knew they were in no position to flush the probe.

In general, though, my relations with my handlers, Corky included, were solid right from the start. One reason: we were all Vietnam vets.

Andy Smith had been a captain in the Army Rangers, doing special operations that included ambushes and recovering POWs held by the Viet Cong. In fact, he occupied a notable place in the history of the war: he was one of the last eleven people helicoptered off the roof of the U.S. embassy in the early morning of April 30, 1975, during the fall of Saigon. He had a crushed hand to prove it—it had been slammed in a heavy door leading to the roof. Andy was an aggressive, get-it-done type of guy, the kind that moves ahead like a freight train. He'd recently been transferred from New York and his attitude wasn't always appreciated by the more laid-back northwesterners, but it suited me fine.

Corky Cochrane, meanwhile, had been an Air Cavalry chopper pilot flying ammo in and body bags out. It had left him permanently wound up, borderline shell-shocked even. Once or twice I took cruel pleasure in sending him back into his past. On one occasion, after he'd left the office for coffee, I hid behind the door. When he came back in, I yelled: "Incoming!" He threw his coffee in the air and dove under the desk. I thought I'd split a gut.

For his part, Larry Brant was the quintessential administrator and go-between. He was so perfectly turned out in both manners and appearance that you knew he had been an officer and had stayed in the rear with the gear. Still, Larry had his place: he was our bridge between the street and head office, and a very good one.

Soon enough, however, I'd learn that not all vets were on the side of the good guys. I'd also find out that having smelled the same smoke could make for a strong bond with even the nastiest of people.

The thirty-day evaluation period was drawing to a close and I was still not much further along in penetrating the Bandidos than I'd been after that first Tuesday night. The terms of my employment were pretty loosey-goosey, little more than an understanding that after a month we would meet to assess the operation and take it from there. I still fully expected to be heading off to Bangkok to join Gary Kilgore and could have left the Bandidos behind in a heartbeat with no worries financially. Still, there was a certain professional pride involved. I wanted to impress the Americans and it was weighing on me that I hadn't yet.

So, late one afternoon, sitting around at the Pioneer with Chuck, I made my move and asked him what the gang thought of me. He replied that the jury was still out.

"Some really don't care one way or another. Others think you might be a cop."

I exploded. "Me? A cop? Who the fuck is saying that?"

Chuck was taken aback. He said it wasn't him, that the idea hadn't even crossed his mind and he hadn't doubted me for a second.

I kept up the theater, demanding to know where I could find the members of the gang that instant.

Chuck said that some of the guys were at his shop. In fact, that was why he was at the bar—they'd told him to make himself scarce while they used his facilities to work on their bikes.

I jumped into the Firebird, peeled out and drove the block and a half to the shop in a matter of seconds. Chuck's shop was divided in two: in front was the retail section, at the back a garage. I screeched around back and into the open garage door, squealing my tires to a halt. Three Bandidos were standing around talking. To say they were surprised would be an understatement. I jumped out and walked up to them.

"Chuck told me you guys think I'm a fucking rat, or even a pig!"

They just looked at me as if I was totally nuts. Getting no response, I continued my rant.

"Where I come from, that's done face to face!"

The same confrontational technique had worked well for me in Hong Kong. But for the act to work, you need a response from the bad guys that you can work with. In this case they just weren't saying anything. Finally, though, one of the guys, who I later learned was Vinny Mann, the chapter president, took a few menacing steps in my direction. Well over six feet tall and solid, with a scraggly beard and unkempt hair, he pointed a finger at me.

"If I thought you were a pig, you would be dead already laying in a ditch," he growled in his gravelly way.

Even if it didn't provide much of a way out, it was at least a response. I jumped at it.

"That's what I heard about you guys—you were solid and didn't play around. That's why I was so surprised when Chuck told me that."

That led to more silence. I knew I was talking too much, but they weren't helping. I relaxed my pose and added, "You can't blame me for overreacting—in my business reputation is everything!"

Vinny muttered under his breath that Chuck talked too fucking much. Then he threw me a lifeline. "It takes balls to do what you just did. I would have done the same thing." Another pause before he continued. "By the way, I *am* checking you out. In the meantime, be cool."

A biker I would later know as Karate Bob—he had a couple inches on Vinny and a foot on me—added menacingly, "Who knows, you may still end up in the ditch."

"It's a hazard of the trade," I said, getting a laugh out of them. Or at least a smirk. Then I went to my car, without a glance in their direction, pulled out—slowly this time—and went home.

Even if I had just scored a few points, I was extremely happy to be out of there. I couldn't help but notice that my hands were shaking.

Back at the trailer, I wrote up my notes about the encounter and later left them in the night drop box behind the DEA building in Blaine. It was the routine procedure we'd agreed to when I'd signed on and wasn't considered too much of a security risk in those more reckless days.

But the response I got from the handlers the next day wasn't standard at all. Everyone had read my report by the time we got together for a meeting, and their reactions were all over the map. Corky was pissed, convinced that I had needlessly jeopardized the case with the confrontation. In my defense I argued that once Chuck had opened his mouth he had taken away my options—I had to act like a bad guy would act. Anything else would have been wimpy, I said. Andy, on the other hand, thought it was not only hilarious but likely

the breakthrough we needed. It was in his rough-and-tumble character to appreciate that sort of rashness.

"I would give anything to have seen the look on their faces," he
kept saying, laughing.

The confrontation did end up being an icebreaker. The next
time I went to the Pioneer, I got a little conversation from Vinny. Once
he acknowledged me, the others followed suit.

I inadvertently scored a second major coup with Vinny not long
afterward. One night we were at the bar as closing time approached
and he told me that I had to give him a ride home. His wife had his
truck and their house wasn't far from the trailer park where I was living. There was a Marty Robbins tape in the Firebird's deck and the
song that came on as we drove away from the Pioneer was "Ballad of
the Alamo." It was a favorite of mine. The story of fewer than two
hundred men holding off a force more than twenty times as strong
was a special inspiration to me. I knew most every detail about it.
What I didn't know at the time was that the Alamo was a very, *very*
special inspiration to the Bandidos. Vinny was surprised to hear the
song but said nothing. I sang along and then went on about how, if the
Alamo happened today, we would be those guys, standing tall until
the end, whatever the odds.

I laid it on thick and Vinny's reaction was hard to read. He just
looked at me in a perplexed but not hostile way. I suppose he was trying to figure me out. The song couldn't be a setup because there was
no way I could have known he would be in the car. He never said a
word about it that I knew of, and when we arrived at his place he just
got out of the car and closed the door, barely mumbling a thank you.
But the story got around, as I would learn two years later in Sturgis,
South Dakota.

The first thirty days were up and there had been no word on the Thailand gig, so we all decided to give the Bandidos job another thirty days.
I was getting into my role and the agency was starting to get a view of
the local chapter they didn't have before. They gave me a $500-per-
month raise and upgraded my Norton, which I'd been riding around
more and more, to a Sportster, the smallest of the Harley family.

Shortly thereafter, I went home for a week of R & R. While in Vancouver, Scott phoned and congratulated me on how things were going. He also gave me an inside perspective on the conversations inside the DEA. It seemed an FBI agent, not Corky, thought the whole case was futile and was convinced there was no way I could get in. This second thirty-day stab had to produce, beyond any doubt, a sense of advancement and actual progress. It was time to approach one of the Bandidos for a business venture.

I picked Karate Bob—I'd learned that he was a state heavyweight champion—thinking that our common interest in martial arts would make us natural partners. Back in Ferndale, I waited until I saw him alone in the bar and made my move. Sitting down, I laid out a plan whereby I would bankroll him to open a high-end martial arts club in nearby Bellingham for which he would be the public face, while I would handle the business end. Without putting any money down, he could have the use of a top-notch facility and make a good chunk of cash from lessons and the like. Money wasn't really an issue for me, I let on; I was interested in the club primarily as a money-laundering vehicle.

Karate Bob heard me out, but to my surprise he didn't bite. He turned out to be a purist and felt martial arts should not be a for-profit business. I was taken aback and, to tell the truth, felt shamed. In some ways it was a setback, insofar as I had lost respect in the eyes of a prominent member. Still, it opened Bob up to further conversation.

My next target was a Bandido named George Sherman, known to all as Gunk. The name suited him well—he was a grease monkey, although he hadn't found any steady work as a mechanic since leaving Florida and coming to Washington a few years previously. He and I had become friendly over a pinball game in the Pioneer called the Black Knight, to which he was addicted. He told me that he was living at the home of another Bandido, Jersey Jerry, but hoping to get his own place once he got some cash.

One evening at the Pioneer I took him aside and asked if he wanted to make a little quick money. He was all ears. I explained that I had a deal happening and I wanted to make sure everything went right. If he would accompany me as protection, I would give him two hundred dollars. He agreed in a second.

A few days later, he and I were in my car in a rest area off Highway 5 between Ferndale and Blaine. I had arranged for an unmarked DEA car to arrive from one direction and an unmarked RCMP car from the other. They showed up right on cue, and a woman got out of the Canadian car and into the DEA vehicle.

I had told Gunk that if she was in there for more than two minutes, it would mean we had a problem and would have to pull her out of the car. He would be paid more if that happened, I'd added. Gunk took the prospect of extracting the woman very seriously, pulling a gun from inside his coat and looking very tense. "Holy fuck, this guy is whacked out," I thought.

It was a very long two minutes and the Mountie used almost all of it. With five seconds remaining, the DEA car's door opened and she stepped out. She walked to her car and pulled out a large package that she then placed in the American's trunk. Both cars pulled out and were gone. It was the easiest two hundred bucks Gunk had ever made and I knew he would soon want more.

It didn't take long for Gunk to come to me with a business proposal of his own. Chuck was closing his bike shop, ostensibly for lack of business. In fact, the gang had decided they wanted complete control over it, so had boycotted it and also warned other bike owners in the area not to patronize the place. Eventually, Chuck just read the writing on the wall, locked the door and left town. Enter Gunk. He had been telling his fellow Bandidos about the job he did with me and saying that I was a big-time crook. So Jerry suggested to Gunk that he hit me up to finance the shop. He did, and I agreed.

It cost the DEA five grand, but it was money well spent. Within a week the store was filling up with stolen parts and Gunk had his own garage and all the work he could handle as a mechanic. The gang's business strategy was at times almost comical: Gunk would hire punks to steal parts off bikes in the area, parts he would then sell over the counter back to their rightful owners.

I played the silent partner and stayed at arm's length. Soon enough, other members started to hover around me, vultures around a cash cow. This led to closer socializing, and before too long gang members began inviting me on small runs—group rides to predetermined locations. These were mostly local affairs—barbecues, parties, bar crawls—but it was clearly a big step into the gang's good graces. Not more than two or three people at a time were invited to join the gang on these runs, and they were usually guys the gang was thinking of recruiting.

More often than not, the other potential recruits would fall out of favor after pissing off a member of the gang somehow or other, usually over a ridiculously minor infraction. For instance, one guy wore a helmet while riding his bike. After a lot of drinking at a campsite we had ridden to, Dr. Jack, a Bandido so named because he worked as a blood separator in a medical lab and was relatively refined and intelligent, asked the poor sap to pass him the helmet. When he handed it over, Jack promptly puked in it. Then he passed it back to the guy with the instruction, "Put it on now if you like your helmet so much."

The guy laughed awkwardly, thinking, praying, that Jack was joking. He wasn't.

"Put it on," Jack repeated. "Now!"

The guy eventually did. And never came on another ride.

One of my most valuable skills on runs and at other gatherings was being able to anticipate when the festivities might turn ugly so that I could slip away unnoticed. Early on I learned that when Vinny began to dance in the campfire with a gun in one hand and a bottle of peach schnapps in the other, it was time to find a hole to hide in. Members weren't allowed to hit other members, and that meant non-members often ended up as punching bags. Since I had no status, I figured "out of sight, out of mind" was the best approach, and it worked.

Not being a drinker helped keep me alert to changes in the atmosphere. It also allowed me to do a lot of observing, even if from a distance. I was especially interested in the treatment of "prospects"— the recruits going through an extended hazing period to see if they had the stuff for full membership—not so much because I was hoping to become one but because they were often my best source of information. Still, once I started getting invited on rides, becoming a prospect myself became an enticing possibility. It wasn't something Andy, Corky and Co. had really dared hope for when I was first hired; just becoming a friend of the gang was a tall-enough order already. But when my being invited to prospect for the club became a realistic consideration, my handlers were seized by the idea.

This occurred about two and a half or three months into the investigation, in the fall of 1981. Thailand, Scott said, was still hung up in paperwork. Meanwhile, Andy was telling me our investigation in Ferndale needed a longer commitment from me to get the funding we required to continue. So, I signed on with the DEA for another three months. In retrospect, I think the funding excuse was a ruse to force my hand and make me forget about Thailand.

Truth be told, even if I'd been given the option of packing my bags and heading off to Bangkok at that point, it would have been hard to do. The more I got to know the Bandidos, the more fascinated I became with them and, by extension, the case. Like me—and like Andy, Corky and Larry—they had almost all served in Vietnam. In fact, like the Hells Angels, their rivals (and occasional business partners), the Bandidos had been formed by disenchanted, recently discharged vets. But whereas the Hells Angels came out of WWII and got started in California, the Bandidos were conceived in the disaster of Vietnam and born on the docks of San Leon, Texas. In this way, I discovered, I had just as much of a bond with most of the Bandidos as I did with the cops. More, in fact, if you took into account my delinquent youth.

All that said, I didn't know if I could put up with the treatment meted out to prospects. It was not only demanding and humiliating—whether it was standing watch all night at clubs and parties, or fetching beers for full-patch members—but also downright dangerous. So I began to study which members to avoid and which ones to stay close to. There was hope: Ronnie Hodge, the Bandidos' national president, had recently ordered all chapters to minimize the brutality on prospects, saying it was deterring a lot of good people from joining. Still, many old-timers saw the old approach as the only way to test the mettle of a man. Nonetheless, beatings were generally kept at a level of punches, no boots allowed. Jobs such as cleaning members' basements and running errands for them had increasingly become the order of the day.

As I drew closer to the gang, I drifted further from my life in Vancouver. My trips became less frequent; rather than visiting a couple of times a week, I would go once every couple of weeks. I didn't have the time, I told Liz—but that was only partly true. A more important reason was that I found going from one life to another just too difficult to keep track of. With the Bandidos, even the slightest slip-up could cost me my life.

Liz wasn't the type to complain or nag, but it was obvious she wasn't very happy with my lengthier absences. Around the time the investigation had got under way, we'd found out she was pregnant again, which only made matters worse. And just before Christmas 1981, when the Mounties finally scrapped any remaining idea of sending me to Thailand—I was obviously no longer available—the strain on our relationship became that much greater. Even if she'd never been keen on moving to Bangkok—and despite the fact that Ferndale was a hell of a lot closer to Vancouver than Thailand—she thought I should have taken the job with the Mounties. Bikers scared her.

Still, we talked on the phone most nights, especially after the DEA moved me from the trailer into a house in Blaine. The house was quite literally a stone's throw from the border, right next to Peace Arch Park—perfect, almost too perfect, for an ostensible smuggler. Liz also appreciated the fact that, if nothing else, I had become a very steady supply of money. The DEA paid me in cash—big piles of cash, about US$4,000 per month—and all my expenses were covered, so I didn't have much use for the money. That meant it all went to Liz. At one point we figured out that the money we were making on the exchange rate alone was enough to cover our household bills.

Once I began going on rides with the gang and socializing with them more closely, the door to actually building a case against them opened up: I started buying drugs from them. Not much in terms of either volume or frequency, at least not to begin with. Rather, a small purchase one day, then, a couple of months later perhaps, another from a different member.

The first Bandido I bought from was Craig, a longtime but low-profile member who worked unloading fishing boats at Blaine's small port. He was always at the Pioneer and was always selling—not small quantities, but not big either, anything from an eighth to a full ounce of coke. He barely bothered to hide it, which was my main reason for picking him. Seeing him at the bar one day, I approached as if I'd been hunting high and low for him.

"Hey, I've been looking for you," I said. "I need an eight ball. Or how much would it be for a quarter?"

My strategy was not to ask him if he would sell to me but rather how much he would sell, thereby making it that much harder for him to say no. Not that "no" even seemed a consideration for him. He simply reached into his pocket, pulled out a quarter ounce and said "Four-fifty" or some figure like that.

A month or two later, I walked into another biker bar in Blaine and saw Bobby Lund, a member of the Bremerton Bandidos, along with a few of the Bellingham gang members. Even if he belonged to the other Washington State chapter, he seemed to like our company more and spent most of his time in the Ferndale area. He was known as a dealer of relatively small quantities. I cornered him and asked, "Is Craig with you guys?"

I already knew the answer: no.

"Have you seen him?" I asked.

Again, no.

"I'm looking for him because I need to pick up," I continued. "Can you do it?"

I ended up buying half an ounce from him then and there.

The next Bandido I bought from was Terry Jones—the only member of the Bellingham chapter to actually reside in Bellingham. The rest lived in Ferndale, Blaine, the tiny town of Custer, halfway between the two, or scattered around the countryside of Whatcom County.

Early one summer evening, I dropped by Terry's house. After a bit of small talk and some playing with his sweet-tempered pit bull, Binky, I said, "I dropped by to see if you had anything."

He didn't blink. By then I was quite sure he was beyond having any suspicions about me. I had been moving very slowly and in a deliberately aloof manner. Had I been full of questions and always trying to buy drugs from any and all, it would have been a dead giveaway. But I kept my business to myself and avoided anything that might have been construed as nosiness. So Terry just asked, "How much were you looking for?" It led to my buying an ounce of coke.

Over the summer I bought again from Craig, Bobby and Terry, each time while wearing a wire. The police always wanted at least two buys in case one was ruled legally inadmissible on some technicality and, more importantly, to prove that the target sold drugs repeatedly and as a business, not just to help out a friend who wanted to score.

I also continued to get closer to the gang, in my non-ingratiating, non-pushy way. I'd go on most of the smaller, local runs but wasn't invited on the mandatory, Bandidos-organized runs—the Four Corners Run, any of the regular summer trips to Texas or to visit other club chapters; they were for members and prospects only. Many I wasn't even aware of: the guys would simply tell me, "We'll be out of town for the next week or so."

That would give me a chance to go back up north and visit Liz and the kids—my son had been born at the end of March. I hadn't been around for the birth; Liz wasn't able to get word to me when she went into labor. Instead, Frank had had to come to Blaine and get me.

"Come on, Twinkletoes—time to dance," he said, and off we headed to the hospital in North Vancouver, where Liz was recovering.

I did go on one major run that summer, to Sturgis, South Dakota. It's an annual gathering that attracts tens of thousands of bikers—all the major gangs but also any number of independents, including such groups as Bikers for Christ and the Blue Knights, which is made up exclusively of active and retired cops. I rode with different packs of Bandidos all the way but wasn't invited to stay with them at the gang's exclusive—and isolated—campground. Which was fine by me, even if it would have pleased my handlers no end. Hanging out with the Bellingham and Bremerton Bandidos was one thing—they all knew me and generally thought well of me. But to be patchless, not even a prospect, amid hundreds of hard-partying, unpredictable, possibly psychopathic outlaw bikers was a risk I wasn't about to take.

Even if I wasn't staying in the Bandidos campground, thus reducing the likelihood of any useful intelligence coming out of the ride, it didn't stop Andy, Corky and three or four other backroom cops from coming along for the fun. Cops are always happy to take a free trip.

As summer progressed, it was clear to everyone in the gang that I was edging toward prospect status, though never, ever was it explicitly acknowledged. I never brought it up—that would have undermined my chances almost as quickly as pulling out a police badge or admitting a fondness for young boys. If you were cool enough to be a Bandido, you had to be cool enough not to be in a hurry, and certainly not whine or nag.

I did, however, begin to cultivate the members whom I recognized as being the most influential. A prospect has to be unanimously approved by all the full members of a chapter, so theoretically everyone has an equal say. But as in any organization, some swing more lead than others, and these were the guys I worked, very discreetly, at winning over.

Vinny Mann was the chapter president and obviously someone I needed in my corner, but I wasn't too worried about him. On the one hand, I felt he was already on my side; on the other, I didn't see him as the real power in the club. Officially, he was outranked by Jersey Jerry—John Jerome Francis—the northwestern regional officer and the national secretary-treasurer. But Jerry was aloof to the proceedings of the local chapter, more interested in the bigger national picture and his own various business interests, which included a video store, the Village Vidiot, and moving some pretty substantial quantities of cocaine and speed.

The real leader of the chapter—and the man I worked most to curry favor with that summer—was George Wegers. He was the vice-president and a force to be reckoned with. Boisterous, outgoing, opinionated, extremely intelligent and very funny, George also had a very serious dark side that could transform him in an instant from a laughing, charming companion to a raging animal. This made him the most unpredictable and violent member of the chapter—and one who generally got his way.

Another reason I needed him behind me was that his best friend and business partner in the club was Mongo (Pete Price), and it became clear that summer that if there was one member of the Bellingham Bandidos who didn't like me much, it was him.

Initially, Mongo had been reasonably friendly, chatting with me at the bar and such. But from one day to the next he stopped saying hello and began shooting dirty looks at me, when he acknowledged my existence at all. The change was dramatic enough that eventually, while hanging around the bike shop, I asked Gunk what Mongo's issue was. "It's as if I pissed in his cornflakes," I said.

"The man had a dream," Gunk said. "He dreamed that you have come to destroy the club. Like you're a curse on us."

I was immediately alarmed. "What, he thinks I'm a cop?"

"No. He just thinks you're here to destroy the club. Stay out of his way and he'll get over it."

Gunk's nonchalance was reassuring—it suggested Mongo had had these kinds of dreams before and no one had ended up in a shallow grave as a result. But I would definitely follow Gunk's advice; I didn't have a problem with staying out of Mongo's way. The Bellingham chapter was known as the Chapter of Giants because of the size of its members, and none was as big as Mongo. He was 350 pounds if he was an ounce, and at least six-four. Top him off with a huge mane of matted flaming orange hair and he made for an imposing package.

No Bellingham Bandido was half as quirky as Mongo, either. In many ways he was almost cuddly and teddy-bear-like, and few members were as loyal. He was also the most philosophical Bandido I'd met, and the only one I knew to meditate. Few, if any, were as highly skilled—he worked in jet engine development at the Boeing plant in Seattle. At the same time, Mongo was intensely irrational. He hated non-whites in general and blacks and anyone in a mixed relationship in particular. He loved the color yellow, but in a proprietorial way—only on himself and his things. (His orange hair was actually the result of a botched dye job; it was intended to be bright yellow.) And he despised anyone riding a bike while wearing running shoes. It all made for an ugly scene when, on a run, we saw a black guy on a yellow Honda with a white girl on the back—and she was wearing sneakers. The couple were very lucky that there was a concrete median between them and Mongo—and that there were a half-dozen Bandidos holding him back.

Steering a wide berth around Mongo that summer, I cultivated George Wegers while also working on Dr. Jack—who was Jersey Jerry's partner and also a fun and sensible guy—and, of course, Gunk, whom I saw more than any other Bandido because of the shop.

It all seemed to be progressing reasonably well when, one evening around Labor Day, Vinny phoned me and ordered me over to his house. His tone of voice and curtness made it clear I had no say in the matter. The whole chapter, along with Bobby Lund and a few other members from Bremerton, were gathered there when I arrived about eight. No one said a word, and whatever misgivings I'd felt when Vinny called were only increasing. I was beginning to think that maybe I should have called Andy and Corky to tell them what was happening. Too late now.

I found myself standing in the middle of the living room wondering why I'd been beckoned. Then Vinny stood up.

"You remember that day when I told you I was checking you out?" he said gruffly.

"Yeah, I remember," I replied warily.

Karate Bob spoke up. "Remember I said you might still end up in the ditch."

"Yaaaaaaa . . ." I began to mentally gauge my distance to the door. Too far.

Then Vinny threw me a denim cut-off with a prospect patch on the back. "Put this on."

I did what I was told in record time. Everybody then stood up and gathered around to congratulate me. Everybody, that is, but Mongo. He just stayed on the couch and moped. As per instructions from Gunk, I stayed away from him. During the next few hours of partying, most of the other guys came around and gave me encouragement and advice for the year I could expect to remain a prospect.

"I'm going to be real hard on you, but if you come through it, you'll be stronger for it," George told me.

Terry Jones came over to me. He gave me a P-38—a small Marine Corps–issue can opener about an inch and a half long with a folding sharp edge and a small hole for a key ring. Every prospect got one. He said I would have to learn how to use it; not being the sharpest knife in the drawer, Terry hadn't figured out that I'd been in Vietnam and would know how to use it already. I didn't say anything. Terry took me to the kitchen and grabbed a can of peas. Within seconds he had it opened. I feigned concentrated interest. You could earn more respect being a fast learner than by boasting that you already knew something. Afterward he gave me a can and I opened it, saying, "Like this?" and "Is this right?" Terry was proud and slapped me on the back. "You'll do all right!"

When I rejoined the crowd, it was Dr. Jack's turn. He gave me my Maglite flashlight. Every Bandido wore one on his belt. They were useful if your bike broke down on the side of the road at night and you couldn't see to fix it. Not that that was likely to happen. Their real purpose was as an intimidating club. All the Bellingham members had the long and heavy D-cell battery version. Dr. Jack gave me a smaller, four-battery C-cell flashlight, which better fit my grip and size.

Then Vinny gave me a leather belt insert to slide my flashlight into. On it were the letters BFFB: *Bandidos Forever—Forever Bandidos*. When I put it on and slipped the Maglite in, it felt like a gun belt. It felt good.

That night was not one of orders or menial tasks, it was a welcoming event. The other shit would start soon enough.

The morning after I was given my prospect patch, I called Andy Smith at nine o'clock sharp.

"I have to see you, and see you right now!" I said to him.

He asked me what was wrong, his voice almost panicky.

"Nothing!" I snapped. "But I have to see you now!"

He told me to come on over. The DEA offices were maybe a hundred yards away from my house beside Peace Arch Park. I walked down the alley sporting my new patch and knocked at the back door. The secretary let me in.

"They're in Larry's office," she said.

I walked in and their jaws dropped as soon as they took in the small prospect patch above the left pocket of my leather vest (or cut, as it was called). I then turned around to shut the office door, in the process showing off the larger patch on my back. It was the first time I'd ever seen Andy speechless. Together with Larry and Corky, he just sat there for a few seconds, stunned. Then all hell broke loose. I spent two hours in the office that morning as we talked about everything my patch would allow us to do.

During that time, Andy had got on the phone and sent the word out to the regional DEA office in Seattle as well as Washington. My acceptance as a prospect was a major deal. For the cops, it was the sign of real, tangible progress that was needed to finally open the vault. Money for the operation would never be a problem again.

Once a prospect, I began buying anything from anyone in and around the gang. Besides drugs—coke and meth, as pot and hash weren't worth the hassle—I bought guns, stolen vehicles and even expensive furniture that had been stolen from an immigration officer's house. My contacts in Canada were insatiable, I let on.

I went into overdrive after playing it so cautiously for so long because the team felt that the investigation could now be derailed that much more easily. Being a "hanger-on," an "associate," a "friend" or whatever I was exactly before being made a prospect meant that I could keep a certain distance. I saw the Bandidos when I wanted, for as long as I wanted. As a prospect, I was at their beck and call, and my presence and services were compulsory at every gang gathering. It created that much more opportunity for me to be exposed, or simply to fall out of favor. And if I was bounced as a prospect from the club, I'd have to make myself scarce—there was no going back to my former status.

Since everything I bought went into the black hole of the police evidence warehouse (or up to Canada, as far as the bikers were concerned), I didn't present any competition to local dealers. That was an upside, especially since George Wegers controlled much of the local trade. At the same time, however, the fact that everything I bought disappeared (except, that is, for the fancy furniture—it was displayed prominently around my house) became a bit of a problem. It seemed unnatural, particularly to someone as hypersuspicious and cautious as George. My not being big on ostentation—no flashing of bulging wads of cash, no big spending on a harem of mistresses—despite my apparently thriving and profitable business, only fed any suspicions George may have had.

Dr. Jack conveyed these concerns to me through an idle conversation we had in his shed while he was fixing his bike. So, after consulting with Andy, we decided to use Jack and his partner Jersey Jerry in our plan to put George's mind at rest. I'd already made one coke buy from them and we were looking for a second. Unfortunately, Jack told me, they were dry. In fact, he added, he wouldn't mind buying a pound or so from me if I happened to find some.

I subsequently approached George and he reluctantly agreed to sell me the drugs I needed. We arranged a time for him to come over to my house. Andy followed George's car from the air in the company chopper as he took a roundabout route to my house. He even drove down a country road and just stopped, waiting to see if anybody was following him. Luckily, he never looked up. When he arrived, I bought the uncut pound for thirty thousand dollars. George honored me by not counting the money in my presence—a faux pas when dealing with a brother. The deal was done in minutes, and I told George I didn't want to be rude but I couldn't hang out with him. My customer was on his way over; George had to leave.

My customer arrived right on time, just a few minutes after George had departed. Or not. Surveillance told us that George didn't leave the area—he just parked at the other end of the alley and waited to see who came by. He must have been surprised when Dr. Jack pulled up to my house. I resold the pound to the doctor for $32,500. He was gone in ten minutes. In case word ever got to George, I wanted to show I had made a profit.

George saw the deal go down and, as he told me later, was very impressed both with my business acumen—buying from one member to sell to another was no problem for him or any other Bandido—and with my maneuvering. The drugs were in my house less than half an hour and I had turned a handsome profit. That started my business relationship with George. It took a long time for him to trust a person, but when he did, it was total trust. The deal also brought Dr. Jack closer to me. And it made a shelter for abused women in Bellingham happier as well: the team donated my $2,500 profit to it and put the receipt in our file.

Another incident that might have made the gang suspicious of me cost me my purple Firebird. One day Jersey Jerry was driving past the Ferndale police station when he saw an identical Firebird parked in the lot. Needless to say, mine was a unique-looking ride and Jerry had to wonder at the likelihood of seeing another just like it. His attitude toward me, I noticed, began to change. Other members in the gang, however, chilled him out. If I were an undercover cop, would I be so stupid as to park my car in full view of everyone in town? It was even more ironic given that the team had decided that the local cops, whether from Ferndale, Bellingham or Blaine, weren't trustworthy and couldn't know of our investigation.

When Gunk told me of the incident and Jersey Jerry's initial suspicions, he was laughing. "You know how we knew you weren't a cop?" he said, referring to discussions the club had had before making me a prospect.

"How?"

"Because if you were a cop, you would have been the worst fucking cop in history. You would have been fired by now."

Clearly, my strategy of not asking questions and minding my own business had worked. And to keep any further sightings of that car from reigniting potentially deadly suspicions, I had to say goodbye to my Firebird. Ferndale's not a big town, but I never did learn whose car that was.

Still, thanks to his dream, Mongo still wasn't convinced about me. Winning him over only occurred when we "tombstoned" an uppity Seattle gang.

The Resurrection was an independent club that was beginning to take up just a little too much space in the area. They'd been around for years, but in the early 1980s they made a few decisions that convinced the Washington State Bandidos that the Resurrection needed dealing with. One was their going from a one-piece patch—with logo, name and city on a single piece of fabric—to a three-piece patch. It sounds ridiculous, but in the arcane politics and symbolism of the biker world, this was a big deal. Three-piece patches—with a central logo, an upper "rocker" with the club's name and a lower rocker with their home city—were the domain of "one-percenter" gangs—that is, outlaw gangs. One-piece patches were for everybody else. One-percenters could happily coexist with non-one-percenters, but not with other outlaw gangs.

Another misstep was a simple result of their growth: the Resurrection were discussing a split into two chapters, one south Seattle, one north. This expansion just couldn't be stomached by the Bandidos.

Their final gaffe—the one that made Vinny say, "Something has to be done about the Resurrection, and now"—was an ill-advised show of disrespect and arrogance. Vinny had made overtures to the Resurrection about becoming a support club. They had not responded. It was time for a visit to make them understand that an enthusiastic answer was required, not to mention polite.

Early on a cold, damp November evening, about thirty Bandidos members and prospects hit the highway to Seattle, mostly in trucks and cars. Twenty members of the Ghost Riders, a support club from southeast Washington State, met us in north Seattle. They pulled the tail end of the procession. Even the president of a support club is lesser in status than a Bandidos prospect and must ride behind him. It was my first taste of power over other bikers.

The Resurrection clubhouse was in a garage-like building in the middle of an industrial park on Seattle's south side. It allowed them to party hard and keep their privacy. It also made them vulnerable. Vinny, who obviously had his spies in their midst, knew that it was their church night and that the subject on the table was the split into two chapters.

We arrived and lost no time. Mongo was our vanguard. He yanked up the garage door, which opened right into the middle of their clubhouse. The Resurrection members—there were at least as many of them as us—were spread around on couches and chairs or just sitting on the floor. They looked at Mongo, as the rest of us lined up behind him, in shock. Bandidos then filed in along both walls and along the back, surrounding them. Three Bremerton prospects and I stood in the open doorway with the Ghost Riders behind us and clearly visible. All the Bandidos pulled out guns and pointed them at the group. Most of the Resurrection guys were terrified. So was I. "Holy fuck," I thought, "they're going to kill them."

Terry Jones had given me a gun when we arrived, so there I was, gun drawn, sweating bullets. I still wonder what I would have done if a member of the Resurrection had made a move and the shooting had started. Standing there with a gun in my hand, I didn't feel like an imposter, an infiltrator or a police agent—I was a Bandido. A very nervous Bandido, but a Bandido all the same.

Vinny walked into the middle of the Resurrection. "I have a list here," he growled. "Everyone on that list sits down. So all of you stand up."

They did as they were told and Vinny started reading names. One by one, about fifteen members of the Resurrection sat down.

"Okay, that's it. The rest of you are to leave, right now. Leave your patch on the floor." The psych-out was masterful. Those told to leave must have thought they were survivors and were only too happy to get out of there. Except for one guy. He looked at Vinny and said, "Fuck you. You can have my patch, but I'm not leaving my bros." Vinny told him to sit down too.

After the rejects were gone, Vinny told the rest they had been chosen to be a prospect chapter of the Bandidos. If all went well, after a year, Seattle would have its own Bandidos chapter.

George Wegers, who hadn't said anything up to now, pointed to the guy who had refused to leave. "And you're the new president."

In a matter of one hour, the Resurrection motorcycle club had gone the way of the dodo. All the "colors"—the jackets and vests on which the Resurrection patches were sewn and which had been dumped on the floor by the departing members—were burned in a steel drum. All except two sets. One would be sent to Bandidos headquarters in Lubbock, Texas; the other would go to Vinny's house to be hung upside down on his wall. The chosen ones were given their Bandidos prospect patches and the Ghost Riders were sent home with thanks. The Bremerton Bandidos also soon departed. The Bellingham crew were the only invaders left. We stood around a bit awkwardly with the remains of the Resurrection, who didn't know whether to be grateful or hostile.

After a while, Vinny came up to me and said, "Hey, you were our only prospect here, and you did good."

"He's not my prospect," interjected Mongo.

Vinny saw this as a personal challenge. "He's the whole chapter's prospect, you got that?" He wasn't so much protecting me as asserting his own authority.

Mongo nodded grudgingly, like a kid who'd been chastised by his father. Still, it wasn't enough, and Vinny decided to deal with the issue once and for all.

"You guys go off and straighten this out and don't come back until you do."

Mongo looked at me and told me to follow him. I got in my truck—before getting rid of the Firebird, I'd bought a 1965 Ford Twin I-Beam pickup—and followed his bike to the back end of the industrial park. I was afraid that some of my cover team might be lurking around, but we didn't see anyone. Or maybe I was actually hoping they would be there. After all, this was a monster of a man with wild orange hair and beard and enough leather on him to dress several cows. The chain going from his belt to his wallet was a real chain, the type you use to lock up fences with. In the other corner—the "how the fuck do I get out of this?" corner—me: a 135-pound, five-foot-six runt.

We parked and Mongo told me that I had one chance to drive out of there and not come back. I told him I wasn't going away. If he wanted to rock 'n' roll, I might not win, but I would never back down. All he said was, "No guns, no knives."

I watched as Mongo took two guns and two knives from various hiding places. He also detached the chain. I just took off my coat and hung it on my mirror. Then he said, "Oh, I almost forgot," pulled up the leg of his jeans and took a small .22 from his boot. Even with Mongo disarmed, I knew I was in a very bad position. The only way I could win was to hurt him very badly, very quickly, and I hadn't figured out how to do that yet.

He looked at me. "You know I can tear you a new asshole," he said.

I said I knew that. Then I added, "It's a hazard of the trade." The line had worked at my first encounter with Vinny and Karate Bob, so why not use it again?

It hadn't lost its charm. Mongo's tone softened.

"Since we're probably spending the night here, we're not in any hurry," he said. "Let's go for a beer first and we can plan this out."

"Sounds good to me," I replied, with obvious relief.

Off we went to the nearest bar. Mongo had got over his dream, but he had a new concern. He thought I saw the Bandidos as nothing but organized crime instead of as a motorcycle club built on brotherhood. That caught me completely off guard. It was like the time Karate Bob refused my offer to bankroll the martial arts club for him. There was more to the Bandidos than just the criminality of some of its members, I was slowly learning. I sat and let Mongo teach and preach to me.

After a few hours we went back to the Resurrection's clubhouse. Some of the gang were sleeping, others were drinking, the remnants of the Resurrection fetching their beers for them. Vinny saw us arrive and looked very pleased with himself. Gunk was still my sponsor as a prospect, but from then on Mongo was my mentor in the gang.

The next day, Andy called me in. During my verbal debrief, I told him and Corky about what Mongo had said. The cops thought it was funny and put no store in it. Though I didn't say anything, I found myself taking Mongo's side. I was beginning to feel that underneath all the violence and leather there was a certain nobility to the bikers. In retrospect, that kind of thinking should have been a warning sign.

It wouldn't have been the only one. Andy also told me I needed to get in touch with my wife. Liz, I think, had phoned him to discuss what this investigation, especially now that I was a prospect, was doing to our family life. I hadn't talked to her in a week or had time to send any money home. And I hadn't visited in at least twice that long. My life in Vancouver seemed to be slipping away. It could have been seen as my work taking over my personal life; in fact, it was my new Bandidos family usurping my real one.

I was starting to rationalize my thinking, saying to myself things like, "She doesn't know what I'm going through." In truth, she didn't know mainly because I wouldn't share the job—its details or its stresses—with her. I now see how unfair and tough it must have been for Liz. Still, even though I made an effort to phone and send money more often, I pressed on with my work.

In early December, a few weeks after the Resurrection takeover, I was supposed to go home for a day or two. My thirty-fourth birthday was coming up and Liz had something planned. But toward noon I got a call from Vinny saying there was a party at his house that night and that I needed to show up. I considered making up an excuse but instead said, "I'll be there." I called Liz and disappointed her again, though she sounded as if she had been expecting it. Then I called Andy and told him about the party. He asked me if I expected any trouble. I said no, so he decided not to put cover on me; as a prospect, I might have to be there all night. I agreed with him.

When I arrived at Vinny's, I helped him set things up, moving furniture around to make room and that kind of thing. Then, just before nine o'clock, Vinny told me to go on a beer run. I jumped in his truck and went down to the local liquor store.

I pulled in just as its employees were pulling out: it had closed for the night. I had to return to Vinny's empty-handed. When I got there, most people had arrived.

"Where's the beer?" Vinny asked.

I explained that I'd got to the store too late. Vinny wasn't pleased. All conversation stopped.

"You don't deserve your prospect patch. Give me that cut," he said.

I was taken aback—I'd expected a reprimand, but not the loss of the patch. I took it off and handed it to him. Then George came out of the kitchen toward me, scowling. "Fuck, here we go," I thought. Things were going from bad to worse.

He said: "Since you're not wearing your patch, here, try this one on." He handed me a leather cut with a full patch on it.

I just stood there holding the patch, looking from one guy to another.

"Put the fucking thing on before we change our mind," Vinny shouted.

Everybody crowded around to congratulate and hug me. Even if I've always hated hugging, it felt great. Vinny asked me if I had anything to say.

"Prospecttttttt! Get me a fucking Pepsi," I bellowed at an aspiring member in the room. Everybody cracked up.

# CHAPTER FIVE

# My Colors Go National

———

As in most outlaw biker gangs, Bandidos prospects usually spend at least a year proving their stuff—and getting drinks for members—before they are considered for promotion. Exceptions are made only in the rarest of circumstances. I hadn't ever expected to be made a full member. At the rate I had been making buys and getting the goods on the Bellingham chapter, I figured the investigation would wrap up and the bust would come down before my year of prospecting was done.

I certainly never expected to be made a full member after only three months of prospecting. I think there are several reasons why I was fast-tracked. The first was that I wasn't a very good prospect to begin with. Not being a grease monkey, not knowing a carburetor from a car horn, I was of limited use to members looking for free mechanical work. I could shine chrome, but that was about it.

At the same time, some of the more influential members began to believe that my being a prospect was costing them money. One of my strategies for discreet ingratiation was to do deals with Vinny, George, Dr. Jack and Jersey Jerry that were slanted to their benefit, and on which they made a good profit. After one incident I realized that such deals could sometimes get me out of unpleasant prospect duties. Vinny called me to say he had a half pound of cocaine that he wanted to unload. Was I interested? I told him I'd love to help but I was scheduled to go clean another member's basement that day. How quickly do you think that job was canceled? But it went both ways. If a member wouldn't let me out of the brush clearing, yardwork or whatever other chore I was supposed to be doing, the guy looking to deal began to feel it was cutting into his sales.

Finally, and perhaps most importantly, I hadn't screwed up in my time as a gang associate or in my three months as a prospect, and had even won over Mongo. The boys liked the fact that I minded my own business but also was reasonably fun to be around. My being a teetotaler didn't bother them in the least.

The brevity of my time as a prospect, and the fact that the three months occurred at a time of year when runs and campouts were few and far between, meant I'd had it easy. That didn't diminish my sincere joy and sense of accomplishment when I received my patch. The best thing was the respect. I felt it from everyone that night. I was now an equal. I partied into the wee hours and then begged off to leave when I felt like it—another thing a full member can do that a prospect can't.

As I was putting my jacket on, Vinny brought out his babysitter. "Here's a birthday present for you. Bring her back in the morning."

The girl was just a kid, fourteen at most. But I knew I couldn't say no. So she got on the back of my bike and I headed for home. When we got there, I told her, "No offense, but I'm tired and going to bed." I threw a blanket and pillow on the front couch. "You sleep there."

Then, after hanging my vest over the back of the kitchen chair, I went to bed.

The next morning, Andy arrived at the office as usual at eight o'clock. My house had been wired to the rafters shortly after I moved in. There were bugs in all the rooms except the bedroom and bathroom, and two hidden cameras covering the kitchen, the living room and the dining room. Andy's morning routine was to grab a coffee and glance at the two monitors. He saw the girl sleeping on the couch and someone's colors—the club patch on a vest or jacket—on the back of the chair. "Ah, a guest," he thought, and phoned the house.

He was calling, as he did most mornings, to verify that everything was okay and to find out whether the tapes from the night before had anything of value on them. If they did, he would review them and set them aside; if not, he would simply press rewind and use the tape again. (It was a habit that got Andy in serious hot water in court. The defense brought up the fact that there may have been things of value on those tapes, and so his actions were tantamount to destroying evidence. It was a valid point.)

I answered the phone and Andy asked who the girl was.

"A friend of Vinny's," I said, in case she was listening.

He asked who else was there.

"No one," I said. "Just us."

"Then whose colors are those?"

"Oh, that old thing? It's just something I picked up last night."

Then I cut off the conversation, saying we'd talk later, and hung up. Knowing he was watching, I put the vest on and woke the girl up. I dropped her off at Vinny's and then went to the DEA office with the cut on. Wearing the colors was a thrill not unlike driving the flashiest car on the downtown strip on Saturday night, everybody looking at you and getting out of your way. That I was an infiltrator just made it that much more of a kick.

I always went in the back door of the DEA building. By the time I entered Andy's office, the boys had the camera ready to take photos to send to the brass. I also asked Andy to keep last night's tape to rebut any defense allegations of impropriety when it came to the babysitter.

It turned out not to be necessary. However, my treatment of the girl did win me an important ally. The next day, when I went to visit Vinny, his wife took me aside.

"Thanks," she said.

"For what?"

"For the girl and how you handled it."

"No problem," I said. "Just please don't let it get around."

From then on I had an influential friend inside Vinny's house, one who proved useful over the next few months, especially when I wanted information about our chapter's relationship with Bandidos' national leadership. Had I asked Vinny any direct questions, he'd have become immediately suspicious. His wife, on the other hand, was only too happy to chat about what she knew. And since most of the calls from national came through their house, she knew a lot.

Getting my patch not only raised my status among the Bandidos, it prompted the DEA to buy me a new bike. It was in part a reward, but there were practical considerations as well. My Sportster was fine for riding around town, but it was useless on long runs—its tiny gas tank had to be fueled up at least twice as often as the bigger Harleys. As a full member, there was no avoiding the longer runs, so a full-sized Harley was in order.

There was another, very practical, benefit to the ride I ended up buying, an FXRT: it came from Jersey Jerry. Buying his old bike brought me closer to him, and he, as national secretary-treasurer of the Bandidos and the Northwest regional officer, topped the DEA's hit list. In fact, like the FBI, the ATF, the RCMP and other forces, the DEA names investigation files after the case's highest-ranking target; in our case, it was Jersey Jerry. So, any way of cozying up to him was good.

The FXRT was a sweet, sweet bike. Jerry had only owned it for six months or so and let me have it for a song—$5,500. Five-speed, rubber-mounted engine with air shocks, it was a full dresser with fiberglass saddlebags and a windshield. I was thrilled even if it was much too big for me. I had to take all the air out of the shocks to lower it and then cut open the seat and remove half the foam just to allow my feet to touch the ground.

Those weren't my only modifications. One of my first highway rides was with George Wegers, taking the I-5 down to Seattle. On the way, we passed two Honda Interstates going north. They both waved to me. I was so upset that I signaled George to pull over and we talked about it. He knew a place in Bellingham that could fix my problem. We headed there immediately. At the garage, I traded the fiberglass bags for old leather ones. Then I held a steel bar in the muffler while George hammered it in, the bar going through all the sound baffles. I kept the windshield but cut it down. When we stepped back, it looked great. I turned it on and it roared at about a hundred decibels, barely legal. No Honda rider would ever wave at me again.

I didn't know why George had asked me to accompany him to Seattle, other than to provide backup. We eventually arrived at an old house on the south side. We parked in the alley and knocked at the back door. A woman answered and George asked if her old man was home.

"He's still sleeping," she said, clearly petrified.

George told her to sit in the kitchen and not say anything. She obeyed meekly. As he walked down the short hallway toward the bed-room, George picked up a golf club that was leaning against the wall. I followed, positioning myself in the hall where I could see George and still keep my eye on the woman in the kitchen. Without saying a word, George started whaling the guy with the club. One unpleasant way to wake up! It took only a few seconds before the late riser was a bloody, whimpering mess clutching his face.

He was able to stumble to his feet and made a break for the door, still in his underwear. I caught him in the chest with a solid kick and he fell back into the room. The woman became hysterical and started rocking back and forth. George leaned over him and screamed, "You have my money by tomorrow or we'll be back!"

When George turned to leave, I glanced at his face. It was con-torted with rage, looking just plain evil. I made a mental note never to be on the wrong side of that look unless I had a gun—a big one.

The storm passed just as quickly as it had come over him. As soon as we walked out of the house, George was all smiles. On the way back to Ferndale, we stopped at a rest area. After we'd dismounted, he came over to me and gave me a small diamond-shaped patch. It had *1%* on it.

It's a patch worn by most of the criminalized biker gangs, indi-cating they're the 1 percent of motorcyclists who give the fraternity a bad name. The origin of the patch dates back to the famous Hollister weekend in 1947, when bad-boy bikers first penetrated the collective consciousness of the United States thanks to lots of sensationalist me-dia coverage. Following it, a spokesman for the American Motorcycle Association said that 99 percent of bikers were responsible citizens and only 1 percent were barbarians. After that, the "one-percenter" designation was embraced as a badge of honor. Most gangs gave the one-percenter patch as a matter of course to all members once they'd successfully completed their prospecting period. Among the Bandi-dos, however, another member had to bestow it, and it indicated a special bond between the two men.

"Can you get someone to sew this on for you?" George asked.

As I spent more time with George and other senior Bandidos, things deteriorated between me and Gunk. He saw himself as my sponsor and it seemed to him that I was ignoring him. I was. We had at least three deals with him, more than enough for the convictions I was there to secure, and so I had moved on. But of course Gunk didn't know that, and he didn't like the fact that he wasn't making any more money off me. He saw my friendship with George as an ambitious attempt to elevate my standing in the gang. Again, he was right.

At the same time, George was a much more interesting and complex person to spend time with. Where Gunk spoke a lot but had nothing much to say, George could hold his own in a conversation about almost anything. Not only did he read the paper, he also read books, which was fairly remarkable among his peers. He wasn't educated, but he was intelligent, curious and ambitious. We'd spend many evenings sitting on the back porch of my house, looking down the alley and south toward California, discussing what we wanted to do with our lives. Even then he was fixed on becoming national and world president of the Bandidos—a goal he would achieve sixteen years later.

George had—and still has—a deeply ingrained hatred for the Hells Angels, the New York Yankees of the biker world. They're either loved or hated—there's nothing in between. But George didn't just hate them: he loathed them, he despised them, he abhorred them, he couldn't stand the thought of them. When the Satan's Slaves of White Rock, B.C.—the Bellingham Bandidos' close business partner in their smuggling activities—patched over to the Hells Angels, George refused to deal directly with any of them again. It hurt his bottom line, but he stood firm.

"Bunch of fucking pussies," he'd say whenever their name came up.

On other subjects, George was more reasonable. He could go on at length about astronomy, physics and U.S. history as well as whatever happened to be in the news. After my evening conversations with George, I would have to write my notes for Andy and the boys. Initially, I would include the substance of our discussions, at least a summary of what we had talked about. But it bothered me to hear the handlers sit around and joke about these conversations. They behaved like children secretly reading someone's diary and making lewd jokes about it. What Andy and Corky and Larry didn't understand was that those moments—those chats with George, or with the equally intelligent but more erudite Dr. Jack—were for me like a ceasefire. Like Christmas Day at the Somme during World War I, when the Canadian and German soldiers crossed into no-man's land to share holiday rations and cigarettes. After hearing the handlers on a couple of occasions mock the gang, their thoughts, feelings and ambitions as conveyed by my notes, I stopped including any details. I'd just write "general conversation" and leave it at that.

I was obviously getting too deep into my role, and actually becoming what I was only supposed to be playing at. Then something happened that brought me back into line.

In the spring or early summer of 1983, the Bremerton chapter hosted a week-long party. It was months in preparation by the Bremerton boys and something I awaited with a sense of excitement. The party would be my first exposure to Bandidos from elsewhere in the United States, especially those from Texas and Louisiana, who had a reputation for being the meanest, the most volatile, the plain baddest of the bunch. In their company, even your patch didn't guarantee your safety, as I was to find out.

The Bandidos rarely traveled in huge packs. They usually set a destination and split up either by chapter or into small crews under the direction of a road captain. On a run, a road captain outranks even a chapter president. His job is to plan routes and rest stops and to reserve motels or campground space.

The war wagon is also his responsibility. It's usually a van driven by two old ladies (not girlfriends, only patched old ladies), carrying all the guns, drugs, tents, tools and spare parts required on a ride. On longer runs, such as the one to Sturgis, there was also a pickup truck with a bike trailer, to carry any bikes that broke down and couldn't be fixed en route.

A road captain also had to deal with police and warn them beforehand that we would be passing through, either without stopping or to spend the night. This was especially important in states such as Texas and New Mexico, where police tended to overreact at the sight of a group of bikers. The system worked very well. In some towns, police actually blocked traffic at the main intersections and just waved us through. When the police did decide to stop us, it was the road captain's job to collect all the licenses and registrations to minimize direct contact between cops and bikers. Dr. Jack was our chapter's road captain. Like all road captains, he could be identified by the small patch above the left pocket of his cut.

Of the Bandidos to make their way north and west across the country for the Bremerton party, the first crew to arrive were the South Texas Nomads. Among outlaw biker gangs, whether it was the Bandidos, Outlaws, Hells Angels or Pagans, nomad chapters were an elite group of enforcers, both within and outside the club. Their relationship to the rest of the gang was not unlike that of special forces commandos to a regular army. So if the Texas Bandidos were the hard cases, the Texas Nomads were the toughest of the tough. Led by Hammer (Thomas Lloyd Gerry), the national president of all Bandidos Nomads, they numbered about twenty and exuded authority. Ordinary members were nervous even talking to them. To a man, they were known to be capable of killing, and they didn't play around. There was a saying back then: "If the Hammer comes down on you, it's over." To the Nomads, fear meant control, and forgiveness was an alien concept.

The South Texas Nomads headed straight to the designated campground for the run, a large property the Bremerton chapter owned across Puget Sound from Seattle. The biker equivalent of a cocktail reception awaited their arrival—and that of any other Bandidos who came in over the course of the day and evening. My job was to make sure there was enough booze and beer for the event. Not being a drinker, and not even knowing how many people to plan for, I had to guess how much I'd need. After Gunk, our secretary-treasurer, gave me money, I sent the prospects out to stock up. At the end of the first day, about a hundred Bandidos had arrived, well within my estimate. It made me a bit blasé when ordering the supplies for the second night of partying.

By the end of that day, over three hundred Bandidos had arrived and the party was in full swing. Until three in the morning, that is, when we ran out of booze. The party ended abruptly and I caught shit from some members for having let the taps go dry.

On the morning of day three, the president of the Bremerton chapter told me someone else was in charge of booze. Then he informed me that later that day I was to go before a Bandidos disciplinary board because of my miscalculation. It didn't really surprise me—I knew the Washington State Bandidos were very nervous about impressing their hard-ass guests. And I knew I'd fucked up. I had no idea what to expect exactly, but I knew to expect something.

That afternoon, in a corner of the property away from both the party and the double-wide trailer where the Bremerton chapter president lived, I found myself standing before a three-man Bandidos court: the president (whom I only ever knew as Pog), Jersey Jerry and, I think, Milo, one of Bremerton's charter members and one of the original Bandidos in Washington State. They sat on a small section of bleachers looking at me. Others gathered around.

The process was informal, beginning with a few simple questions everyone knew the answer to.

"You know why you're here?" asked Pog.

"Yes."

"When did you realize we were going to run out of booze?"

"As the evening progressed, I guess."

"You had no contingency plan?"

"No."

"You have anything to say for yourself?"

I could have pleaded teetotaler's ignorance of how much a person could drink in an evening, but I decided that was lame.

"No," I answered.

"Well then, you know we have to deal with that?"

"Yes."

At that point two guys came at me from behind—Gunk and Dean from Bremerton—and began beating on me with both fists and boots. I put my hands to my sides and stood for as long as I could, which wasn't too long. It was a "minor punchout" in the Bandidos scale of measurement, but still a good shit-kicking. Just no broken bones—those were for major punchouts. When I came to my senses, my cut was lying next to me with the bottom rocker cut off.

I was shocked when I looked at myself in the mirror that night. It looked as if I had been hit by a truck. One eye was totally shut and the blood from the punches covered my face. I cleaned up as best I could and stayed away from the bonfires. I thought everybody knew, but apparently the guests were never told. I was reluctant to call Andy and the boys. I didn't want to be pulled.

On day four, about a hundred of us went on a ride through the Cascades and down to Wenatchee. En route we dropped into a bar, Three-Fingered Jack's Saloon. As I walked across the porch toward the door, Hammer called me over. He was standing outside the door with Sir Spanky (Glen Alan Wilhelm), the national sergeant-at-arms. Spanky looked like Tom Berenger in *Platoon*. He always wore a three-point bandana on his head and just reeked of violence and mayhem. I never saw him smile. When he looked at you, it made your skin crawl. All in all, he was a bad motherfucker. Put him next to Hammer calling me over and it was less than reassuring.

"What happened to your bottom rocker?" Hammer asked.

"It's a long story," I said, not stopping.

"Then take the fucking time to tell me!"

I stopped and told him about being responsible for the booze shortage and the subsequent punishment. He just nodded and waved me into the bar, giving no indication whether he thought I deserved more pain or had got my due.

The next morning, the main camp broke up for the second phase of the partying. Groups would spread out and visit the local members' homes. That's where I scored my points.

Hammer and his girlfriend came to the house that afternoon with a group of Bandidos who were checking out Blaine and the Peace Arch Park, and they didn't leave for two nights. My place was cleaner than most and I had the immigration officer's nice leather furniture—I guess Hammer saw it as the best accommodation going. With Hammer there, my house soon filled up with a constant parade of guests, and I got to know as many influential out-of-state Bandidos as possible. I had two local patched old ladies working the stove and the barbecue, along with girlfriends of miscellaneous visiting Bandidos. There were steaks, hamburgers and hot dogs for everyone. And the fridge never got low on beer—I'd learned my lesson and filled the outside shed with dozens of cases.

That's when I met Sly Willie (William Boring), a seriously nasty member of the Lubbock chapter who later unwittingly helped the investigation expand into Texas. Willie was one of the first recognized cases of Agent Orange poisoning among Vietnam vets. He was dying, and from what I could tell it only made him meaner. I also made the acquaintance of a pair of brothers from Louisiana. They were swamp-raised Cajun boys by the name of Lejeune. The older brother, Henry, known as Coon-Ass, was a Nomad; the younger, stupider brother, David, was a member of the Shreveport chapter. When they came over the first time, I recognized their accents and spoke to them in French. They were blown away.

Six months or a year later, Coon-Ass became famous in the club for beating himself silly. At a club gathering in Lubbock, he'd been admiring the new gun of his chapter president and managed to fire off a round that went through the president's foot. At the disciplinary board later that day or the next, he was asked whether he had anything to say before his inevitable punishment. "I'll take care of this myself," he replied, and began punching himself and smashing his head against walls, tables, anything available. He beat himself to a pulp in front of a couple dozen of us until two guys had to pull Coon-Ass off himself.

By the second-last day of the get-together, my house had unquestionably become *the* party spot. That evening Vinny and a bunch of the local guys showed up and immediately announced to all assembled that he had a declaration to make.

"Bandido Alex has shown a lot of brotherhood in the last few days," he declared. "We think he should get this back."

And he pulled out my bottom rocker. It had clearly been organized in advance—Vinny's wife had brought a needle and thread and within minutes she had sewn it back onto my cut. Gunk didn't bother to hide his displeasure, but that didn't make me any less happy. Later I learned that the idea had come from the Texas boys.

Influence and pressure from guys like Hammer was not something to ignore.

During the party week, I hadn't seen the handlers at all and had only talked on the phone to them briefly. They, however, had been keeping a close eye on the festivities—and me—thanks to the hidden cameras in the house and the assorted other wires. Andy had noted that I was bruised and battered and especially that my bottom rocker was gone. But he and the team reasoned that whatever had befallen me was in the past and that relations between me and the gang seemed again to be perfectly harmonious. What was important was that I was still alive and, judging from the members coming in and out of the house, seemed to be doing very well. Later, in court, the DEA would be criticized for not covering me properly at the party and for letting me go so long without contact. At the time I felt Andy made the right call; in retrospect, they should at least have followed me to Bremerton.

Whatever damage that decision may have done to the case was far outweighed by the evidence we caught on videotape. Many of the guests would step outside to talk business. Unfortunately for them, we had security cameras and audio covering both the front and back doors. Even if the bikers conversed *sotto voce* about their business, their discussions were usually picked up. Among other information gleaned from those conversations that would eventually prove devastating to the gang, police learned that Hammer was purported to have been involved in a murder in Arizona the year before.

Still, most important to the investigation were the friendship and business contacts I made with out-of-state Bandidos. These led to Terry Jones and me making our own cross-country trek just a few weeks later, in mid-June. My main goal was to buy some guns from Sly Willie—he had an Ingram MAC-11 and a converted AR-15 for sale. We'd discussed the purchase at my house in Blaine and I'd even given Willie a deposit on the weapons, though it was really a loan; he was broke and needed money to get back to Lubbock.

Before Terry and I could set off, safe passage through California had to be negotiated with the Hells Angels. Times were tense between the big biker gangs. The Outlaws, born in Chicago and strong across a wide swath of the country from Illinois to Florida, and the California-based Angels had been at each other's throats for a decade. Through the early 1980s, the Outlaws had a "shoot-on-sight" policy regarding their western enemies. In fact, the Bandidos owed much of their remarkable growth in the mid-1970s to the enmity between the Outlaws and the Angels. The Bandidos had cunningly offered to serve as a buffer between the gangs and, out of Texas, expanded northward into Colorado, Montana, South Dakota and New Mexico.

But by the early 1980s, the Hells Angels were beginning to resent the space being taken up by the Bandidos—especially those in Washington State. Were it not for the boys from Bellingham and Bremerton, the Angels would have had a clear run from the Mexican border all the way to Alaska.

Making matters worse, another Texas-born gang, the Banshees, were on a rampage in the Southwest and had killed several Angels in Arizona and California. This wouldn't have reflected badly on the Bandidos were it not for the fact that some Banshees—if only in Texas and Louisiana, as far as I understood—were renegade Bandidos.

Finally, the Angels were feeling especially put upon in those days because the Outlaws and Pagans, another major gang from back east, had recently brokered an alliance, and an upstart gang, the Mongols, was causing the Angels grief in L.A., their own backyard.

That, in short, was why Terry and I needed a safe-passage guarantee.

Off we went to Jersey Jerry's house. As northwestern regional officer he would have to make the necessary phone calls to California on our behalf. He also handed us business cards with several coded phone numbers to be presented to anyone from the Hells Angels who challenged us. As far as Oregon was concerned, there was no negotiating with the Gypsy Jokers. While the Jokers were reluctant to do anything that would put them on the wrong side of the Hells Angels, they were a lot less diplomatic with the Bandidos, who had driven the Jokers out of Washington in the early 1970s. Jerry's advice was simply to keep our heads down and hope that no Jokers took notice of us.

Andy, perhaps feeling a bit guilty for leaving me so exposed during the party week, wanted some reassurance that riding through Oregon wouldn't get me killed. So, on the day we were to ride through Oregon, the DEA orchestrated a series of raids and searches on the Jokers to keep them occupied. All their bikes and vehicles were hauled in for safety inspections, and their dogs were dragged into the ASPCA to ensure they were up to date on their shots. The child protection and health departments went through their houses. It was classic Andy, and not for naught—the raids recovered illegal firearms, drugs and stolen goods, justifying the police action. So Andy and his crew had a fun day and Terry Jones and I sailed through the state without seeing a single Joker.

We spent the first night at a motel in northern California and then blasted all the way to Phoenix. There we took a room at a motel on the outskirts of town. We drove our bikes into the rooms for security and then ordered pizza and kicked back. About an hour later, I heard the roar of Harleys coming into the motel court. I looked out the window and saw four nasty-looking bikers coming toward our room. In a flash I was into Terry's room, gun in hand, telling him we might have a problem. He was unperturbed. "Don't worry, they're friends," he reassured me.

The bikers turned out to be Banshees, and we spent the evening with them, partying as if we were brothers—which, in due course, I learned we were. They took us to a private house and I saw Bandidos paraphernalia everywhere. That initially confused me. This wasn't stuff you could buy at a Harley concession or a flea market—biker gangs do their utmost to tightly control distribution of anything with their logo on it, whether it be belts or jackets or official T-shirts, even tattoos. Quitting the gang without returning this stuff, or wearing it without being a member, is a serious, serious transgression in the biker world.

Then one of the Banshees confided to me that he was anxious for "this gig" to be over so he could put the "fat Mexican"—an affectionate term for the Bandidos patch—back on. That's when the penny dropped: the rampaging Banshees were really undercover Bandidos. Apparently, they were provoking the Hells Angels on their eastern flank to distract them from any expansionist plans elsewhere, particularly to the north. I later learned the backstory: a year or so previously a group of New Mexico Bandidos had wiped out the Arizona Banshees but kept their colors, which they then donned for activities that, for obvious reasons, the Bandidos couldn't be associated with. It was all an eye-opener for me.

But not for Terry. He passed out from too much fun, so I told the guys to keep him there; I'd go back to the motel and pick him up in the morning. They drew a map for me to find my way back. En route, I pulled over and called Andy. We met behind a Denny's and I gave him the scoop and the map for the house location.

By four a.m., I was fast asleep. Before dozing off, I'd thought of calling home, but Liz and the kids would be asleep—I'd call tomorrow. Earlier that day Andy had called Liz, telling her he was doing it at my request, to say that I was in a deep situation and couldn't call myself. He also sent her five hundred dollars in my name. Of course, I hadn't asked him to make the call or to send the money; I was too involved in the operation to think of calling or of being that considerate. Things would get worse before they got better. Not only could I not take time off—I didn't want to, I was too wrapped up in the case. But I wasn't just chasing the Bandidos in order to bring them down; I was fascinated by them. As much as I loved Liz and the children, the Bandidos allowed me to be a version of myself that I really enjoyed.

Our first home turf stop—at least officially—was Albuquerque, New Mexico. Like most Bandidos coming through, we bunked at the home of Chuck, real name Charles David Gillies but known as Ha-Ha for his twisted sense of humor. When we got to his house, the front door was open with just a screen door closed to keep the bugs out. We found Chuck on his hands and knees looking under the living room couch with a flashlight. The room was filled with about a dozen large aquariums, each containing one or several exotic snakes, some of them disconcertingly large. Ha-Ha waved us in and gestured at us to take a seat in a couple of straight-backed kitchen chairs in the room. He continued his hunt. After a couple of minutes I finally asked, "What are you looking for?"

"My fucking one-step got loose and I want to catch it before my ferret does," he answered calmly.

Before Ha-Ha had finished his sentence, Terry's and my feet were a foot off the ground—we both knew one-steps from Nam. They are short, very thin and extremely venomous jungle snakes. They liked climbing into boots, and if you were stupid enough to put such a boot on without shaking the snake out first, you'd likely last only a step or two before collapsing in a toxin-induced shock. Death would arrive in about twenty minutes if the antivenin was not available.

Ha-Ha finally gave up his search.

Terry knew Chuck well, but it was my first time in his, uh, fun-loving company. We exchanged a few pleasantries and then he said to me: "You're a small guy—you must be pretty fast?"

"What do you mean?" I asked.

He leaned forward and asked again in a louder voice, "Are you fast?"

"Yeah, I'm fast enough!" I shouted back.

"Get him, Thor!" he yelled.

At that, a large Doberman came bounding out of the kitchen at a dead run toward me.

"Fuuuuuuuuuuuuuuuuuuuuuuuuccckk," I said as I flew out of my chair and out the screen door, cutting my hand on the latch in the process.

Behind me, Ha-Ha (who had mercifully called off Thor) and Terry were slapping their knees in hysterical laughter. "He is fast!" sputtered Ha-Ha.

The next day, Chilly Willie (James T. Chilton), president of the Denver chapter, and one of his members dropped by and our stay turned festive. After the drugs came out, I pulled Ha-Ha aside and told him I was impressed by the quality of his shit. Did he have a couple ounces of speed I could score for the trip? He said sure, we could do the deal later that day.

I managed to sneak away, rendezvous with Andy and the team behind a nearby restaurant, and get wired and cashed up. Back at Ha-Ha's, we went out to his shed and he lifted up a small rug, removed a couple of floorboards and took out two ounces of speed. There were maybe thirty or forty bags still in there. I asked him to keep the deal private, it was no one else's business. Chuck agreed. Then I begged off and met up with Andy again. I gave him the drugs and took off the wire. We had our first out-of-state drug buy. The case had officially gone national.

When I got back to the house, I found Terry and Chilly out in the shed taking a bike engine apart. I reminded Terry that we should get going soon to Texas. He agreed and went back to the house with Ha-Ha for some business of their own.

As soon as I was alone with Chilly, he asked me out of the blue if I wanted to buy a gun. It was a semi-auto .380. Seems Chilly thought it was too small for him but figured it might work for me. I said sure and gave him four hundred dollars. The gun itself was legal and a sale like that, without the required paperwork, would have been a very minor infraction in New Mexico, except that Chilly, thanks to a recent conviction, had a court order not to buy and sell firearms. I figured that brought it up to a felony charge.

There was no time to bring the gun in—Terry was ready to get going. Still, when he and I stopped to gas up, I managed to make a call to Andy. He deemed it a non-prosecutable buy. Useful to establish credibility with Chilly for another time, but not much else.

"You just bought yourself a gun," he said, before adding that he would work expenses to make sure I got the money back. I could live with that.

Before leaving Albuquerque, we stopped to get something to eat. That's when Terry told me we wouldn't be riding to Texas alone. We had to do a favor for Chilly, he explained. On our way out of town we were to stop by a house on the edge of Albuquerque to pick up a couple of strippers. The girls had been brought to New Mexico by Chilly and were to be delivered to a Lubbock Bandido known as Frio (William Jerry Pruett) as a gift from Colorado.

Frio was VP of the Texas Nomads and definitely on the most-dangerous-men-in-the-club list. According to a story circulating in Bandidos circles, once, on a run, Frio had arrived at a campsite so drunk that he fell off his bike. The Kid, a Bandido from Montgomery, Alabama, thought it was funny. Frio, however, didn't appreciate the

Kid laughing, so when he got up he pulled his gun and shot him in the forehead. They buried the Kid at the site. I don't know if the story was true, but the Kid was never seen again.

The girls were waiting for us when we arrived. They were quite thrilled about the trip. They'd sent their stuff ahead by bus the day before and only carried small packs. They were wearing hip-hugger jeans with rips in the right places and tank tops. I pointed to the shorter one, with waist-length jet-black hair, and said, "You're with me."

In retrospect, it wasn't a good position to be in. It could be argued we were committing a felony under the Mann Act by "engaging in the interstate transport of females for immoral purposes." It would probably come out in court and perhaps hurt my credibility. But at that moment it didn't even cross my mind.

Jasmine, the one who was to ride with me, reached in her bag and took out a wad of bills. "Chilly said to give this to you guys for the ride."

I counted out the cash—there was two thousand dollars—and gave half to Terry. My mind was reeling. That was way too much money for gas and food. Terry wasn't the least bit concerned. He just asked the girls if they had their bottles—a requirement for riding in the desert: the passenger sprays a mist of water in front of the driver to prevent sunburn and heatstroke. They nodded and Terry gave them the signal to climb on. We were off.

We had the kind of day on which biker fantasies are built, riding helmetless and side by side in our jeans and colors on a desert highway. The chrome of our Harleys shining under a cloudless blue sky. And the two scantily clad beauties on the back. I'd found many aspects of Bandidos culture seductive, but this trumped them all.

I wasn't the only one smitten with the image that day. Families in station wagons took our picture as they passed. Likewise, single men and old couples. At one point, even Andy snapped away as he flew past in an unmarked car with a female cop driving. I was just glad for the spray: Jasmine liked to ride with her hands on my thighs, and by the time we pulled into a truck stop for supper I didn't need to be misted so much as hosed down.

We parked in some shade and gave the girls money to get us something to eat. Terry and I kicked back on the grass and relaxed. About fifteen minutes later, Terry's girl came back by herself.

"I thought you guys should know, there's a couple at the store and the guy is wearing colors." That sure got our immediate attention.

"What club?" Terry asked.

She didn't know. I asked if the guy's patch had a separate bottom rocker. "Yes, it said Texas."

Terry told her to go back and invite them over, without telling them we were Bandidos. She went off and Terry asked me if I had a gun. I patted my pocket. I actually had two—the new .380 and a small .22 derringer I always kept in the back of my belt. Our idyllic mood was replaced by apprehension. It never ceased to amaze me how, in the biker world, things could go from one extreme to another in seconds.

Soon we could see our girls making their way back to us carrying bags of food and pop. With them walked two strangers. The guy looked about forty and his companion ten years younger. Her step was slower than his and seemed to be faltering as they approached, but he didn't look nervous at all. He was about six feet tall with long hair and a beard. His tattooed arms were burned brown by the sun. I made a note of the large knife tied to his belt. As they neared us, Terry said, "Aces and Eights."

Aces and eights was the hand Wild Bill Hickok was holding when he was shot in the back while playing poker in a Deadwood saloon. It became known as the dead man's hand. It had also been adopted as the name of an independent biker club in Levelland, Texas. There were only about forty members and I surmised that they had to be pretty tough just to survive so deep in Bandidos territory. I wasn't up on the policy concerning these guys, but Terry was. Although he wasn't the sharpest tack, he was knowledgeable about (and hung up on) certain details, including the protocols between his club and all others.

The man introduced himself as Ratchet and shook hands before sitting down on the grass. His companion sat closer to the girls, who were smart enough to recognize the diceyness of the situation and move well out of harm's way. Terry got right to the point.

"Well, Ratchet, you must be aware that you can't be flying colors outside of your territory unless it's under Bandidos invitation. Do you have an invitation?"

Ratchet said he knew the rules and no, he didn't have permission. It was like being pulled over by a cop and not having proof of insurance. Ratchet, in fact, had been part of the negotiations that ensured the survival of his club two years earlier. He knew he had fucked up and seemed resigned to it.

"This is a clear violation of that agreement," said Terry.

"We're not going far, so I didn't think it was a major deal."

"Well, you were wrong," said Terry in a more serious tone.

Ratchet was still surprisingly calm. "I can see that now. So what do we do?"

"One thing is sure, we can't let you ride out wearing them."

Ratchet looked straight at Terry. "You know I can't let you just take them."

Terry sighed. "I know."

It was an absurd situation. Neither Terry nor Ratchet wanted a confrontation or fight, but both seemed resigned to the fact one was inevitable.

That's when I joined in. "Let's look at this from a different angle. Suppose you took off and forgot to leave your shit"—slang for colors—"at home. Meeting us here becomes a good thing: you could ask us to bring your colors back home for you. I'm sure we would be willing to do that."

Ratchet looked at me and I could see his mind working. Just to make things entirely clear, Terry said, "Hey man, he's giving you a way out. Take it."

Ratchet slowly started to nod and everyone was relieved. He took his vest off and handed it over to Terry, who folded it with exaggerated respect. "Don't worry, we'll take good care of your colors and leave them in Lubbock for you to pick up."

Ratchet got up and nodded to his old lady. They both walked off and the crisis was over. The girls brought the food closer and we relaxed again. Terry threw the colors to his girl, telling her to put them in her bag.

"He'll never get those back," he said to me.

That turned out to be a prophetic statement. Six months later, the Aces and Eights had become a Bandidos support club, those same colors were hanging upside down in our Lubbock clubhouse, and Ratchet was lying face down in a hole in the ground, according to a fellow Bandido.

Jasmine asked if we were going to spend the night at the truck stop. I liked the idea. Driving in the desert at night was cold and dangerous because of all the snakes and lizards sleeping on the asphalt. No fun at all. So we told the girls to go get a couple of rooms. By sending them, we'd given Jasmine and her friend the option of getting separate rooms if they wanted to. It wasn't that we'd suddenly become gentlemen: the girls were Frio's property. We were just deliverymen—deliverymen with Bandidos patches, but deliverymen all the same. The girls came back with one key each; I guess they had decided.

"We're in room fourteen," Jasmine said, taking me by the arm. I didn't put up any resistance at all—and of course I rationalized it expertly afterward. Not taking advantage of a beautiful and available woman would have gone against the biker norm and raised suspicions.

We dawdled even more the next day. Still, the trip ended much too soon. By late afternoon we were in Lubbock. The town is famous for three things: it's the birthplace of Buddy Holly; it was the largest and longest-lasting "dry" city in the U.S. (until 1972, when it finally allowed liquor to be sold within city limits); and, even if the club was born five hundred miles across the state on the coast, it's the spiritual home for the Bandidos. Why exactly, I've never known.

By the early 1980s the Bandidos had acquired almost every house on one of the streets in the Mexican part of town. Police and townsfolk called it Felony Flats. No members actually lived there; rather, the homes were more like frat houses used for parties and as crash pads for visitors.

Upon our arrival, the first stop for Terry and me wasn't Felony Flats but Frio's house. We dropped the girls off and visited for a while. Frio was hospitable and friendly and it was all very pleasant—until

Frio's hospitality took a perverse turn. As thanks for delivering the strippers, he offered Terry one of his daughters, a young girl about fourteen, maybe younger. Terry passed, saying we had other business to attend to. He told me later that he had been afraid Frio would take it as an insult, which could have turned nasty for both of us. But all Frio said was, "It's your loss, she's really good. I trained her myself."

We left there as soon as we could after that. Even Terry was disgusted.

Then we headed for the Felony Flats home of the Gimp chapter. Every member of that group was missing an arm or leg, some thanks to traffic accidents, some from the war. Individually they belonged to different chapters, but they were allowed a secondary group of their own. They even had their own small patch on the lower left side of their cut that said *Cripple Crew*.

There we found a party in full swing. The occasion was an odd one: everyone was under orders to return to their home chapter, and quick. Us included, we learned—even if we had just arrived. So it was something of a goodbye party. There was no explanation offered, and we knew better than to ask for one. Instead of relaxing or hanging out, we took care of business. We turned in the Aces and Eights colors to Sir Spanky, the national sergeant-at-arms. Then Terry took off to arrange a flight home for us and organize prospects to trailer our bikes back to Washington.

I, meanwhile, went out and called the number Andy had given me. After I told him we'd be heading back to Washington the next day, he said we should meet up immediately. When we did, he wired me up and gave me a pile of money—seven thousand dollars cash—instructing me to try to get a deal or two before I left town.

First I dropped by Frio's place again. I was sure he would have something to sell me. His place was more warehouse than home. Among other things, there were electronics, still in their boxes, littered around the living room. Frio was in a merry mood, not drunk but getting there, along with a Bandido known as Killer Kelly.

Kelly was a psychopath of the first order and known in the club to be an eager killer. I wasn't interested in lingering in his company. So, soon after I arrived, I asked Frio if he knew anyone local who could sell me shit to take home. He said I wouldn't have to go any further—he happened to have half a pound of speed right in his house. I bought it for five thousand dollars. And thanks to the wire, I got good conversation on tape from both Frio and Kelly. They were both done, nailed in a direct sale, and I left there happy. These guys were real assholes—a vice-president of the Nomads and a known killer—and taking them down was a pleasure for me and a major coup for the cops.

Then I went by Sly Willie's, but not without calling first. Willie was famous among the Bandidos for having planted Claymore mines around his house and having wired his whole place with explosives. According to our original plans, I was supposed to pick up the machine guns I had agreed to buy. I told him I still wanted the guns but couldn't take them back right now, since I had to fly home the next day and didn't want to carry them on an airplane. We agreed to complete the transaction on my next visit. But while I was there, he urged me to at least try out the Ingram MAC-11, which I did. With the briefest squeeze of the trigger, I fired about two dozen rounds into a pie plate nailed to a wall inside his closet.

# CHAPTER SIX

# Bringing the Bandidos Down

———

It would be years before I found out why we had been ordered to leave Lubbock so soon, so unceremoniously, after our arrival. It all had to do with the Banshees—the leftover real ones, not the Bandidos in disguise.

Despite having been wiped off the map in Arizona, Alabama and most of Louisiana, the gang still had a profile in Texas, especially in the Houston and Dallas regions. Considering Texas was the Bandidos' home state, the surviving Banshees were a source of embarrassment and aggravation. So when, on May 1, 1983, a group of Bandidos ran into a group of Banshees at a drag strip in Porter, just north of Houston, violence was guaranteed. The conflict ended with two bikers dead—the president of the Banshees had his throat cut, and a Longview, Texas, Bandido was shot in the face—and a good handful more with stab wounds.

The clash prompted Bandidos president Ronnie Hodge to call a meeting of national officers to plan retaliatory action. That meeting, on May 6, led to the club sending out teams to gather intel on the Banshees—where they lived, where they hung out, who their associates were. Those teams reported back at another meeting on June 13, at which the club made further plans with their typical military precision. Various Bandidos across the state were to acquire the different components for bombs—timers, blasting caps, wire, explosives—so as not to arouse suspicion; the club would set up a safe house in Dallas with abundant emergency medical supplies in case they sustained any injuries.

They held a final meeting in Lubbock on June 20 and 21, which had just ended when Terry and I pulled into town. Being on a war footing, the Texas Bandidos didn't need the distraction of visitors, and so ordered us and all other out-of-towners home. They moved into action two weeks later, on the Independence Day weekend, but the results were humiliating. Rather than wiping out the Texas Banshees, all the Bandidos succeeded in doing was blowing up a van and causing some structural damage to the Banshee clubhouse. Even worse, years later, long after my time with the club, the botched attack on the Banshees would end up being quantumly more devastating to the Bandidos after a member turned. Eventually, twenty-three were arrested for their involvement, many of them pulling stretches in prison as a result.

When Terry and I touched down at Sea-Tac Airport in Seattle, I had no inkling, of course, of what was under way back in Texas. Up in the Northwest we were a world away. I even managed, shortly after our return, to get five days off and spend a bit of time in Vancouver getting to know Liz and the kids again.

After that, I settled back into a routine of buying drugs and weapons, accumulating evidence against my fellow Bandidos and our associates. One of my targets was a gun dealer from Bellingham named Rex Endicott. He sold to all the Bandidos in the area—and all the cops, which came to cause a problem. Some of his sales were legal but many were not, Washington State being relatively demanding as far as firearms permits were concerned. And even if his sales to cops were generally legal and those to Bandidos generally not, that wasn't a hard and fast rule. Many cops bought their "throwaways"—the extra guns they all carried in case they needed to plant a piece on someone— from Rex.

Terry Jones had introduced me to Rex before our ride to Texas, and when we got back I called him up. I had a reputation for being interested in almost any kind of firearm, the nastier the better, and Rex accommodated that. Among other weapons, he offered me a heavy-duty, belt-fed Bren machine gun that came complete with bi-pod— the kind often featured in WWII movies, mounted in the back of a jeep.

Even if the price tag was two thousand dollars, Andy and Larry were eager for me to make the buy, especially Larry, who thought that Rex and his house were a public menace. The old house, right in downtown Bellingham, was wall-to-wall weaponry: guns, bullets, grenades, mortar shells, flares. Not only was it hugely attractive to thieves, the place would have taken out the whole block had it ever caught fire. But even if he was in violation of all sorts of zoning, storage and commercial regulations, Endicott's close ties to local and state police had so far saved him from being investigated or charged.

After my verbal debrief with the DEA boys, I wrote up my notes and went home, expecting to get a green light to make the Bren buy. But the next day I got a call from Andy telling me to come in for a meeting. Something was up.

The atmosphere was tense when I got to the office, but no one would discuss anything until the FBI arrived. Eventually Corky came in with another agent, a man I'd met a couple of times but who was involved in the Bandidos investigation only in a supporting function. That afternoon, he stopped being a wallflower. Without so much as a greeting, he looked at me and said, "I think you're lying, just to score points with this office!"

I looked at Andy and asked, "What the fuck is he talking about?"

The DEA at the time was still a relatively young agency—it had only been created in 1973—and the FBI frowned on it as bush league. I had the feeling the G-man was trying to intimidate not just me but also Andy and Larry.

"I know Rex," he said. "He's my neighbor. He and his wife were just over at my place for dinner a few nights ago. He's not a crook! And I'm not alone—me and half the cops in this area would vouch for him. Rex is a good man, and you're just trying to score points with the DEA by going after him."

The Bandido in me quickly rose to the surface. I was up out of my chair and in his face.

"Put your money where your mouth is, asshole!" I shouted. "You give me two thousand dollars today and I'll have that gun by tonight."

Larry stood up to calm the situation and back me up. "Then it's settled—I'll call ATF and get an agent here to accept the evidence."

I asked Andy to let me use the phone right now to set up the appointment with Rex. I wanted the jerk-off from the FBI to hear the tape for himself. Everybody sat quietly while I made arrangements to meet and purchase the Bren that night in a supermarket parking lot in Bellingham. After Andy replayed the tape, the FBI guy never said a word. I just looked at him and headed toward the door, telling Andy I'd call him later.

I arrived in a wired-up old van, and after carrying the machine gun from Rex's pickup to it, he and I got down to talking. I questioned him about his relationship with the cops, asking if he was ever privy to information that might be useful to the gang. He said they talked around him and, yes, he would let us know if anything came up that was useful to the Bandidos. I had him count out the money on tape. He was in the bag.

The buy had gone off without a hitch and there turned out to be an unexpected bonus: we now had tape of Rex offering to sell out the cops who were so fond of him. Afterward, I went to a motel room Andy had rented for the occasion, turned the evidence over to the ATF and made my notes. The FBI guy wasn't there. I wasn't heartbroken to learn after the case wrapped up that he was under investigation by the FBI's Office of Professional Responsibility—the agency's equivalent of an internal affairs department—for his friendship with Rex and several other bad guys.

I was in deep with the gang and had been for a while. No member had any lingering suspicions about me or my game. In fact, if anything, the police were the ones who were beginning to have doubts—I was still acting just a bit too much like a real biker for their liking. There was just one thing that made me stand out from my Bandidos brothers: they all had at least one woman on the go, usually several. I, on the other hand, was resolutely single.

It wasn't a big issue, but I knew that some members found it odd: here was a reasonably handsome guy with a lot of cash and no interest in women? I hadn't mentioned a wife or girlfriend in Canada—though that wouldn't have carried any weight with them anyway; monogamy is for straight society, not for bikers. And availability certainly wasn't an issue: bikers seem to attract groupies in the same way professional athletes and rock stars do. A couple of times, members had remarked on my apparent celibacy in my presence. No doubt it was discussed

more extensively when I wasn't around. On one or two occasions I'd
hooked up with a woman while in the company of other Bandidos,
more for deniability than anything else. In the end I'd just dropped
them off at home. But in the summer of 1983, I'd been hanging with
the Bandidos for almost two years and, after one too many raised eye-
brows or wisecracks, I figured it was time to get an "old lady," in biker-
speak. Or at least a steady girlfriend. After all, when I'd been made a
full member, I'd been given a patch that read *Property of Bandido Alex*.
It was time to pull it out from deep inside my bottom drawer.

The companionship on runs and having someone to help me
out with duties at home and at the campsites would be great, and from
an intel point of view it would also be valuable to have someone who
might feed me gossip she picked up from other girls. There would be,
of course, an inherent danger in having someone so close to me. My
dealing with the cops would have to be much tighter—Andy couldn't
just casually call me for an update like he did most mornings. And the
monitoring equipment in the house would be a risk if my girlfriend
became a regular visitor and, say, decided she wanted to have a peek
around the attic.

Those were the potential professional problems; there were just
as many on a personal level. Having a girlfriend would make disen-
gaging from the Bandidos all that much harder when the time came,
especially if I'd grown attached. And what kind of danger would I be
leaving her in when the operation ended?

These were all serious questions. But after lengthy conversations
with both Andy and Liz, we decided that the benefits outweighed the
risks, especially insofar as it would make me seem less of an oddball in
the gang. Liz was surprisingly amenable—we just agreed that it wasn't
me who would be getting a mistress, it was "Bandido Alex." Andy was
more skeptical. I found his reluctance strange and figured he was
doubting that I could keep up my act with someone I went to bed
with and woke up beside (what if I talked in my sleep?). Later, I realized he was more concerned about the degree to which I seemed to be
embracing the Bandidos life. What if having an old lady pushed me
over the edge? I guess he saw that the line between me and me—

between Alex Caine and Bandido Alex—was getting thinner all the time.

One of George Weger's many girlfriends had an attractive, single, older sister. One night that summer George invited me to his house when the sisters were both there, having a good time. George was drinking straight vodka, as was his custom in those days; the girls were drinking something brown—bourbon, rum, whatever. I hit the Pepsi. It was clear I was being set up with the older of the two even before George took off on some business and left me alone with the girls. We continued to party, but the sister didn't really interest me, even if she was a looker. I knew that she had been Vinny's second girlfriend for a short time and that the parting between them had not gone smoothly. Pursuing her might cause more problems than it would solve.

Instead, I decided to chase Vickie, a barmaid at the Pioneer. Although a lot of guys had chased her, none to my knowledge had succeeded. I moved on her like a tornado. Before too long she was a regular on the back of my bike and at my house in Blaine. (She lived with her mom in Ferndale, so we didn't hang out there.)

Vickie's good looks and her fun yet cool temperament gave me prestige with the other members. Having spent so much time in the company of the Bandidos at the Pioneer, she knew when she could be loud and rambunctious and when to keep quiet, or to simply leave the room because club business was being discussed. The fact that many had gone after her but none had scored also earned me points, and perhaps a bit of resentment. Vickie, meanwhile, was happy to have hooked up with someone not too offensive from the gang: it meant she was now off-limits and therefore safer at parties and gatherings, as well as at the Pioneer.

The women in the club played a major role in many ways. Some were breadwinners, others organized events, carried drugs and guns or otherwise acted as couriers. They had to be solid and above reproach to begin with, and even then they still went through a training period. Vickie was a bit of an exception; she already knew the Bandidos culture, the dos and don'ts. Most others, however, came in cold.

They had their own mentor or sponsor and underwent a mild sort of prospecting. There were those who didn't make it: some members were told to get a new primary girlfriend if it had been decided that the one on whom they wanted to bestow their property patch came up short. For Vickie, approval was just a formality.

There were a few basic rules that a woman who wore a patch had to subscribe to: don't flirt or play around, and never challenge your old man in front of his brothers. In return they were accorded substantial respect. In all the time I was with the club, I never saw a member disrespect a patch-wearing old lady. Unless she was his old lady, that is. It was like a wolf pack in that way: everyone knew their place. Those old stories about old ladies pulling trains—sexually satisfying many members in one sitting—and being passed around were just that, stories. And as Vickie had learned, it was the girls without the patch who were in danger at campsites and parties.

Vickie came with me on several local runs that summer, but not to Sturgis, South Dakota, the mecca for American bikers and Harley-lovers thanks to the giant run—and week-long party—it hosts every August. Despite Vickie's absence, Sturgis was memorable for me that year, largely because of one episode. I was sitting around a campfire with a dozen or so other Bandidos. Steve, a national VP who came from Washington but had moved to Texas, looked at me and said, "I hear you know something about the Alamo?"

"Yeah, I do," I answered, without looking up from the fire. I was surprised that that night with Vinny from almost two years earlier was being brought up.

"Tell me," said Steve. There was silence around the fire and everyone waited.

"Back in 1836, Houston said to Travis, 'Get some volunteers to-gether and go defend the Alamo,'" I began. And kept going for a least twenty minutes. Other than the rise and fall of my voice, all you could hear was the crackling of the fire, which I poked from time to time to add emphasis. I finished by saying I had to go check the guard ros-ter, threw my stick in the fire and disappeared into the night. No one said anything. It was my best performance. My only real concern was the kinship I felt with those guys that night. I truly felt like one of them.

Sometime in the weeks after we returned from Sturgis, the officers of the chapter got together to choose a new road captain and a new secretary-treasurer. These were the only positions that had a term limit—the road captain because members worried that his contacts with police had the potential of compromising him if allowed to continue too long, the secretary-treasurer because he handled the club's cash. At the next regular church meeting, the new nominees were put forward, pending ratification by all the club members. I was the choice for secretary-treasurer and, since no one opposed the idea, I got the job.

The next day, Gunk came over to the house and handed me the books, the bank account information and thousands in cash, as well as separate records of individual members and what they owed the club from loans, missed dues and the like. Gunk also outlined my responsibilities. Besides managing the club's expenses, I had to collect the dues—a hundred dollars per month from each member—and meet with Vinny and George every two weeks. The chapter as a whole required a full report every month. Finally, it was my job to liaise with the national club on financial matters, which included cutting a check to Jersey Jerry once a month for chapter dues. I wasn't tremendously surprised by the new role thrust upon me—someone had to do it, and better a member with half a brain—but neither was I particularly thrilled by all the extra work.

Andy and the boys, on the other hand, were ecstatic. This would be the cops' first good look at the club's finances. And even if the accounts I was overseeing were overwhelmingly local, the secretary-treasurers from across the country got together at least once a year to discuss the club's larger finances. Those meetings were a source of excellent intel, but they were also nerve-racking: each secretary-treasurer was subjected to a polygraph test, administered by a member who had been with military intelligence in Vietnam.

When the time came, the questions mostly had to do with finding out if anyone was skimming cash, and I could answer those honestly. But we were also asked whether we'd shown the books to anyone outside the club. I had, of course. Still, I managed to pass.

My sec-treas responsibilities gave the police a peek into the bureaucratic and administrative workings of the club, but didn't lead to the legal bonanza my handlers had hoped for. Instead, my appointment produced a lot of what cops call "nice-to-know" information—interesting but not legally actionable. My time with the gang produced a lot of that. It all contributed to providing the cops with a solid sociological profile of life within the club. Some of this was pretty innocuous stuff, such as club rituals and the various quirks of character of some of the members.

For instance, Mongo's fondness for repeatedly telling the same long joke. It was rude, crude and not all that funny to anyone else. That didn't stop him wanting to tell it. So when he'd get the urge, George and Karate Bob would go out to the sidewalk and bring some poor passerby into the Pioneer to listen. They would sit the scared-stiff visitor down and stand behind him with arms crossed as Mongo launched into the joke, complete with gestures and falsetto voice. It involved a man, a woman, a dog, some perverted sex and a turd in a purse. The guy was usually so nervous that he'd laugh at the wrong places or just stare blankly at the end of it. Then Mongo would lean over him and ask, "Didn't you think that was funny?"

I saw it happen at least three times and it was all in good fun. The visitor always left unharmed, if shaken.

The club members' capacity for intimidation and casual violence wasn't always so easy to stomach. George Wegers was the prime, psychopathic example. One night he was driving with Mongo and they passed a couple kissing on a corner. It threw him into such a rage that he pulled over, beat the guy to a pulp and hit the girl several times. Then he got back in the truck and continued on his way. And I once saw Steve, the VP who asked me to hold forth about the Alamo, pistol-whip a prospect because the guy answered a question too slowly.

As that incident suggests, members sometimes found themselves on the receiving end of their brothers' violent wrath, despite the rule against members pounding on each other. Unfortunately for Gunk, there was also a rule against wearing your colors while in a car or truck—they were only for bikes. In four-wheeled vehicles, members were supposed to put their cut on the seat next to them or behind. On one occasion Gunk was observed having neglected to take his colors off. Vinny and Jersey Jerry spoke to him about it at the Pioneer, and Gunk, half drunk, was deemed not sufficiently remorseful about his transgression. Vinny and Jerry responded by hauling back in synchrony and belting him on either side of the head simultaneously. Gunk hit the floor like a sack of potatoes. If he had any brains before being hit, he sure didn't afterward.

It all made for an atmosphere where the possibility of violent outbursts lurked constantly, like rain clouds in the Pacific Northwest. And seduced as I was by many aspects of the Bandidos lifestyle, I wasn't immune to the temptation to resolve things violently. On one cold, damp evening in late 1983 about ten members and several girls were at the Pioneer, just chilling out. When we had arrived, the place was empty except for two cowboy types drinking at the bar. Nobody I recognized. I was standing nearby with another member, joking and laughing with the barmaid. Vickie was in the corner with two other girls, playing a pinball machine. Gunk and several others were sitting across the aisle from us, close and within earshot. Everything was relaxed and peaceful. Until, that is, one of the cowboys started bugging the barmaid.

"Hey, where's my change?" he asked accusingly. "I had two quarters sitting here and now they're gone."

"You pushed them to me, so I put them in the jar," said the barmaid, taken aback.

The exchange was loud enough to catch everybody's attention. I had money on the bar, so I pushed a couple of quarters toward the cowboy.

"Here," I said to him. "Now get the fuck out of here."

He didn't. Instead, he turned toward me and leaned so that his face was just a foot or so from mine.

"Fuck you, asshole," he said menacingly.

I couldn't believe the guy. Everybody had heard him, so I was obligated to go on the attack. But that wasn't part of my computation, at least not consciously. Rather, my reaction was purely visceral. I pulled my flashlight out of its holder in an instant, whipped it around and brought it down on the side of his head. Immediately, blood began gushing.

I backed up in a fighting position and said, "Come on, asshole, I'll rip your fucking head off."

He was already done for and his friend was smart enough not to be too loyal or tough. "Sorry, I'm really sorry," the bleeding cowboy muttered as he staggered, trying to remain on his feet. Gunk, on the other side of the guy and apparently unaware I'd already clobbered him, didn't want to let it end so quickly. He and two others grabbed the cowboy, but when he swung the guy around to nail him, he saw blood and left it at that.

By this time everyone had gone, automatically, into cover-up mode. One member had immediately secured the front door so no one new would come in. The girls started gathering our stuff from the tables. Within five minutes we were out of there. Some of the guys headed home, but a handful of us hit the I-5 and went down to Bellingham to another bar. We stayed there and talked over the incident like people doing a post-mortem on a championship football game.

The local police quickly learned that Bandidos were involved, but they didn't know which ones. The feds weren't so in the dark: the morning after the incident I told Andy all about it, and was required to make detailed notes on the entire evening.

We spun it in my notes and later in court as a last-ditch action to prevent more grievous injury to the cowboy from the other members. In other words, I had clubbed the cowboy to save him. An interesting concept and, of course, one that never crossed my mind at the time. He had insulted me and I had made him pay the price, as any Bandido would.

The wives and girlfriends of the gang members were all quite surprised when they heard it was me who had hit the cowboy. They had never seen or heard of me being like that. "Hey, he's a Bandido and he's a crazy Frenchman to boot," Vinny told his wife. "That asshole's lucky to be alive."

Later that night at the bar, Dr. Jack and Jersey Jerry came in.

"I was impressed when I heard what you did," Jack said. "Then I found out the guy was a retard."

"I thought that would give me extra points," I replied, laughing along with him.

Both Vickie and the barmaid would one day testify in court that the incident was unnecessary and instigated by me. They weren't lying. It was just more evidence that I was becoming my character to a dangerous degree.

By 1984, I had long got the goods on all the Washington Bandidos. Two times over. So I began concentrating on expanding my contacts and dealings with the Bandidos community elsewhere. It meant I was on the road almost constantly: Texas, Louisiana, New Mexico, Colorado, even, for good measure, a few trips to the chapter in Rapid City, South Dakota. Sometimes I'd go by truck, more often by bike. Sometimes there would be a pack of us, sometimes just a couple, with or without our girlfriends. Always I'd be doing deals with as many different members as possible. With the investigation this widespread, when the law came down, it would come down hard.

On one of my trips to Texas I made a purchase I hadn't planned on, one that didn't do anything for the investigation but helped me make amends. Amends that had been due since Christmas morning, 1970.

It was early summer and I had traveled down to Lubbock with Dr. Jack, Terry Jones and Bobby Lund from Bremerton. One evening we were hanging around a house on Felony Flats when a teenaged girl came in. I recognized her as a Native girl Sly Willie had bought from her drunk or junkie mother when he had come up for the Bremerton party weekend more than a year earlier. He had brought her around to my house in Blaine before leaving Washington, and I'd reported it to Andy and the boys, hoping something could be done and fast.

"Just pull him over with a busted tail light or something. He's going to have a gun—and a minor in the front seat!" I'd said.

They'd toyed with the idea but discarded it. Even if they made it look like a routine traffic violation, they thought it could jeopardize the whole investigation. At the very least, they argued, it would cost me the only good contact I had in Texas at the time and scuttle the purchase of the guns. After that call, I suppose, they just forgot about the girl. I did too.

Now, more than a year later, here she was in a long Chinese gown with a slit up the side and done up to look Asian. Still, the heavy makeup didn't completely hide a black eye. It was clear she was on her way out for a long night of turning tricks.

I was shocked when I saw her, and perhaps it showed. Her blank look lifted for a second and there was a glint of recognition in her eyes. "I want to go home," she said to me. Out loud, I think. As crazy as it sounds, I may have got the message just from the look she gave me. In any event, it struck me to the core.

I asked who owned her and she told me: a Texas Bandido named Wheeler had bought her from Sly Willie.

"Go get changed and be back here in half an hour. I'll take you home," I said, and she was off like a shot.

Wheeler was in the other room. I went in and called him outside. I was determined to keep my promise to her even if it meant blowing the whole case.

"I want that Indian girl," I said.

He looked at me closely. I think he must have recognized my determination and understood that "no" was not an option. My eyes and tone indicated only one thing: matters could turn very ugly very quickly if he refused to sell her. He was clearly evaluating whether she was worth the trouble.

"Do you have any cash?" he said.

"Yeah."

"A thousand dollars and cover the price of a generator I have to pick up tomorrow."

"Done," I answered.

Then he looked down at my feet. "I really like those chaps you have. Are they Brooks?"

I took them off and threw them on the ground. He almost said something further, then thought better of it.

I took out a wad of cash, peeled off a thousand dollars, threw in two hundred extra for the generator, and handed it to him. It was buy-money for drugs and guns that Andy had given me. I'd found a more important use for it.

On my way out, I told Dr. Jack something had come up and I had to leave for home. He looked at me curiously. "Fine, I'll cover for you," was all he said.

When I got to the bike, the girl was waiting for me, dressed in jeans and a T-shirt, a small knapsack beside her. "Let's go," I said. She climbed on and we were gone.

I know I should have called Andy or handled it some other way, but I was a man on a mission and nothing else mattered. I thought about that runner I'd picked off in the Vietnamese village so many lifetimes ago. Maybe, just maybe, I was beginning to make up for it.

As I went about my work collecting evidence and assuaging my conscience, the higher echelons of the outlaw biker world were maneuvering and negotiating in anticipation of a major shakeout. Not that this was obvious to the lower ranks, even those of us who were chapter officers. Secrets tend to be well guarded in biker gangs.

The first inkling I got that anything was afoot was at a special church meeting convened immediately after a trip I made to Texas. It was held at Vinny's place—a sprawling one-story wood house on a large, very private spread outside of town. It was ideal for such meetings. When I arrived, there was already a crowd: the Bremerton chapter was there along with the ex-Resurrection prospect chapter and, lo and behold, the Yakima chapter of the Ghost Riders. About sixty guys in total, plus dozens of old ladies wearing their property patches, milling about outside.

Vinny emerged and called the meeting to order. All the Bandidos patches went inside, leaving everyone else outside, including all the prospects. Jersey Jerry took the floor.

"Everyone knows or has heard rumors of the coming sit-down between the HA"—the Hells Angels—"and the Outlaws. It will be happening at Sturgis at our campsite. We'll be in a dangerous situation, truce or no truce. If the shit hits the fan, it could get really ugly. We will have to draw up plans to cover all possible situations. National will be letting us know.

"We in the Northwest have other problems to consider. We are the break in the Hells Angels' chain. We must become immovable. A small chapter in Bellingham is not enough. There is talk at the national level of ordering the whole chapter to move to Bremerton or even another state—basically trading our territory to the HA so they have a clear run all the way to Alaska. Of course, I don't like the idea, but national seems to think there might be something in it for the club as a whole."

The news had the room buzzing immediately. It seemed the national leadership of the Bandidos had been negotiating with their counterparts in the Angels and Outlaws, discussing the division of the entire country between them. And it appeared the Bellingham chapter was in the balance, and about to become part of the horse-trading. On top of that, the Angels and the Outlaws looked to be about to settle their differences formally at Sturgis, with the Bandidos acting as mediators.

Several people stood and gave their opinion and a consensus quickly emerged: we weren't going anywhere if we could help it. George had a plan. He suggested we patch-over the Ghost Riders' best chapter and bring up the ex-Resurrection prospect chapter in Seattle to probationary status. There was a lively debate, especially from guys such as Bobby Lund and Milo from Bremerton. They were old-school and had less to lose; all they really had were their bikes and their way of life. Rules and traditions were important to them. They objected to the probationary status for the ex-Resurrection. I got the impression there may have been bad blood between them and the Resurrection boys.

After more than an hour of discussion we broke for beer. I could see on the faces of the people outside that they were dying to know how it was going. We said nothing; instead, after a quick drink we went back to talking.

Eventually, all of George Wegers's suggestions were adopted, an indication of his growing power. The Ghost Riders could patch-over straight across, but would be denied their one-percenter patch for a year. The Seattle crew—the ex-Resurrection—got their probationary status with no state bottom rocker and certainly no one-percenter patch. Their bottom rocker would say "Probationary," although a small Washington patch under their left pocket was allowed. Neither group would be allowed to give property patches to their wives or girlfriends for at least a year, although a property belt was permitted after six months if the old ladies from Bellingham and Bremerton voted her in. Nobody wanted an untested or troublemaking woman sporting a property patch.

Sturgis was still weeks away, and just as well—the big sit-down was a complicated thing to organize, not least because of the egos and suspicions of the heavyweights in the Hells Angels and Outlaws. The basic ground rules were simple: The Bandidos would serve as the hosts and mediators. The two antagonists were required to send their top people, people who could make decisions, not just second-stringers who would need to get agreements vetted and green-lighted by someone else. Each group would be allowed an escort of no more than fifty patches—no prospects, no women.

The Outlaws were sure that Hells Angels president Sonny Barger wouldn't show up, and indeed the club's point man, George Christie, had been negotiating with the Bandidos not to send Barger. Barger's presence, he contended, would attract all kinds of heat on the summit and be counterproductive. The Angels offered instead to have Barger connected on an open phone line to make decisions. But Bandidos founder and former president Don Chambers, who had recently been paroled after doing ten years on a murder stint, wouldn't have any of it. An open line would just be an invitation for the cops to listen in.

The Outlaws, who were sending their entire national chapter, interpreted Barger's reluctance to attend the summit as proof that he was chicken—and happily went on about it to anyone who would listen. "He's gone Hollywood," they'd say, meaning he'd become soft and obsessed about his image. Among Bandidos, meanwhile, the word was that Barger was afraid of assassination, though we too thought he was more interested in his image than in club issues. Of course, all this talk made its way to California, putting the Hells Angels in an awkward position.

Then the Angels did a strange thing. The club had given up doing the Sturgis run years previously for reasons that were unclear.

Then, in 1982, two years earlier, after the Outlaws had said the Angels didn't do Sturgis because they were there, the Angels—including Barger—took up the challenge and attended. But the following year they'd been no-shows again. So in 1984, with the Outlaws again suggesting the Angels were afraid to attend, the Hells Angels took the bizarre step of producing a newsletter bringing the Sturgis run right to the forefront—and quoting the Outlaws' challenge that the Angels wouldn't show up.

The newsletter made no mention of the secret summit; still, the Bandidos and the Outlaws were pissed. No one understood what the Angels' agenda was. The Bandidos thought it was Barger trying to create a situation that would blanket the run with law enforcement, thus making it safer for him or, alternately, giving him a reason not to show up. The Outlaws just saw it as proof that the Angels weren't real one-percenters anymore: that newsletter might just as well have been a press release—next they'd be holding news conferences and hiring booking agents.

Whatever the reasoning was, it aggravated an atmosphere already replete with distrust and duplicity. But as early August approached, the bigwigs kept negotiating. Eventually, it was time to pack up the bikes and head to South Dakota. Still no one knew for sure whether Barger—or any Angels for that matter—would be showing up.

Sturgis always starts on a Monday, but one-percenter clubs rarely arrive early or even on time—they like to make a dramatic entrance. On this occasion, however, we weren't too concerned about appearances. An advance party of Bandidos arrived on Sunday evening. We set up camp on Bandidos-owned property twenty minutes outside of town and the next day met up with some envoys from the Outlaws in Deadwood. The Outlaws were arriving en masse and would also be staying in the Bandidos campground. Whereas usually they came to party, with their women, booze and drugs, this year they were at Sturgis entirely on business. They wouldn't be staying on after the meetings concluded. We gave the envoys directions to our spread and, after they left to rejoin the rest of their contingent, headed back to our campsite.

True to their word, when the Outlaws arrived, there were about seventy-five of them in total, the national leadership plus their fifty patched escorts. They set up close to a small man-made lake that formed the back boundary of the property. Between them and the road were all of us—400-odd Bandidos from around the country, many with wives and girlfriends. The Outlaws were well protected.

And with good reason, it seemed. The Hells Angels entirely ignored the fifty-escort limit. They began arriving that day at a separate campsite ten or fifteen miles from ours—and just kept on coming. Eventually some six hundred or so members and associates showed up.

Suspicions rose with each Hells Angels arrival. Did they see the summit as an opportunity to wipe out the competition in one fell swoop? The Angels' show of force prompted the Bandidos brass to triple the number of guards posted around our site. It also brought us closer to the Outlaws. No one trusted the Angels, and here was proof that our skepticism about them was well founded. Neither of us was the top dog and both of us disliked that pooch intensely. So while we were on high alert that Monday afternoon and evening, we did find time to hang out and party with the Outlaws among us, guys who, more and more, were looking like our natural allies.

The meeting was set for twelve noon Tuesday. Sir Spanky, the Bandidos' national sergeant-at-arms and head of security for the summit, had parked an Airstream trailer in the middle of our camp. He surrounded the trailer with two rows of Bandidos Nomads, arms crossed, facing outward, who would keep any unauthorized person from getting too close. No one in the camp had been allowed to drink or get high that day; everyone was stone cold sober.

Along with a dozen other Bellingham members, I was assigned to man the front gate, perhaps fifty or seventy-five yards from the trailer. The gate itself was about a quarter or half a mile down a dirt road off a secondary highway. When we were at Sturgis, the cops were often spread out all along the paved road, peering through binoculars, but they couldn't come down the dirt road since it was Bandidos private property. The police also went out in boats on the little lake in behind, snapping away with long-lens cameras. On days when guys were bored, they would go to the water's edge and throw rocks at the boats. This was not a day for such sport, however; things were tense.

I heard them before I saw them. Their arrival sounded like rolling thunder and sent a chill down my spine. I looked around and saw the tension I felt reflected on everybody else's face. Eventually they came into sight, an endless line of Hells Angels and associates slowly making their way across the horizon on the secondary highway. They were in no hurry, riding two abreast at maybe fifteen miles per hour. When they turned down the dirt road, they slowed even more and a cloud of dust started to rise and soon engulfed even the lead bikes. It was quite a sight—and sound, getting louder every minute. As they drew closer, the front bike reappeared through the dust. The riders of the second pair of bikes were each holding a flag; one was the Hells Angels' death's head, the other the flag of California. The rider all alone at the front of the parade was riding a full dresser—windshield, saddlebags, the whole shebang—and wore no head cover except a pair of goggles. As he drew closer, he looked larger than life, and for good reason: it was Sonny Barger.

About thirty feet from the gate, Barger raised his hand and slowed to a stop. As if choreographed, the whole line stopped with him, everyone turning off their engines simultaneously. Then— nothing. No one moved, there was no sound except those of summer bugs and birds. The Hells Angels just sat on their bikes, looking at us looking at them. The moment was suspended in time. I was impressed, I'll admit. As much as I disliked the Hells Angels, they sure knew how to put on a show.

Then I noticed Spanky standing behind us. He had brought up fifty or sixty reserve Nomads to beef up the line. We all watched together as Barger got off his bike and started the long walk to the front gate. The twenty or so lead guys followed. The other Angels dismounted but stayed with their bikes.

Spanky ordered the gate opened. The Angels, Barger included, were patted down by the Bandidos Nomads as they entered the camp one by one. Once they were all inside, Spanky yelled, "Shut the gate," and told Barger to follow him. We all moved aside to let them by. The group headed toward the Airstream, the Nomads escorting them.

Barger's companions didn't seem too brave as they walked through the camp. They kept looking from side to side—I suppose they were as suspicious of us as we were of them. But the die was cast; whatever was to happen was going to happen. We took our positions back at the gate.

Five Angels and five Outlaws, along with a Bandido or two, went into the trailer for preliminary talks lasting between a half-hour and forty-five minutes. Then the meeting moved outside and the other executives from the two clubs joined in. There were no altercations—well, at least no physical altercations—except for a brief scrap between an Outlaw escort and an Angel. The Angel had strayed a little too far from his group and a little too close to the Outlaws. The two went nose to nose and bumped each other with their puffed-out chests. It was stopped within seconds by Bandidos security. Still, the incident served to raise the tension several notches.

By that time we'd been relieved at the gate by the Amarillo chapter and ordered to our section of the camp at the top of the hill. We sat in twos and threes in front of our tents, talking about what might be going on below. Even from a distance we could see nervous fidgeting and fists being clenched around the trailer. But we could only speculate for so long about what was being said, and things began to get a bit boring—a state of affairs not improved by the fact that all the women had been sent to town for the day.

I knew that that night would be a rowdy one, so, after telling Terry to make sure he came for me if something happened, I crawled into my tent for a snooze. I was soon dead to the world. The next thing I knew, Terry was kicking my boot.

Anyone who's ever fallen asleep in a tent in the sun knows what it's like to wake up parched, covered in sweat and not in the best of moods. My little pup tent didn't offer much protection against anything—I had bought it at a surplus store, used. (As I would tell my Bandidos brothers that summer, "It was the best of times, it was the worst of times, it was the summer of my discount tent." Dr. Jack was hugely amused; most others stared blankly. Terry Jones just said, "Oh, you should have told me. I have a spare tent in my garage. I could have lent it to you.")

After a few moments I got my bearings. It was about four p.m. and, sure enough, the Hells Angels were heading back to the gate and the Outlaws to their camp. From our tents on the crest of the hill we watched as the Angels mounted their bikes after being let out through the gate. Sonny gave the signal to everyone to start their bikes. Then he raised his hand once again and brought it down. The roar was deafening. He pulled a U-turn and rode past the line in the opposite direction. All the others followed, driving up to the gate and turning at the last minute to go the other way. It was like a precision drill on a parade ground.

When they turned on the paved road, the cops, who had beefed up their numbers, pulled them over and held them there for an hour, checking papers and taking names. Shortly after the road had cleared, the Outlaws, who had set about striking their camp immediately after the meeting, mounted up and headed out too. The cops stopped them and put them through the same routine. I saw a few Outlaws wandering around Sturgis and Deadwood in the following days, but only in twos and threes. The main group had left for Florida—there was no partying for them.

After the summit ended, there were no announcements or declarations—that isn't the biker way. Instead, there was just the sense that the goal of the meeting—a truce between the Outlaws and the Hells Angels—had been accomplished. The Bandidos had come out of it well. Order had been maintained, no one had been killed, the encounter had gone smoothly. That made us all feel good and, after the tensions of the summit, put us in even more of a mood to party than was usually the case in Sturgis.

If the words "Sturgis" and "party" appear in the same sentence, you almost invariably have to add "Buffalo Chip Campground"— certainly anyone who has been there on that August weekend would agree. It's ground zero of the action and fun. Beer flows in rivers. Rock 'n' roll blares from outdoor speakers only to be lost in the din of roaring, rattling exhaust pipes. Tough-looking men dressed like pirates in black leather drink, laugh and drink some more. Hard-looking women, in leather chaps and little else, straddle the saddles of

Harleys or walk around, among the miles of parked choppers, looking hot.

It could be argued that it's at Sturgis where the great American fixation with breasts reaches its zenith. After "Nice bike" the most common phrase heard is "Show us your tits." Not that most biker chicks have to be told to lift up their fringed leather bra. Even with their clothing in place, they show more cleavage than a convention of crouching plumbers.

Being a Bandido in Sturgis is good any year—you're biker royalty. That year, it was even better. We had come there with a challenging and delicate job to do, got it done, and now we could party. We gave it our uninhibited best for three or four days and then, having had our fill, packed our things and headed home. I rode with Dr. Jack and a few others and we took our time along the way, visiting friends and seeing the sights. It was on the trip home, and more particularly sitting around the campfire chatting with Jack, that I began to get an idea of the scope of the summit discussions.

The Angels–Outlaws peace treaty was actually a relatively small part of the proceedings, Jack said. The really significant development was the partitioning of the entire United States between those two clubs and, of course, us and the absent fourth player, the Pagans.

Whatever their differences, the four major gangs had a common concern: the independent one-percenter clubs, most of them regional, some with a presence in several states. These indies, it was now felt, were taking up too much space. It wasn't that they were growing; rather, the larger clubs were expanding and, in so doing, bumping up against the smaller ones. And not liking it much. There was a long list of these independents: the Dirty Dozen, the Chosen Few, the Hessians, the Iron Horsemen, the Coffin Cheaters, the Mad Hatters, the Ching-a-lings, the Vargas, the Mongols, the Rebels, the Henchmen and the Booze Fighters, as well as our old friends (and enemies) the Gypsy Jokers, the Ghost Riders, the Banshees and the Aces and Eights.

Under the agreement, the strongholds of the major clubs were enshrined as their exclusive domain: California, Alaska and Hawaii for the Hells Angels; Texas, New Mexico, South Dakota and Washington for the Bandidos; Florida and Illinois for the Outlaws; Pennsylvania,

Maryland, Delaware and Connecticut for the Pagans. In these states, the major clubs would not just be given the green light to get rid of any independents, they would actually be required to do so.

Then there would be states such as Oregon, Arizona, Louisiana and a few others where the indies were traditionally dominant and which served as useful buffers between the big boys. These states would be reserved for the indies—but they had to get rid of their three-piece patches and change them to one-piece. Similarly, they'd be required to remove any one-percenter designations. And while no major club would be allowed to set up shop openly in these states, adopting an indie as a "support club" would be tolerated. In practice this meant any indies that were big enough to be noticed, like the Gypsy Jokers in Oregon, were required to affiliate or face extermination. Still, there was no turning a support club into a probationary chapter in buffer states.

The rest of the country was basically up for grabs. This led to frenzied expansionist drives by the four big gangs and a dash for cover by dozens of independents. Some took the easy way out and affiliated with one of the big four clubs immediately, becoming probationary chapters and eventually patching over. Other indies stayed put and resisted. Several disbanded. A few decided that their future lay outside the country and moved offshore—the Coffin Cheaters to South Africa and Australia, the Rebels also to Oz and, eventually, the Gyspy Joker diehards to England, Ireland and, again, Oz.

Two exception states were Idaho and Montana. Even if they didn't serve as a buffer between antagonistic gangs, they were given that designation. It was a Hells Angels demand: if the Angels weren't going to get Washington State to complete their north–south axis of influence, then the Bandidos had to be denied an east–west chain stretching from South Dakota to Seattle. Of course, that was fine by us in Bellingham. After all, we had been sitting on the endangered list just weeks earlier, half expecting to be traded away by the Bandidos national executive.

In this way the Sturgis summit was similar to the famous 1957 mob summit in Apalachin, New York. Except in that case organized crime was only divvying up New York City; at Sturgis, it was the whole United States that was parceled out.

Some aspects of the agreement were easier to implement than others. For instance, the Banshees were still causing the Angels grief in southern California. So the Bandidos selflessly undertook to solve the problem—without, of course, fessing up to the fact that the Banshees were really their own members operating undercover. Other aspects of the agreement resulted in years of hostility and gallons of blood being spilled, especially in the free-for-all states. Sometimes the ugliness broke out between members of the big four and holdouts from the independents; sometimes it was the big four dueling for dominance among themselves.

Then there was the spinoff skulduggery. The Bandidos may have assented to California becoming the exclusive playground of the Angels, but that didn't mean they were keen on making it easy for them. So the Bandidos secretly began making nice with the L.A.-based Mongols and doing everything they could to quietly help them resist the Angels' eradication plan.

For their part, the Outlaws set up a gang called the Black Pistons in Florida and then, pretending to be dutifully cleaning out their backyard, pushed them north—where, of course, the Black Pistons were the vanguard of the Outlaws' expansion drive.

Big surprise: the "buffer treaty," as we came to call it, began disintegrating the moment everyone left Sturgis, and well and truly collapsed within two years. But by then it had resulted in a complete shakeout in the biker world, one that led to a consolidation of power for the big four, extinction for many indies and a great deal of confusion for cops around the country.

By then, of course, I'd made like many of the independents and got away while the going was good.

Back in Washington after the Sturgis summit, I was increasingly faced with a problem that had presented itself months earlier. Since we had the goods over and over again on everyone in Bellingham and Bremerton, I was no longer doing deals with them. Initially, it had been easy enough to come up with an excuse for not buying a few pounds of coke here or a stolen car there. After a while it became more difficult. It became downright uncomfortable when, over the course of a week, Vince or Gunk would call me repeatedly, pitching deals to which I would have to say no.

A solution arose six or eight weeks after Sturgis when Steve, the national VP from Lubbock, called me up from Texas, out of the blue.

"Hey, you remember my trailer?" he asked. I did. "Well, you think you might know somebody across the line"—up in Canada, he meant—"who might be interested in buying it?"

It sounded ridiculous to me. Even if the trailer was stolen, there was no reason to drive it across the country just to unload it. It wasn't as if Texas didn't have its share of trailer dwellers.

"I suppose I could find someone, depending on how much you want for it. But why go to all the trouble?" The last thing I wanted to do was buy a crappy trailer; at the same time, I didn't want to say no flat out. "You know, if it's money you need, I could make some arrangements," I added.

"No, it's no big deal. And I'm okay for cash," he said, and then got onto the real reason for calling. "There's a bar we're opening up down here and we wanted to know if you're interested in investing."

"Now that sounds more interesting. Let me check things out and I'll get back to you."

I didn't ask for any details. In the biker world, like that of many crooks, things are done backward: you don't ask for specifics until you say yes. There's a simple reason for this: if you're given the details and then say no, then you know too much. Knowing too much, and then saying no, was what got me into the infiltration game with Hobo.

If it had been up to me alone, I would have said yes on the spot to Steve. This was a golden opportunity to expand the investigation while also getting out of Washington with my rep intact. Still, my investment would obviously need to be approved by my handlers and their bosses. There was no saying yes and then changing your mind with the Bandidos, especially the hard-asses from Texas.

As soon as I hung up, I called the office and gave them an outline of the situation. "I need to know really quickly if this is a go or not," I said, suggesting we meet immediately. They put me off to the next day, however, saying they'd have to verify "jurisdictional control" and look into other questions.

When we finally met, we all agreed that the Texas invite was a gift from on high. It meant that I'd likely be able to transfer my patch to the Dallas or San Antonio chapter (Lubbock didn't have its own chapter despite being the center of Bandidos-dom—go figure) and be in a position to go not just national but National—nailing the top leadership.

"We're on, but it's going to take a little time for us to get everything together," said Larry Brant.

"So long as I know it's going to happen, then I'll say yes. But I want to be sure," I said.

At that, Brant hedged a bit. "Well, you can definitely say yes because either it's going to happen or else we'll bring the case down. It's one or the other."

It made sense to me. Little did I know, however, that behind the scenes Larry, Andy, Corky and the rest of the crew had major misgivings about a central part of the investigation: me.

Two or three months earlier, we had been sitting around the office discussing the case of an FBI undercover agent who had spent two years infiltrating the Hells Angels. He'd got relatively close to the gang but was never made a member. Still, it had been a successful case, one that led to a bunch of arrests and prosecutions. The undercover should have been happy and gone home. He did for a spell, but he couldn't leave his undercover persona behind; he was happier in that skin than his real one, it seemed. We were talking about him because he had just been arrested for shoplifting food. According to his wife, he hadn't been home in weeks and was broke. Still, he was unable or unwilling to go back to his real life. When he was busted, he'd used his old undercover identification, even though flashing his badge might have got him off.

I'd taken the guy's side somewhat, saying the Feebs should have made sure he had psychological help. I even asked point-blank if the DEA had any such help available. That had prompted Andy to make a scene.

"Come on!" he said. "An agent worth his salt doesn't need that kind of shit. The guy's a wuss!"

That silenced me on the subject, but Larry, it seemed, had filed my concern away. There had been other red flags: the Bren machine gun outburst with the G-man, the cowboy beating, my increasingly sporadic contact with my family back home, the fact that I'd taken to wearing my colors into the office as often as not. But Larry's reluctance to commit to a move to Texas was my first real indication that he and the others thought I might be getting in too deep.

Nonetheless, I had got the green light to say yes to investing in the bar, and the next day I phoned Steve from my house. I told him I was in and he confirmed that it would be a strip bar—no surprise since that was the only type of bar bikers were usually interested in.

"And how much money are we talking about?" I asked.

"Fifty large," he answered. It was less than I'd been expecting. I thought he'd want at least $100,000. Still, it didn't stop me from making a gambit.

"Listen, I don't want to be a silent partner. If I'm in, I'm in. I want an office at the club and access," I said. By access, I meant the right to look at the books and total involvement in day-to-day operations of the club. It was a big request, but being a silent partner wouldn't have got me any prestige or provided me with an excuse to move down to Texas.

"No problem," Steve said. Maybe he was so amenable because he was desperate to get his hands on my cash; or maybe he just saw my demands as inevitable. After all, a biker businessman likes to follow his money, and if there are any side benefits to an investment, and there usually are with peeler bars, he likes to take advantage of them.

Everything was unfolding as we wanted it to, and I phoned Andy with the good news. "We're good to go," I said. "Steve's cool with me moving down there and being totally involved. I just need to be down there in a day or two with the money."

"Great. But I need to get together with you alone and talk about something."

At the office early the next morning, before the rest of the staff arrived for work, Andy dropped a bombshell. Head office had approved the move to Texas, but they were refusing to allow him to stay with the case. It was an administrative thing, he said. He was stationed in Washington and they didn't want to go through the hassle of transferring him to Texas. Needless to say, he wasn't happy about it.

"We built this thing together and I want to stick with it to the end," he said. Appealing to my loyalty, he continued, "There's only one way I can see them changing their minds: you tell them you won't go if I don't go."

I would be only too happy to issue the ultimatum. Andy and I worked excellently together and always had. After more than three years, we were finishing each other's sentences and I had no interest in developing a new working relationship with an unknown, especially some Texas yahoo with more testosterone than brains.

After I told Andy I'd lay it on the line with the brass, he smiled broadly. "Okay, then. They want to meet with you tomorrow."

That pushed it all back a day, but it was fine with me. Texas, however, wasn't being so patient. The night before, I'd gone up to Vancouver to discuss the move with Liz. I'd presented it as the mop-up to the case and found a silver lining that appealed to her: Louise and Frank, Liz's parents, had moved to Florida about six months previously and I suggested that she and the kids could join them for as long as Texas lasted. After all, Texas and Florida were a lot closer than Texas and B.C. The trip to Vancouver had meant that I hadn't been around for Steve's calls. So he had phoned Vinny, asking where I was.

"Steve has been calling for you," Vinny told me later that day when I dropped by his place for a visit. "Where the fuck you been?"

"I'll get on it," I said, but I wasn't going to phone Steve until I had something solid to tell him—a departure day, a flight number. Too much vagueness didn't go over well with bikers like Steve.

The only Washington Bandido I'd told about my Texas business opportunity was Dr. Jack. I would have told George, but he was in prison, doing time on some charge from before I'd come onto the scene. I wanted someone of influence in the Bellingham chapter to know that my getting involved in the bar was the result of an invitation to invest, not me looking for other action behind the backs of the local boys. Jack had been encouraging, but he also warned me to be careful of the Texas Bandidos—there was a treacherous streak to them, he said, telling me a cautionary tale. Apparently, a few years previously, some of the guys in Texas had made the acquaintance of a rich businessman and wannabe bad-boy biker. They'd fed the guy's interest and dangled in front of him the prospect of becoming a member. First, though, he would have to do what all members did, they told him: make the club the exclusive beneficiary in his will. The idiot went along with it and of course soon found himself dead in the desert. They wouldn't go to such lengths with me—after all, I was a patched member—but I got the picture.

What I didn't realize was that Andy and Co. could be equally duplicitous, though it was probably for my own good.

I went into the meeting where I was going to issue the Andy ultimatum armed and wearing my colors—not a good start in retrospect. I had no plans to start banging my fist or anything; I would just calmly lay out my bottom line and leave it at that.

The local boys were there—Andy, Larry, Corky—along with two suits from the Seattle DEA office and a regional director of the FBI. We began with casual chitchat about the move to Texas and the opportunities it would offer. Soon enough, though, either Corky or Larry—I forget which one—said, "Too bad Andy can't go along with you."

I feigned surprise. "What do you mean Andy can't go?"

"What? Didn't Andy tell you?" came the reply. "It was decided Andy would be more useful up here and that we'll transfer the handling to a local guy."

First I got inquisitive—Why couldn't Andy come? Was the decision final? Who would the new handler be? Then I played the digesting act—staring at my feet, stewing on the news, thinking about it. Finally I went into the rejection role. "Well, I'm sorry, but if Andy isn't going, neither am I," I said simply. It was a pretty good performance, I thought. Little did I know that I was the one being played to perfection.

The suits then said it wasn't just an administrative decision and started questioning Andy's competence and his performance as handler. That got my back up.

"If you don't know he's capable, why are you so sure I am?" I said, my voice rising.

"We're not so sure," the suit said. "But you're all we've got."

That pushed me over the edge and the Bandido in me came out full force. I exploded to my feet and started stabbing at the suits with my finger, screaming, challenging, maybe even threatening them physically. I was in such a blind rage I can't remember what I said. All I recall is that I was yelling and swearing until, all at once, a light came on in my head. I just stopped and looked around. No one had moved from his chair, no one was saying anything. Confused, distraught, I turned and walked into Andy's office and just sat there in a daze, scared of who I'd become.

After about five minutes, Andy and Larry joined me. I told them that I knew I needed help, that I was getting lost in the character. They agreed and then gently let me in on something: one of the suits was actually a federal deprogrammer who had worked extensively with cults. The whole meeting—and more—had been a test to see how I was handling my double life. There had never been any plan to pull Andy from the investigation. It had just been a ploy to push me over the edge and get the sort of reaction needed to assess my state of mind. The ultimate goal: to gauge whether I was still receptive to following orders, and find out whom I was really working for—the cops or myself. I had failed the test.

We agreed that the thing I needed most right then was rest and time to reflect. So I went home, got a change of clothes and checked into one of the motels on Blaine's main strip. For two days I just disconnected from the Bandidos life, staying inside the whole time. I had three or four visits from the deprogrammer, who turned out to be a civilian employee of the FBI. They weren't formal "sessions" as such; he would just drop by for casual chats, sometimes bringing food. I also spent hours on the phone with Liz, reconnecting. Those talks did me a world of good. But just as important was the time I spent staring at the ceiling, thinking things over, getting my bearings back.

Finally, on the evening of the second day, I felt I had my shit together enough to go back to work and get the Bandidos job over with. The end was overdue. I had no idea, however, that it would come so quickly.

Looking back on it, I suppose my meltdown-turned-breakdown sapped not just my drive to make the case as big and devastating to the Bandidos as possible, but the drive of the whole office. The scene hadn't cost me any respect or admiration from Andy, Corky and Larry; on the contrary, it seemed to open their eyes to the pressure I'd been working under and engender within them a certain deference. But I think it was also a reality check. We'd taken the case way beyond anything we'd originally imagined or even dared to hope for, but it couldn't go on forever, nor nail every Bandido or badass biker everywhere. It was time to wrap it up.

Even calling in the deprogrammer must have been a difficult decision for Larry. Here was the biggest case ever to come to his office. It had been a huge success and, in going national, put his career on the fast track. He could have just let things play out, sent me to Texas and hoped for even bigger returns. Instead, he saved my life, I'm quite sure. And, in doing so, maybe even saved the case. Had I not been around to testify, racking and stacking those Bandidos we already had wouldn't have been the breeze it turned out to be.

The afternoon of my third day at the motel, I called Vinny to check in. His reception was cold.

"Where the fuck have you been?" he asked. Apparently some of the local boys had been trying to contact me for a couple of days, not to mention our friends from Lubbock. "They're waiting for you in Texas," he continued. "You got to get down there and take care of business."

"I know, I know. I'm just getting things organized. I'm going down as soon as possible."

"Things are already organized," Vinny said. "There are some guys from Texas in Seattle right now and they're going back and they want you to go back with them."

He gave me the name of a motel in a scuzzy part of Seattle and a phone number to call when I got down there. "Get down there tonight," Vinny ordered.

It all screamed setup to me, and not just because it was the first I was hearing about some Texas Bandidos visiting. I immediately called Andy and shared my concerns with him. He thought I was overreacting and said even if things did turn ugly, he and the boys would be covering me, I had nothing to worry about. His reassurances were comforting, but not very; I hadn't got as far as I had in this investigation without relying on my instincts, and things still felt wrong. I went, but on high alert.

I drove to Seattle, Andy et al. presumably not far behind, checked into the motel and made the call. I didn't recognize the voice that answered, but whoever it was seemed to have been waiting for me. He said someone would be coming straight over to pick me up to take me over to where the Texans were. This was definitely not right.

In less than ten minutes, two guys arrived at my door. One I recognized from the Resurrection, by then a full-patch Seattle Bandido. The other guy I'd never seen before. Another former Resurrection member was standing guard near the car.

At the car I hesitated for a moment before getting in. It wasn't long, but long enough for my worst fears to be confirmed: the guy I didn't recognize pulled out a semi-automatic nine-millimeter and said, "Get in." That cleared things up. I did as I was told.

Had I not, they might have knocked me out and stuffed me in the trunk. Instead, I sat in the back seat on the passenger side, waiting for Andy and gang to descend. I noticed that the driver didn't lock the sedan's doors from up front and thought that might help me escape if absolutely necessary. Still, I was sure it wouldn't come to that. Another indication that these guys weren't real professionals: it was the guy in the passenger seat who held the gun, making me an awkward target.

We drove for I don't know how long through Seattle, I wasn't even aware of what direction. At first I just wondered whether these three clowns would put up a fight when Andy and the team took them down. Then all I could think about was how long it was taking for Andy to act. I waited and waited until I decided I couldn't wait any longer—sooner or later we were going to arrive at where we were going and my options would then be even more limited.

As we took a left turn, I noticed the guy with the gun was looking ahead. That was all I needed. In an instant, I had the door open and was rolling out. God, it hurt. Still, the second I came to rest, I was up on my feet and running down a dark alley. Without looking back, I tried every door I came to. I didn't hear anyone behind me, but if someone was chasing me I, frankly, didn't want to know about it. Finally, a door gave when I tried it and I rushed into the pitch blackness within, slamming the door behind me. Then I stopped and just stood there about five or six feet from the door, waiting, my heart pounding.

Five minutes, ten minutes, twenty minutes passed, each going by excruciatingly slowly, with no sound of feet, no one pushing open the door. I relaxed a bit, sitting down on a concrete floor, leaning against a wall, but still not venturing out.

I stayed there at least an hour, maybe two, maybe more. I may have fallen asleep for a few minutes, but I'm not sure of that either. Eventually, everything aching, the cold of the concrete and the damp of Seattle in late fall having sunk into my bones, I got tired of waiting. Inaction leads to failure, I told myself, and I pulled my legs toward me and got to my feet.

I listened at the door. Nothing but the sound of my own breathing. I opened the door a crack and peered into the alley. A fine drizzle had turned the alley pavement into a mirror, reflecting the light bulbs above the doors.

Nothing. No movement or sign of life.

I opened the door wider and stepped out into the night. No one came out of a shadow, nothing sprang to life. I was really alone. I walked quickly to the street where I'd bailed from the car so unceremoniously earlier that evening. It was deserted. So I started walking toward the lights of downtown. A cab came my way and I hailed it. It didn't even slow down. No wonder: my clothes were ripped and I was covered in cuts, scrapes and blood.

Eventually I came to a pay phone and called the emergency number I had been given at the very start of the operation. By then I'd figured out I was on the south side and gave the intersection. The voice told me to wait there. It took fifteen minutes or so before three Seattle PD black-and-whites, sirens screaming, arrived. I got into the back seat of one, no encouragement of a semi-automatic required this time. I went with a couple of the uniforms to the nearest station; others went to the motel to retrieve my truck.

Andy, Corky and the tactical squad were at the station when I arrived. They told me they had been on the car the whole time but had somehow missed seeing me roll from it. For whatever reason, the bikers hadn't stopped and chased me; perhaps by then they had figured out they were being tailed. Not long after I bailed from the car, Andy and company had pulled it over. Of course, the three goons weren't talking, and Andy, astonished not to find me there, didn't want to ask them directly—it would blow any cover I had left. They were being held on some trumped-up charge (and eventually were charged with kidnapping and forcible confinement).

After I had my cuts and scrapes attended to, a tac squad member drove me back to Blaine while another drove my truck. We all went straight to the DEA office and into a discussion about what the next step should be.

As far as Corky was concerned, the investigation was completely done for. "We're going to evac you right now and take you across the line," he said. Back to Canada.

Andy wasn't so unequivocal. Sure, I had fallen afoul of the Texas nasties—that was a given. Still, he wondered if the local boys might stand up for me. For my part, I wanted it all to be over, but at the same time I agreed with Andy. No one, to our knowledge, suspected I was working for the cops. As far as they were concerned, I had simply fucked up; I'd promised cash to a member of the national and then not delivered as quickly as he'd expected. Maybe he had lost a little face, but it wasn't that big a deal one way or another.

Sure, they had sent what seemed to be a hit squad to deal with me and I was lucky they'd gone with the B team—had they sent Milo or guys from Texas, I would never have seen it coming. But that didn't necessarily mean that, given the chance, I couldn't still talk my way out of trouble by appealing to the common sense and loyalty of influential members in Bellingham.

In hindsight, that's what I should have tried to do as soon as Vinny ordered me down to Seattle and my date with destiny—gone over to his house, surprised him, explained my little disappearing act by saying I'd been nabbed at the border or something. Convinced him to argue my case with Texas. That's where our imagination failed us, that's where our diminished drive led us astray.

Sure, it was Vinny who had tried to set me up in Seattle, but

Andy and I decided that talking to him was still worth a shot. Even if it turned out that the investigation was beyond saving, trying would at least let us know for certain.

Finally, if Vinny lost it and said something along the lines of, "You should be dead by now!" or "What! You're still alive!" it would tie him into a conspiracy to kill me and perhaps be enough for other charges against him.

So, under close cover, I returned to my house up the alley from the office—thanks to the cameras and surveillance, we were sure no one was waiting for me outside or with a garrotte behind the door—and phoned Vinny. We didn't do it from the office because the fifteen or twenty members of the tactical team made it difficult to concentrate. I needed some breathing room to relax and get my wits about me. Furthermore, if things went badly with Vinny, I would have a few minutes to pack some belongings before being evac'd.

In the house, I sat down in the living room, turned on the TV and collected my thoughts. It wasn't long after midnight on what had been a seriously long evening. Finally, I called Vinny. His surprise at hearing my voice was obvious. There was a pause. But he recovered relatively quickly and without saying anything incriminating.

"I thought you were gone to Texas," he said. "Where are you?"

"At home. I haven't left yet," I answered.

"Well, you've got to stop by here to change your trailer hitch before you go," Vinny said, completely out of the blue.

Had I woken him up? Was he dreaming? There was some logic to his remark. When we drove to Texas, we often brought our bikes along on a rail trailer. Those trailers generally took a smaller ball on the hitch. But I wasn't trailering anything down to Texas—if I was going, I was flying, and Vinny knew that.

"Noooooo," I said.

He immediately lost his patience. "Anyway, I want you over here right now!" he barked.

That's when I knew it was well and truly over.

"Yeah right!" I answered. "Not in this lifetime."

I hung up and called Andy. He had heard the whole conversation through the wire. It was time to get out, we agreed. I grabbed my colors, the club's accounting books, a few clothes, three guns and a few other odds and ends, and headed down the alley.

Back in the DEA office, we watched a half-dozen or so Bandidos arrive at my house—a couple on bikes, the rest in a car and a truck. Vinny, Gunk, Craig and a few others came into focus on the four small monitors. They kicked in the front door, and Grinder, the dog I had given Mongo a year or so earlier but which he had returned to me when he discovered it wasn't purebred Rottweiler but half shepherd, attacked. Vinny shot him in mid-air. I was beside myself with anger and remorse that I'd neglected to bring the dog with me. Then they started going through the house, searching for anything that said Bandidos or was otherwise linked to the club. There wasn't much.

The tac squad used the gunshot as a reason to go in. Gunk was halfway up the ladder to the attic, where all the video and communications equipment was stored, when the team arrived. The Bandidos said that one of their members lived in the house and that they'd just been partying a bit heavily. The gun, they maintained, went off by accident. After being held and harassed for several hours by police, the bikers were let go. It was November 3, 1984. It wasn't time yet for the big bust or to let them know I'd been working for the cops. But it was time for me to get out of Dodge.

# CHAPTER SEVEN

# KKK to the Rock

———

That night, I went home to North Vancouver. An agent drove me, as much to get my guns across the border by flashing his tin as to make sure I arrived safe and sound. I'd phoned Liz earlier in the evening and she was still up, expecting me and as relieved as I was that the investigation had finally come to an end.

I stuck around Vancouver barely long enough to have a shower and do my laundry. During my therapy break a couple of days earlier we'd agreed that I'd take my family on a week-long Hawaiian vacation on the DEA dollar as soon as I was out of Blaine. It happened sooner than expected, but we weren't complaining. The beach time was just like it was supposed to be—hot and sunny—but I've never been much of a tropical vacation kind of guy. I'll swim if I have to—if I fall in or get pushed—but you won't catch me taking a dip or splashing in the surf for pleasure. The kids and Liz loved it, however.

Within a few days of returning to Vancouver, Liz and the kids were off to the sun and sand again, this time to visit Louise and Frank in Homestead, Florida, as we'd planned when I was still hoping to transfer my patch to Texas. Obviously, Texas wasn't in the plans now. Still, Liz, the kids and her parents had been looking forward to getting together, so they went ahead with the visit. As far as I was concerned, the time alone would let me learn to be me again. I had always been on the more emotionally remote side of things; my time with the Bandidos had only made me more so. So while superficially things were fine with Liz, there was a distance there, a gulf, that I would have to work to get across.

For a week or so I had relatively little contact with the outside world. I'd check in every day with Andy and the boys to see how the preparations for the arrests were going. The rest of the team had a lot

of paperwork and bureaucracy to get through: unsealing indict-
ments, writing up and swearing out affidavits, applying for warrants,
determining whether charges would be federal or state—that kind of
thing. It required constant back-and-forth between my handlers and
the assistant district attorney. I, however, was just a spectator.

Given how long the investigation had gone on, I didn't have any
friends in Vancouver anymore, and Liz's friends sure weren't going to
drop by if she wasn't there. I was still in biker mode—standoffish and
then some—and that kept regular people at a distance. The only
exceptions were Liz's sister Sue and her husband, Phil, who lived just a
few blocks away and dropped by almost every day. I suspect their
visits were a favor to Liz, whom I spoke to daily, and who no doubt
wanted someone keeping an eye on me. I didn't mind. Phil was a Bob
Dylan wannabe and would sometimes hang around and play guitar.

Slowly, I could feel myself getting back to normal, or at least a
workable facsimile of normal. One morning I woke up, had breakfast
and then hauled all my biker stuff out and into the middle of the living room floor. There I packed it all up into two boxes, sealed them
with duct tape and shoved them into the back of the closet. I was putting my Bandidos baggage away, literally and, I hoped, figuratively.

The Bandidos, however, weren't getting over me like I was getting over them. I found this out an evening or two later when Sue and
Phil dropped by.

The brother of a Mountie I knew owned a security company
that kept a few guard dogs, and the day after Liz and the kids left I'd
borrowed a Doberman from him. I wasn't necessarily expecting trouble
and, frankly, figured I'd appreciate the company, but I knew biker
gangs didn't take kindly to members disappearing on them, especially
with their colors. As it turned out, the dog almost got Phil killed.
Looked at another way, he may also have saved my life.

Every night about eight, I would take the dog out into the yard
and chain him up so he could do his business. The house we were
renting was on a corner lot, so except for a thick hedge surrounding
the backyard it was exposed to the street. That night Phil wanted a
breath of night air and offered to take the dog out for me. He had just
clipped the dog to his chain when a shot rang out. Phil went down.

Luckily for him, he had been crouching down and the bullet went through his thigh rather than into his chest. Luckily for the shooter, the dog had just been attached to the chain—otherwise he would have had his teeth in the shooter's ass in no time. The gunman had been on the other side of the hedge, only about fifteen feet from Phil, when he'd fired his .38 revolver.

Police were on the scene in minutes, but they never caught anyone. The next day, after the Mounties swung into action on behalf of the DEA, I was driven to the airport, escorted through security and put on a flight to Florida, feeling more than a little rattled and leaving poor Phil in hospital to have a metal pin put in his leg.

In Florida, Liz and I rented a place across the street from Frank and Louise. We were there indefinitely now, not simply for a prolonged pre-Christmas visit. I continued my regular calls to Andy and Co., helping out as much as I could with preparations for the busts. I made a trip or two back to Seattle and Texas to consult with police and prosecutors. As the big day approached and the arrest and search warrants were nailed down, the DEA's attention turned toward the mechanics of the raids: who had the biggest arsenal or kept the meanest dogs, who was likely to go peacefully and who would probably act stupid and dangerous. I spent hours with different tac team leaders and analysts making drawings that showed exits and doorways, bedrooms (the raids would be made, as usual, in the early morning), possible hiding places and the like. I was thankful to have been trained by the Mounties when it came to making notes. On the inside of my notebooks I had sketches of all the houses I had entered.

Finally, early in the morning of February 21, 1985, the hammer was brought down by more than a thousand cops in nine states and one Canadian province.

The big show happened outside of Lubbock, where the gang had a trailer compound ringed by two chain-link fences, which themselves were separated and topped with razor wire. Andy, wearing camo pants, an orange Bandido Busters T-shirt specially printed up for the occasion, a white silk scarf and a pair of goggles, rode a borrowed armored personnel carrier right through the fences, followed by legions of police. Behind the police, the press poured in. Guess whose picture made the evening news? For a long time after that, we referred to Andy as Rommel.

In Lubbock and elsewhere, the busts went overwhelmingly smoothly. Most of the bad guys didn't put up much resistance. Those who did were quickly subdued.

I'd told the tac team rounding up the Bellingham chapter that Terry Jones would probably come through the living room from his bedroom with a gun cocked and ready. I also advised them to ignore Jones's dog, the pit bull Binky. He was harmless and would hide. To avoid having to shoot Terry, the tac team hit his house in such a way that he was immediately surrounded, and he surrendered. Binky did indeed hide, after peeing on the floor.

I'd also predicted that Dr. Jack would cooperate so long as the cops treated his wife with respect. When they hit his house, they were polite, and didn't enter the bedroom until his wife had a chance to dress. There, and most other places, things went well. There were a few cuts and bruises, and in Fort Worth, Texas, a trooper was shot but not seriously wounded by one particularly hotheaded biker. Beyond that, nothing too dire. No dead bikers or associates. Other than Binky, however, the dogs weren't so lucky.

At the end of the day—actually, probably before noon—law enforcement agencies had arrested ninety-three patched Bandidos, two British Columbia Hells Angels and dozens of gang associates. Seized were some drugs and an impressive arsenal of weaponry: more than one hundred machine guns, three hundred other firearms and a bunch of explosives. In terms of arrests and charges it was—and remains—the biggest bust of outlaw bikers in U.S. history.

All the bikers faced multiple charges, some federal and some state, some RICO. In certain jurisdictions—Washington, Texas and Louisiana included—the law gives an accused the right to confront the person who has denounced him, in this case me. So, following the takedown, I spent about a week flying across the country facing my old friends in small interrogation rooms. They or their lawyers were allowed to ask me questions relating to their charges.

Vinny was the first up. He stared menacingly at me as his lawyer asked stupid questions such as, "Are you sure that this is indeed the man who sold you cocaine?" At one point Vinny abruptly reached for the ashtray and the two cops in the room jumped in surprise. I just thought it was lame. I looked at my erstwhile chapter president and felt nothing—no pity, no allegiance, no anger. Yes, he had tried to kill me, but he was just doing what was expected of him. I didn't take it personally. For his part, he didn't say a word. He just glared.

When it came to Dr. Jack, all he wanted to know was why I turned. The club could have helped me through whatever problems I had, he said.

"Jack, I didn't turn," I told him. "I was hired from the start to get you guys. I was never the guy you thought I was. That guy never existed." As I was saying it, I realized it was as much to reassure myself as to convince him. He picked up on it.

"Sure he does," he said. "Somewhere inside you're still Bandido, and you'll never change that."

Jack ended up taking a plea and got four years. I never had to testify against him. Most others also took the easy way out, pleading guilty to reduced charges either before or after preliminary hearings, and got similar terms: Vinny, George Wegers (who was in prison at the time of the takedown), Jersey Jerry, Terry Jones, Sly Willie.

As is almost always the case, the soft sentences were a bit of a letdown after all the work. Even those, such as Gunk, who pleaded not guilty got off lightly. They were almost all out of jail by 1988 or 1989.

A couple of things, however, made me happy. Everyone we charged went down, with the exception of the wife of Rex Endicott. That was fine with me, because as far as I knew she was innocent. At her trial, her lawyer asked me if I thought she was involved. I testified that I had never said anything in front of her and didn't think she knew anything.

It also pleased me that Mongo was never charged with anything. At one point in the investigation he needed money and had offered to sell me some coke that George had given him. I passed on it and lent him some cash instead. Even if he had a psychopathic streak, I knew he was in the Bandidos because of the brotherhood, not the criminal opportunities it presented. I also felt a sincere affection for him and his quirky ways, despite his racism and occasional viciousness.

From almost any way you looked at it, the investigation was an unmitigated success. We might not have gone in the direction we'd originally intended—rather than getting the goods on the dealings between the Washington State Bandidos and bikers in Canada we'd infiltrated the American gang nationwide—but we far exceeded any expectations we had when we started out. All the bad guys we arrested were convicted and sent to prison. And, special bonus, no one had been killed or maimed.

Still, in terms of dealing a real blow to the Bandidos, it's hard to find evidence that we made much of a difference. When I arrived on the scene, there were two chapters in Washington, in Bellingham and Bremerton; while I was there, two more were created, in Seattle and Yakima, by co-opting the Resurrection and the Ghost Riders. These days Washington boasts at least a dozen Bandidos chapters. Elsewhere their expansion has been just as impressive. At best our investigation slowed them down a bit—that's all.

And for me, on a personal level, the case was a mixed blessing. Sure I made good money and had a lifetime's worth of excitement and crazy experiences. Sure it provided no shortage of good stories for grandkids (if I ever have them) or bar-stool neighbors (if I ever take up drinking). But I've never seen my "victory" over the Bandidos as a triumph of good over evil. They changed me more than I did them. In many ways, they were the closest thing I'd ever had to a family. Maybe that's why, after more than twenty years, I still have my patch and my Bandidos membership card. So I guess Dr. Jack was right.

I remained on the DEA payroll through all of 1985 and into 1986, until the case's last court date was over. This was before the days of direct deposit, so while I was in Florida, collecting my pay involved going into the DEA office in Miami. There I made the acquaintance of Frank Eaton and Tom Rice, two agents who had their hands full trying to keep Florida from becoming completely snowbound thanks to the Colombian cocaine cartels.

They quite quickly saw what was clear to everyone: neither Florida nor inactivity was for me. They tried to interest me in working with them on the Colombians. Even if I was bored with the beach and mall routine, I didn't bite. I had heard some very nasty things about Colombians. I may have been out of the Bandidos frying pan, but I wasn't yet ready for the Colombian fire.

I was then offered an FBI–ATF job infiltrating the Ku Klux Klan in Mobile, Alabama, and finding out if there was any truth to rumors that members were not only involved in illegal weapons and drug dealing but also had what the feds called "subversion"—what today might just be labeled terrorism—on their minds. A bunch of good ole boys dressed in white hoods and swigging bourbon sounded more my speed at the time than Uzi-toting Colombians, so I took the gig. I didn't ask Liz what she felt about it, but I doubt she was displeased to have me out of her hair.

All I was given was the address of a pawnshop on Dauphin Street in Mobile and the name of its owner, Willie, who had been identified as a prominent member of the local KKK chapter. So, using a different name as a precaution, I rented a room at a motel two blocks away from the store and started hanging around the neighborhood. In particular, I became a regular at a little greasy spoon next door to Willie's store. I did that for two weeks or so, until I was reasonably sure Willie had noticed me. Then I finally went into the pawnshop. It was a cramped but neat place, with a pronounced specialty in guns and other weapons, including crossbows, bayonets and knives. There were the other staples of the trade—guitars, amps and other electronics, a jewelery counter—but Wille's money was evidently in firearms. A bunch of military memorabilia—badges mostly—testified to his personal interests.

Willie was friendly in a Southern way, and solicitous in a store-owner kind of way. But he wasn't unguarded. Initially our conversations were superficial, hardly more revealing than chats about the weather. We'd talk about fishing, guns, music. I also made it clear right from the start that I was a rabid racist, something that clearly put him at ease.

"There are a lot of fucking niggers in this town!" was one of my first observations.

"There sure is," he answered. "You can't get away from them."

After that, almost every chance I got I would hint at a hatred of blacks. A school bus would drive by and I'd remark, "You got busing in this town?" Or we'd be talking about cars and I'd say that I used to own a Delta 88.

"That's a good car," he'd say.

"And a big one. You can stack ten niggers back to back in the trunk."

After maybe three increasingly lengthy visits, he felt that he knew me well enough to spout off with his own racist views. He wasn't like some of the nutcases I met on the job who still had ambitions of "cleansing" the United States. His was a more pessimistic view: blacks were everywhere and would remain so; all whites could do was keep apart from them and stand their ground.

At the back of the store there was a TV and a chair on the merchant side of the counter and a couple of stools on the customer side. I would sit back there with him and just hang out. Willie wasn't overly inquisitive about my origins or reasons for being in Mobile. I just let on that I was a drifter, a bit of a ne'er-do-well, someone who couldn't find a place to fit in. Having just come off the Bandidos case, I suppose I emanated enough hardness that Willie didn't need much convincing.

Before long, maybe a couple of weeks, we were spending time together outside the store as well. By this time he had admitted to being a KKK member. Contrary to what the feds had told me, he didn't occupy an important position in the Klan; in his early thirties, he was still too young for that. Nonetheless, he looked as if he'd had a tough life already—he was short, wiry, stooped, with a mouth full of crooked yellow teeth. The look of having been raised poor in the backwoods. But Willie did serve an essential purpose for the local Klan: he was counted on to be a recruiter of new, younger blood. And so he began taking me along with him to barbecues and on errands, and on other occasions when I would meet his KKK friends. Most of them were as straight and upstanding as could be—"pillars of the community." And often very well off. Several had boats at a local yacht club, and we'd sometimes join them for picnics on islands in Polecat Bay.

Eventually, after a little more than a month in Mobile, I was invited to a Klan meeting where, along with about twenty or so other new members, I took what Willie called "the oath of the initiates." We met in a pasture beside a gravel road outside of Mobile. There were a couple of beat-up trailers where mostly older, gray-haired members changed into their robes and hoods and where I put on a borrowed set. Willie hadn't explicitly asked me whether I wanted to join up, but I knew what was happening. I'd been over to his house a week or two earlier and we'd watched *The Birth of a Nation,* the classic Klan film from 1915. And he'd given me a scrap of paper with the oath scrawled on it to memorize.

" 'In the name of God and my country, I promise to defend with valor and integrity the aims of the order,' " I duly recited. " 'To keep its secrets, to obey its orders, to help the members in times of danger and need, to recognize the authority of its leaders, and not to be a traitor to its rules.' " To me it sounded like a Boy Scout mantra, but proclaiming it publicly won me trust and gave me access to other Klansmen.

Soon after the initiation, I got down to business. My first deal was with Willie himself. I let on that I was connected to bikers in Florida who had an appetite for serious weaponry, and he sold me a converted AR-15 with a grenade launcher attached to it. It cost me $1,500 and I promptly turned it in to my ATF handlers, whom I would meet on a weekly basis in Pensacola, across the Florida state line.

Almost immediately after that deal I bought a MAC-10 machine pistol from a friend of Willie's, again, I claimed, for a biker customer. That led to a blur of gun deals—about a dozen with various Klan-connected individuals—over the next two or three weeks. I'd put out feelers to buy drugs but hadn't got anywhere. Similarly, the concern that these clowns had any serious potential or eagerness for "subversion" seemed exaggerated. So, after a couple of months in Mobile, the FBI and ATF decided that we had gone as far as we would likely get. At least there was enough evidence to shake up the Klan on a local basis. I was pulled and the ATF descended.

The cops had my notes and photos, maybe video from the cover team that followed me on my transactions. Still, I expected to be called for court, at least to a preliminary hearing. But in the end, nothing. I don't know whether Willie and the boys pled out or if the charges against them ended up being dropped for some reason. From my perspective, it was a short, sweet and moderately successful operation in what was now, without a doubt, a career of infiltration.

During my two months or so in Mobile, I hadn't once gone back to Homestead to visit Liz and the kids. I called them every other day or so, but not as often as I'd been speaking with Andy and the gang. Any time I'd left the Mobile region, it had been to tie up Bandidos loose ends—the big bust had occurred just days before the KKK job started, so there was a lot of work to do.

Once I vanished from the scene in Mobile, I made a beeline for our Florida home, but not to linger. Instead, after pausing for barely enough time to pack our things, Liz, the kids and I headed north again. It wasn't that Willie and the gang had me all that spooked—they didn't seem as if they had the reach or the nastiness to come after me (especially since I was white). But I had told them I spent a lot of time in the Miami area, there were the children to consider, and I wasn't attached to living in Florida anyway. In fact, I hated it. It was always hot, humid and buggy, the only attractions the malls and the TV.

Liz was perfectly happy to move again too. Living near Frank and Louise was fine, and useful as far as child care was concerned, but both of us found Florida tedious. We also pined for Canada—it just seemed to suit us better. Vancouver was obviously out; Ontario wasn't an option because that's where Ottawa is, and I've always had a thing against it; we'd tried Quebec and it hadn't worked for Liz. So we decided on eastern Canada. We chose Saint John, New Brunswick, for no other reason than it was the city in eastern Canada closest to the U.S. border. In fact, once we got on the I-95 just outside Miami, we never had to turn—it took us the whole way.

Neither Liz nor I had ever been to Saint John, and neither of us knew anyone who lived there. That was just the way we wanted it. We arrived late one May evening in 1985. It was still distinctly chilly and we suddenly thought that maybe the heat of Florida wasn't such a bad thing. Still, the locals were acting as if it was high summer, sitting on their porches with their pant legs rolled up.

We took a room at a motel on the edge of town and the next morning bought a paper and started to look for a home. It wasn't long before we found what looked like a good place at a reasonable price—the upper floor of a duplex in a leafy central neighborhood of older Victorian houses. The owners, a pleasant Lebanese family with several mostly teenaged children, lived around the corner.

Mahmoud, the father, came over to show us the place along with a young man he introduced as his soon-to-be son-in-law, Bashir. We worked out a deal for the place. I had a Rottweiler puppy I had bought in Florida and that was a bit of an issue, but eventually we agreed that I'd give Mahmoud a damage deposit. We all got along perfectly well, with no hint at how complicated things would get between us in the years to come.

Liz and I had brought a bunch of stuff up from Florida in our pickup and a U-Haul trailer, and we spent the first few days in the new place unpacking. Then, as soon as the phone was installed, I called up Scott Paterson to let him know my whereabouts and tell him I was available for work again. Several months later, after Liz, the kids and I had enjoyed a relaxed summer, he called me back to say that a Mountie from Newfoundland wanted to talk to me.

Without telling me any details of the job or how long it might last, Corporal Pete Peterson asked if we could meet in Halifax in two days' time. For me it was a three-hour drive away, for him a flight from St. John's. I said sure—something that didn't make Liz very happy at all. She liked Saint John and didn't want to be forced to move again soon. She was thinking of settling down and raising our kids there, beginning a more normal life, maybe even embarking on a career of her own.

I too was getting tired of the tension, turmoil and inherent instability of my job. Still, I loved the work. So she and I talked late into the night and decided that I would take only small cases with long breaks in between while Liz upgraded her education. No more three-year, complete personal transformations, like the biker gig. I still had several Bandidos court cases pending and was being paid a monthly stipend, so there would be no money concerns for a while.

When I left for Halifax, it was a warm and bright early fall day. Liz was taking the kids to the local United church to check it out and meet the minister. She wasn't religious; in fact, that's why she chose the United Church of Canada. In many ways it's the least dogmatically religious of churches. Certainly it can't be called doctrinaire or severe. Liz opted for it because it seemed like a good way to meet people in a somewhat sleepy, traditional town such as Saint John. Especially if you wanted to put down roots.

I met up with Peterson at a Halifax hotel. He was with a member of the Royal Newfoundland Constabulary, Newfoundland's quaintly named provincial police. They were both big-hearted, friendly guys—typical Newfs—but in a somewhat pathetic predicament. There were ten dealers of note in the province and the cops wanted them off the streets. But after putting all their pennies together, the local RCMP and the RNC only had enough money for a ten-week investigation. That was one dealer per week—a tall order.

I took the job nonetheless and the next morning returned home for two weeks of prep and planning while the cops got their ducks in a row. Try as I might, however, I couldn't figure out a good story with which to get in. Newfoundland isn't a big place—a half million people or so—and its largest city and capital, St. John's, is just a fraction of that, back then maybe 100,000. To boot, the island is a long way from anywhere. That means that everyone knows each other and new faces stand out and are talked about endlessly. Add to that the fact that I was going there in gloomy, gray October, when the tourists would have long since headed home, and I had to be prepared to be noticed early and often—no slow blending in this time. Unable to come up with a plan, or even a good excuse for why I was visiting the Rock in the fall, I finally resigned myself to flying by the seat of my pants.

I arrived at the St. John's airport and retrieved the little green car that the cops had left for me in the parking lot. Task number two was finding a place to live. In the meantime, I checked into a motel on the edge of the city. When I entered its reception area, workers were putting the final touches on a fountain meant to spruce up the lobby. It actually looked pretty nice, and the owner behind the counter was certainly proud of it. We chatted for a while and she told me they would be testing the fountain later that day. She encouraged me to attend the little ceremony.

"Sure thing," I said before going to my room, settling in and calling Peterson to let him know I had arrived. We arranged for a late night meeting. When I went back through the lobby on my way out, everybody had mops and buckets, hard at work cleaning up a flood. It seems that before turning the fountain on, they had drilled holes into its basin to run wiring for the lights.

I spent the first week to ten days on the Rock finding my way around and locating the investigation's targets and the joints they hung around in. Of the ten dealers, I chose first to target a Latino by the name of Carlos. He was the person most in need of money, and that, combined with the fact that he was an outsider himself, made me think he'd be the least likely to check me out too closely. He was a young street hustler type, short and slight—not unlike me fifteen years previously—and he shared an apartment with a Latin American family who had somehow washed up in Newfoundland. I rented a small place myself on the same street and the cops wired it with audio and video. Then I started to stalk Carlos, looking for an opening, a break.

One day he drove by my place in his old, red and white Monte Carlo. I noticed it had a For Sale sign in the rear window with a phone number. Perfect. I called and arranged for Carlos to come by and discuss the car. My only prop was an empty cocaine vial showing traces of a white powder along the rim and bottom (baking soda, of course) sitting on the table. As soon as we sat down, I grabbed it and put it in my pocket—making sure, of course, that Carlos saw it. Then I told him I needed a car for the few weeks I would be in Newfoundland but couldn't have it in my name. I didn't want anything fancy, something I could easily walk away from. He was keen to work out a deal for his car, but I backed off, saying it was too flashy for my purposes.

"Why you selling it, anyway?" I asked.

"I need the money."

"Well, if you need money, maybe we can figure something else out," I said, casting the line. I was improvising, but it seemed like a good bet.

"Depends."

"Well, I need a guy Friday. You know what that is?" He didn't, so

I explained. "Someone who can help me out, show me around. Introduce me to the people I should know, steer me clear of the people I don't want anything to do with. 'Cause the last thing I want before my big deal comes through is to get mixed up with the wrong people."

With the mention of the term "big deal" he lit up. He immediately figured I had money—I never said that the Monte Carlo was too expensive—and he wanted as much of it as possible.

"I can get you anything you want—anything," he said, even though I hadn't hinted at wanting to score.

Once I was in with Carlos, I was as good as in with everyone else. After all, this was Newfoundland and everyone knew everyone. As Carlos introduced me to the other dealers in St. John's, I developed a cover story that I was on the Rock to organize the transportation to Quebec of thousands of pounds of hash from a ship due any day. The hash was to be trucked across the province and then ferried to the mainland. But if Carlos or anyone else was inclined, I could siphon off a few pounds, I let on. Sure enough, they were keen, and soon, thanks to Carlos's fixing and connecting, almost all the targets on the list were putting in orders or at least expressing serious interest.

As the days passed and the hash boat didn't arrive, I told Carlos and some of my other new contacts that, actually, I might need to score some coke off them in order to keep some of the people involved in the transport of the hash—drivers and the like—content. They were scattered around town, keeping a low profile, I suggested. And getting bored and edgy with all the waiting.

Soon I was buying an ounce here, half an ounce there. After four weeks on the island I took a week off and went home to relax. Upon my return, Pete Peterson had organized the takedown. I spent two more weeks taking care of loose ends, keeping the targets excited about the impending shipment and making secondary buys. By then I had nine of the ten guys on the list. The tenth was away from Newfoundland and wouldn't be back for a while.

Finally, I announced to Carlos that the drug ship had arrived and had him get word to the other targets that we would meet at the Newfoundland Hotel to organize the final details of the sale and transfer of the hash. And, of course, I'd need to collect a down payment. The police duly installed a video camera in the TV above the minibar in the hotel room.

"Serve yourself," I told them as they arrived, and they all fixed themselves drinks and let the police get full-frontal footage of them. Then, when everyone was sitting down, I expressed some concern about whether they could handle the amounts they had ordered. "I don't want to pull two hundred pounds off the load and then only have buyers for one hundred," I told them.

That achieved its intended goal, prompting them to brag about all their drug-dealing experience. These guys were tough enough for an isolated market like St. John's, but any one of them would have struggled in the larger criminal circles I'd learned to negotiate. We talked delivery and they gave addresses. By that point I'd collected the down payment cash. So, after an hour of self-incrimination from them all, I'd had enough—I gave the signal and the police came crashing through the door. Like Jean-Yves Pineault six years earlier in Hong Kong, I hit the deck immediately. But there was no trouble. We had them, their money and their networks all on tape.

Three weeks ahead of schedule, I was on my way back home, thinking, "How stupid were those guys?" Ignoring, of course, the other question, "Why couldn't the cops catch them without my help?" I liked Peterson and his colleagues too much to think about that.

Eventually, seven of the targets, including Carlos, took guilty pleas. The other two were convicted at trial.

Back in Saint John, I found Liz ever more involved in the United Church. She wasn't getting religious—she was still too sensible for that—but she enjoyed the people and the community. Gradually, over the winter and spring, she began to see a role in the church as a possible career. Nursing, which she'd studied at the University of British Columbia, had long since lost any charm, and the United Church was a welcoming place. It had been ordaining women since 1936 and was far and away the most liberal of the established Christian churches in North America.

We agreed that come September 1986 she'd enroll in religious studies at St. Thomas University in nearby Fredericton—the first step in becoming a minister. First, though, she would need to be nominated as a potential candidate for the ministry by her local church. That wasn't as easy as she expected. Some of the more chauvinist members of the congregation resisted—just because they'd been ordaining women for fifty years didn't mean everyone liked the idea—as did some people who'd been wondering about her sketchy husband.

I was still disappearing fairly regularly to deal with what remained of the Bandidos business, and few people felt they had a handle on me. Liz was very persistent and won most people over, but the senior minister of the local church—it was big enough to have two ministers—was openly against her nomination. Eventually I had to get involved. Suffice it to say that my powers of persuasion hadn't been hurt by my time with the Bandidos. Nothing more than words were exchanged, but it still didn't take long to convince the minister to stop blocking Liz's plans.

I didn't work at all through 1986 or 1987—at least not in what had become my career. The phone was ringing—both from Scott Paterson in Vancouver and Andy Smith in Washington—but I wasn't biting. I almost took a job referred to me by Pete Peterson out in Newfoundland, working the recently created Halifax chapter of the Hells Angels. The job was nearby and it was something I knew. But I ended up saying no—I just didn't feel like it. I was still collecting DEA pay, and I was enjoying being an active, involved dad for a change. I became a Beaver and Cub Scout leader, cooked and cleaned, and generally just got a kick out of being a househusband. It was all new and all so different, though I wasn't doing it for the novelty factor. As of September, Liz was a full-time student, so the role needed to be filled and I loved every minute of it.

Around that time my son, then four or five, entered Fredericton's Third Annual Earthworm Race. The local CBC-TV station decided to profile his efforts despite the fact that his worm, Squirm, seemed to die before it reached the finishing line—the edge of a table. "I did my best and my worm did my best," he told the CBC interviewer with utter seriousness. I had a misgiving or two about appearing in the item, but eventually did so in dark glasses and a hat. I figured that if a bad guy tracked me down thanks to Squirm the worm, it would almost have been worth it.

Even if we weren't hurting for money, I still kept my "ear to the tier" as they say in prison, my eyes open for almost any interesting opportunity. It was in my blood and the instinct had served me well, from getting by on the streets of Hull to pretending to be a Bandidos businessman.

For instance, one day I was watching TV and a guy knocked at the door. "Your stuff's here," he announced, pointing at an eighteen-wheeler parked in front.

"Okaaaaay . . ." I said, not knowing what he was talking about.

All my things from Blaine and Vancouver had been shipped out to me by the DEA, taking me entirely by surprise. I had simply written that stuff off, left it behind like a shed skin. Now I suddenly owned four TVs and three VCRs, not to mention far too much furniture (including the leather set stolen from the immigration officer's house). It made for one big yard sale.

It also allowed me to make $15,000 from the RCMP. The DEA had included in the shipment the candy-apple red Harley FXRT that it had bought for me for $5,500 from Jersey Jerry. I had no need or desire for it. In fact, I didn't even want to look at it—those kinds of bikes tend to attract trouble. A couple of months later, Scott phoned me up saying the RCMP were launching an undercover biker probe out west and needed a convincing Harley. Did I know where they might get one? I sure did. Since they didn't have funding yet for a full investigation, I agreed to sell it to them on a conditional installment plan: $5,000 down, $10,000 more after thirty days if the project took off. If it didn't, the bike would come back to me. The Mounties paid up and I never saw the bike again. I have no idea whether it led to a successful investigation or not.

Other money-making schemes were more straightforwardly entrepreneurial. Thanks to the guy who shot Phil, we'd spent the Christmas of 1984 in Florida, and I'd been shocked by the ridiculous prices down there for real Christmas trees. So, almost two years later, I decided to get in on the racket myself. I borrowed a good-sized trailer from my landlord, attached it to my pickup and drove up to northern New Brunswick, where I bought about 250 tightly bundled trees for two dollars each. Then I hightailed it down the I-95 to Homestead, where Frank and I set up a stand outside the store of a gun dealer he knew. A few weeks later I was back in Saint John in time for Christmas with more than ten thousand dollars in pure profit.

In the eighteen months we'd been in Saint John, we'd become reasonably good friends with our landlord, Mahmoud, and his family. It would have been hard not to, they were such hospitable people. Even though we were just their tenants, they had invited us to the wedding of their eldest daughter, Natalie, and Bashir a couple of months after our arrival. And we occasionally got together on Sundays, after Liz and the kids had been to the United church and Mahmoud's family had gone to the small Lebanese Maronite church.

Our friendship wasn't without its dramas. While I was selling the trees in Florida, Mahmoud had had a blowout with his second daughter, April, and had hit her. She fled the house but, being in her teens, had no money or vehicle and nowhere to go. So she came to our place. We'd moved to the downstairs unit of the duplex by this time and, sure enough, shortly after April arrived seeking refuge, her father, his eldest son, another male relative and a couple of Lebanese friends were at the door. They angrily demanded that Liz surrender April, but Liz stood her ground, helped out by Thumper the Rottweiler, no longer a puppy.

The family mob eventually backed off and April didn't leave our house for a week, several days after I'd returned from Homestead and gone straight over to my landlord's house to set things straight.

"This is how we deal with things in our culture," was the gist of Mahmoud's explanation.

"Good for you," I said. "But next time you lay a finger on your daughter, I'll call the cops."

Still, Mahmoud was a decent guy and didn't hold my intrusion into his family affairs against me for long. A good thing, since in due course I was to become part of that family.

Liz received her religious studies diploma from St. Thomas University in the spring of 1988. Her next goal—and the last major hurdle before

she became a United Church minister—was a Master of Sacred The-
ology degree. For that, she would have to attend McGill University in
Montreal for three years.

We were clearly on completely different tracks. Largely alone
with the kids for the first six years of our marriage, she had had her fill
of domesticity and was eager to go beyond the family, into the world,
and into a meaningful career. Studying in a big, vibrant city like Montreal can only have fueled that urge. Not that she was living a wild coed
existence—she was studying for the ministry, after all, and the living
situation we arranged wasn't exactly conducive to late nights and partying. In return for room and board, she moved into the Verdun home
of an elderly woman, kept her company and kept an eye on her well-
being. Still, what Liz was aspiring to was very different from what I was
interested in at that point. I had been adventuring in the world since I
was a child; now I was intent on playing an important role in a very
different, much more tightly focused adventure, one I'd never really
had—a family.

So even if the phone kept ringing, and even if Liz and I had an
agreement that allowed me to take short infiltration jobs now and again,
I'd lost the desire. In some ways, I guess I was burned out. And anyway,
once Liz was studying in Montreal, I was tied to the house and Saint
John, at least during her school terms.

The DEA money had stopped coming, but even so, we were getting by. I made a bit of cash teaching martial arts, but it was really just
a hobby. Much more lucrative was a gig I had for three years or so
starting in 1987 or 1988 selling disability insurance for Canada Life. I
did well enough at it that we moved from our apartment to a spacious
house we rented outside of downtown. After a year or so there, we
took the plunge and became homeowners ourselves, buying a brand
new house a block or two away that was built on the grounds of an old
drive-in movie theater. For me, coming from the cramped quarters of
my childhood in Hull, it was a dream house: big front and back yards,
all sorts of room in the basement, bay windows, two-car garage—
almost too much room. My daughter loved it just as much. It was the
first place we'd lived in with a second story, and she'd always dreamed
of having her bedroom on an upper floor.

By then Liz was in her final year of studies at McGill, and in fact not at McGill much at all. Most of the last year was a practicum, spent working out of a church that needed the help—usually a church with a small or poor (or both) congregation. The church Liz was assigned to was in the blink-and-you've-missed-it town of Massey in northern Ontario. If Montreal was far from Saint John, Massey was at least twice the distance. So no surprise that we saw even less of each other, especially given that two of the major holidays for me and the kids—Christmas and Easter—were the busiest times of the year for a minister.

That certainly didn't help our marriage. Nor did the fact that Liz was clearly beginning to believe in all the God stuff. It became a running argument between us—or at least a point of contention, since we never had knock-'em-down, drag-'em-out arguments, which may have been a problem itself. I would tell her, "I don't mind you becoming a minister, I just don't want to live with someone who believes that shit." Needless to say, she didn't appreciate my emphatic atheism.

Finally, in February 1990, when Liz was on a visit home from Massey, we sat down and had a long-overdue talk, one we'd been planning for a while. It wasn't loud and ugly—just the opposite. But the upshot was the same. She couldn't live anymore with my incapacity for emotional intimacy (which I've never really got over) and certainly didn't see me as an appropriate spouse for the minister she was soon to be. I couldn't handle me and the kids playing second fiddle to God and her new religious career. So we decided to split.

Over the next few weeks, we figured out the fine points. It was easily done. My demands were simple: I wanted the two kids, the cat and the dog, and the station wagon to take us wherever we would go, because I certainly wasn't going to stick around in Saint John. She could have everything else—the house, the furniture, the bank accounts, the retirement savings.

By April, I'd herded the kids and the animals into the packed wagon and headed back to the only place I could think of: Hull.

Aunt Cécile had lined up an apartment for us in the north end. I would have liked to return to the old neighborhood, but it didn't really exist anymore, thanks to all the office towers and autoroutes. I got the kids into an English school and set up a home as best I could. But I didn't look for work—there was no time for that, and I wasn't planning on sticking around anyway. This time I didn't see Hull as anything but a place to regroup before heading out into the world again.

Liz was ordained in two different ceremonies not long afterward. The first took place in Montreal, the second in Sackville, New Brunswick. I drove the kids to both so they could attend. I stayed in the car. However smooth our split had been, our veneer of civility, politeness and consideration covered a certain amount of hostility and recrimination, which, not surprisingly, welled up often in the months following the separation, especially because I didn't have a lot else occupying my mind.

Soon enough, however, a major distraction came along. One of the few people I stayed in touched with from Saint John was my landlord's youngest son, Andrew, who was in his late teens at the time. When we'd arrived in town, he'd been having a lot of trouble with bullies at school. I taught him a few tricks to defend himself and he subsequently became my most diligent martial arts student. Like the rest of his siblings, he was caught between his traditional parents and contemporary Canadian culture, and saw me as a sounding board for his problems.

I'd given Andrew my number in Hull and he'd phoned a couple of times to chat. Then one day he called with a pressing problem: he wanted to rescue his sister Natalie from her violent and unpredictable husband, and he needed somewhere for her to hole up. It wasn't news to me that her relationship with Bashir had turned seriously ugly. I think he abused her physically, psychologically and verbally from shortly after their wedding. And it wasn't the first time that Andrew had asked me to intervene.

The summer before, Natalie had decided enough was enough. She'd told Bashir, who had been a judo competitor in the superheavyweight category—which meant he was very big, about 240 pounds—that she was leaving him. He didn't say anything; he just left the house they lived in on a large wooded lot about fifteen miles outside of Saint John. When he came back an hour or two later, she repeated her intentions. This time Bashir grabbed her by the hair and dragged her out the back door and over to a freshly dug pit at the edge of the woods, a stone's throw from the house. There, he stuck a gun to her head and said, "You ever try to leave me, I'm going to shoot you and throw you in this hole."

Natalie had called up Andrew, to whom she was very close, and he had contacted me. It wasn't culturally acceptable, it seemed, for the men in her family to get involved, but it was tearing Andrew up and he wanted something done. The next day I went over to Natalie's house when I knew Bashir would be home alone.

"Get out here—I want to talk to you," I ordered when he came to the side door.

He did as I instructed—it helped that he had always been wary of me, despite my being half his size—but we, needless to say, didn't do much talking. When he came at me, I did what had worked for me in other fights with big guys: I dropped into what's called "number one horse stance" to make myself even lower and get under him. As he tried to get hold of me, I moved toward him, grabbed him by the crotch and shirt, and let his own momentum flip him over. At that point, he was effectively done for.

"If you ever do what you did to Natalie again, I'll fucking come back here and bury you myself," I told him before leaving.

Apparently, things improved for a while after that, but now, almost a year later, here was Andrew phoning me again, planning Natalie's escape.

Because of the size, influence and ruthlessness of Bashir's family in New Brunswick, Andrew wanted to get Natalie and her four kids out of the province immediately. I contacted a women's shelter in Ottawa and they soon had a place waiting for the five of them. They arrived by the end of that week. I was the only person Natalie knew in the area and she needed someone to talk to, so naturally we almost immediately began seeing a lot of each other. Since I knew her family and the situation she was running from, I was able to be more than just a simple shoulder to cry on.

About a week after her arrival, I accompanied her and the kids to a meeting with her parents at a hotel in Montreal. They knew

Bashir was dirt and they hated him and his family, but they tried to convince her to go back anyway. In their world a woman was her husband's property; also, his family were the biggest wheels in New Brunswick's Lebanese community and it was important not to be in their bad books.

Natalie refused, and after her parents returned to Saint John they got an intimidating visit from the men of Bashir's family. Eventually, Mahmoud told Bashir where Natalie and the kids were, right down to the address of the shelter. (At the meeting in Montreal she had made the mistake of telling them where she was living.) Within a couple of weeks his family had a court order giving Bashir exclusive custody of his kids—because Natalie had fled the province—forcing her to hand over the four children, the youngest of whom was under two, the eldest not more than six.

Obviously, Natalie was devastated. She was also soon homeless— the shelter was for women and their children, and she didn't fit the criteria anymore. I invited her to move in with us in Hull. We had room because of an emptiness that had opened up in my life. In the middle of all the drama with Natalie's escape, my son, Brian, had told me he wanted to go and live with Liz. He was eight at the time and seemed to have thought it over. As much as it hurt, I decided to respect his choice; when I had been his age, not only was I not given any say in such matters, I wasn't even told a decision had to be made, or what it was. So I phoned Liz and she came and got Brian right away. Handing him over to her was about the toughest thing I've ever had to do.

There was nothing romantic between Natalie and me at the time; we were just two hurting units helping each other get by. We were both shell-shocked by recent events and stumbled through our lives for a few months. Neither of us was under any illusion that Ottawa or Hull was a place we wanted to stick around. Still, it took until early December and the start of winter for us to make our move. And where else would we run away to but Vancouver? I wasn't too worried about the city being unsafe. Vancouver was a big place, five years had gone by since my former brother-in-law had been shot in my yard. I'd keep my head down.

I traded in the old station wagon for a much smaller Pontiac and somehow managed to cram Natalie, Charlotte, the cat and dog, me and a few possessions into it. On our way across the country we stopped in Massey to see Brian. By then he had decided he wanted to come back to live with me and his sister, but we had made a deal before he left: he would have to stay a full year with Liz and give it a real chance to work. Otherwise, I would have happily made room for him in the Pontiac.

My sisters Louise and Pauline had moved to Vancouver some years previously, but they didn't have room for us all. So I tried Liz's sister Sue. She had split up with Phil—he of the bullet in his leg—and was living out in suburban Burnaby with their three kids while Phil had spiraled into the life of a junkie on Vancouver's Lower East Side. Sue had the room in her house and the generosity of spirit and welcomed us in a heartbeat.

We stayed there through the holidays and into January, when we found our own place in Burnaby. By then Natalie and I were a couple. That month I also rented a studio space above a store on Commercial Drive in East Vancouver and started teaching kung fu. Every other time I'd opened a club or given lessons, I'd done it just to keep in shape and as a hobby. Now I was going to do it as a business. Some of my first students were Liz's two other sisters—one of whom was overweight, the other anorexic (it sounds like the beginning to a bad joke, but it was true). One of them brought along a black friend who was already a black belt in tae kwon do and worked in security. He in turn brought in a bunch of friends, most of whom were also black. Then a stripper who was a regular brought in a gay friend, who loved the fact that his sexuality was of no concern to me or anyone else at the club. And he recruited a bunch of friends of his. We soon had a crazy quilt of clients, and the club was all the more vibrant for it. Before four months was up, we had run out of space and were moving the club to larger premises at the corner of Hastings and Slocan.

Natalie helped out in the running of the club, doing the books and paperwork and, after a while, giving more fitness-oriented martial arts classes to women clients. She also developed classes and other activities for children, which became an important part of the business. These included a day camp during school holidays and an informal child care program for emergencies. We even lent out the club for birthday parties on occasion. Some of these things we charged for, others not. One way or another, the variety of events brought people circulating through the club, integrated it into the community and made joining up an easier decision for many people.

The club could have consumed every waking minute we had, and frequently did. It paid off in terms of revenue and client base. But I had other demands on my attention, in particular my brother Pete, who had fallen on hard times and came to live with us after spending two weeks in a drug-induced coma. Initially, he was incapable of making any decision—even something as simple as one egg or two— let alone of continuing to make a living playing music or taking care of himself. But gradually he recovered his wits enough that he was semi-functional, and I had his old guitar sent to us.

Pete had saved my ass in his time—in particular on one occasion in northern Ontario during my hitchhiking days. I was in a restaurant in the town of Dryden when a redneck about my age started riding me. It was only after I straightened the guy out in a physical way that I was told he happened to be the son of a local cop. That made me less than interested in standing on the side of the road with my thumb in the air, so I went to a gas station and called up Pete in Hull. Together with Rita, later to be the mother of his four sons, he drove more than a thousand miles—almost twenty-four hours—while I hid in the rocky woodland outside of town waiting for them. So, in a sense, helping Pete now was just paying him back.

If I couldn't ignore Pete and his problems, there were some things competing for my time and attention that I could take a pass on. After arriving back in Vancouver, I had got in touch with Scott Paterson and given him an update, as was my habit any time I went somewhere new. We got together once or twice for coffee. Then, a couple of months later, around the time Pete washed up in Vancouver, another Mountie called and said he wanted to meet.

A day or two later I was in Confederation Park, meeting him and his partner. Within five minutes he had handed me a roll of bills. Seven hundred and fifty dollars.

"What's this for?" I asked.

"Just to show we really appreciate you taking the time out to meet us."

I wasn't going to say no to that. I did, however, say no to the job. It was a drugs-and-bikers thing, but the problem was the location—right there in Burnaby.

"You don't shit in your own backyard," I said. "I never work where I live." I went on to explain that we'd just settled in and got the club going and that I really wasn't interested in uprooting the kids and Natalie all over again. The Mounties accepted that and weren't too upset, even if it turned out to be a pretty expensive no.

A few months after that, Scotty called me again, but this time it wasn't work-related. His old RCMP partner, Larry Ricketts, had recently reunited with his wife and moved with her to Victoria to make a fresh start. They'd bought a puppy for their son and were intent on making things work. But tragically, the boy had been killed in a traffic accident not long after they'd moved.

I phoned up Larry to offer my condolences, and he was appreciative. He also told me that his wife didn't want the dog around anymore because of the memories and associations. Soon enough, Thumper had a girlfriend and we had a litter of little Rotties.

More importantly, however, my renewed contact with Larry led to him phoning again a year later. And to me eventually, finally, getting back in the game.

# CHAPTER EIGHT

# Les Hells and the Para-Dice Riders

———

The first Canadian Hells Angels chapter opened in Montreal in 1977, and the gang has dominated the province's biker scene ever since. By the early 1990s, however, domination was no longer enough—they wanted to be the only game in town. At least in Montreal, the province's biggest city and home to pretty much half its population. So, with several puppet gangs as their foot soldiers, *les Hells,* as they're known, began a brutal campaign to monopolize the drugs business, especially the big money-maker: cocaine.

Other organized crime groups, most of which were French-Canadian family mobs based in the various working-class neighborhoods around Montreal, first tried to accommodate the ambitions of *les Hells* and work with them. When that didn't work, the families began resisting. To little effect. Finally, in 1993, they banded together and started to fight back, under the banner first of the Alliance and eventually of the Rock Machine, a biker gang created for the exclusive purpose of resisting the Hells Angels' predations.

Initially, police didn't much mind criminals taking out criminals—it made for fewer bad guys to deal with. But as 1994 turned into 1995, bombs increasingly became *les Hells'* weapon of choice. A successful explosion could accomplish three goals: kill their enemies, destroy a place of business (and point of sale) and send a very strong message.

Then, in August 1995, a piece of shrapnel struck and killed an eleven-year-old boy when a booby-trapped Jeep exploded across the street from where he was playing. Police suddenly were forced to jump to it. So was born *l'Escouade Carcajou*—the Wolverine Squad—a special task force uniting the RCMP, the Quebec provincial police (known as the SQ after its name in French, the Sûreté du Québec) and various municipal police forces, principally Montreal's. To accomplish its work, Carcajou was handed what amounted to a blank check from the Quebec government.

I didn't know any of this when I got a call from Larry Ricketts in October 1995 asking me to speak to Corporal Pierre Verdon, a Mountie colleague of his from Quebec. After a brief conversation, during which I said little more than that I was interested in going back to work, I was on a plane for Montreal. There, in a hotel room on the South Shore, Verdon and a colleague of his from Ottawa, Staff Sergeant Jean-Pierre (J.P.) Lévesque, gave me the details of the job.

They wanted me to penetrate the Sherbrooke chapter of the Hells Angels. It wasn't deeply involved in what Quebecers were already calling *la guerre des motards*—the Biker War; that was really in the hands of the Montreal chapter, the recently formed Nomads and the Montreal-area puppet clubs. Instead, the Sherbrooke chapter was considered to be the money chapter, and that's what the Mounties wanted me to focus on. Rather than nail the members in drug buys or other front-end illegal activity, they hoped I would find out where their money was going and maybe get them to invest in a scheme I came up with.

I liked that angle, and the job appealed to me on several other levels as well. Sherbrooke was not unlike Hull in many ways: neither small town nor big city; mostly French but with a solid English minority; blue-collar. I was also up for an adventure. I'd not done an infiltration job for a decade and had been totally immersed in my martial arts club for five years. Now, with the business effectively running itself thanks to our two talented and dependable instructors, taking time away was conceivable.

Natalie and I had had a child of our own about six months earlier, so I didn't expect her to much like the idea of me returning to my old job, which I'd told her about after we got together. Her reaction surprised me. If it meant we might have a chance of moving back east, she was all for it. The new baby had reminded her how much she missed her other children, whom she hadn't seen—or been allowed to see—for five years now. Heading back east wouldn't get her access—only lawyers could do that—but she'd at least be closer. So, with her blessing, I accepted the gig on the understanding that I'd initially commit to only a three-month probe, and then she and I would decide whether moving east made sense or not.

I flew back to Montreal a week or two after that first visit, this time to get to work. There I had a day of meetings with Carcajou squad members and got outfitted with a credit card with a $25,000 limit.

"Don't use it!" said the SQ sergeant, Guy Ouellette, who gave it to me. He then lectured me as if I were a criminal who had just agreed to become an informant. "You do anything illegal—*anything*—we'll find out about it and you can expect to be charged."

After that, he repeated the same message about five times, but using different words.

"I know my fucking job," I finally said aggressively, just to shut him up. Speaking French again—and swearing in it—was a pleasure.

The next day, Pierre Verdon drove me the ninety miles or so from Montreal to Sherbrooke. We didn't talk that much on the way and the silence gave me time to plan my entry into the world of Sherbrooke's Hells. This time, I decided, I'd come in seriously crooked. I had with me an eight-by-ten glossy studio portrait of a girl called Rachel, who had been one of the Élite team, a short-lived escort agency I had set up way back when for the Thai pilots case. I made up a story in which she was a stripper-turned-snitch due to testify at an upcoming trial; I was the guy charged with taking care of her. Exactly what that meant, I'd leave up to the imaginations of the people I spoke to. If they thought "hit man" or "contract killer," I'd be doing my job. Of course, I wouldn't be stopping people on the sidewalk to ask if they had seen the woman. Instead, I would concentrate on three bars and a motel, all of which I knew to be biker-owned.

On my second visit to the main biker bar, a strip club called Barbie on Wellington Street, I confided in the doorman. He wasn't being too discreet about his affiliations: he was wearing a Hells Angels T-shirt.

"Listen, out of respect for you guys, I should tell you what I'm here for," I said, before pulling out a shrunken-down copy of the photo and giving him the CliffNotes of my interest in her. "*C'est un rat,*" I said, adding, "She's from here and word is she's coming back here."

I counted on him not to ask too many questions, and he didn't. Instead, he just took a long look at the photo, said she wasn't working there and hadn't been around, and promised he'd keep his eye out for her. "Check in occasionally," he said.

I went back a few nights later, only to find a different doorman out front. But things looked positive when I went to order a drink— the barman brought me a Pepsi without my having to ask, and when I went to pay he just waved me off. I guessed they had been talking about me and regarded me favorably.

Like the doorman, the barman turned out to be a patched member of *les Hells,* and I spent a bit of time chatting with him that night. Again I flashed the photo, and he, of course, said he hadn't seen her. It wasn't much, but still, things were looking good. I had made contact.

Then the jerk from the SQ, who was his force's main expert on bikers and had never met a microphone he didn't fall for, decided to mouth off at a press conference about Carcajou's goal in the Sherbrooke area. He said the task force had a comprehensive plan to crack down on the illegal activities of the Hells Angels, their puppet clubs and associates and to go after them ruthlessly. Then he added, "And we've recently inserted an agent in place for that very purpose."

That was it—in one sentence the goofball had torpedoed the whole project. I called Verdon as soon as I saw the item on the evening news. "I'm out of here," I said.

He fully understood. If anything, he was angrier than I was. While I packed my bags and got the hell out of Sherbrooke, Verdon went on the warpath within Carcajou.

I initially thought it had just been a combination of stupidity and motor mouth that had led the cop—who went on to become a successful provincial politician—to make his blunder. Later, though, I came to suspect otherwise. For years, the ill will between the RCMP and the SQ had been pretty much as bad as that between the Hells Angels and their criminal rivals. The creation of Carcajou didn't make things any better, at least not initially. The police seemed to be investing as much effort in undermining their rivals within the task force as in going after the bad guys. And since I was brought in by the RCMP and was clearly their infiltrator, I'd been a target of the SQ.

I headed home to Vancouver, the family and the club with one thing clear in my mind: the investigation may have ended as prematurely and as unsuccessfully as any I'd been involved in, but that was the work I wanted to be doing. Another thing became clear during the following weeks: it was back east that we should be living. Natalie would be closer to her kids; I would be near to Verdon, who seemed as likely a source of future employment as any of my police contacts. Scott Paterson had retired by then to set up his own security company, and Ricketts's new job was in uniform and administrative; it didn't put him in a position to require my services.

We moved early in 1996. The car was just as overloaded on this trip as it had been coming the other direction five years earlier. The occupants, however, were different. My son, who had come back to live with us after the year with his mother, was thirteen now and was a passenger. But my daughter, who was fifteen, had decided she didn't want to go through the pains of moving and making new friends all over again, and she opted to stay with her mom's sister and her family. Then, of course, we had the baby. Of the animals, only the cat made the return trip. Thumper had had to be put down because of hip problems and Teela, the female Rottie that Larry had given me, turned out not to be very good with young children, so I'd passed her on to someone else. I'd also given the club to the two instructors who, by that time, had been effectively running it for several months anyway.

Our plan was to spend a month or so in the Ottawa-Hull region and then move on to Saint John. The time in Hull didn't have anything to do with nostalgia on my part—I was over that. Rather, I'd spend it building a bit of verifiable background for use in future infiltration assignments. In particular, in consultation with my new Mountie friends, I'd get involved in a business that had been known to attract organized crime in the past: I'd promote a concert or two. How hard could it be?

My brother Pete, who had recovered enough to go back to Hull and back to playing music, provided an entree and the Mounties covered a few expenses—a car and a cellphone, for instance. Since I wasn't an RCMP employee, I got to keep any profits I made from my ventures. (There weren't many, but I didn't lose my shirt either.)

Of course, that sort of background-building ended up taking more than a month. I eventually stayed six months in the region, while Natalie and the kids went on to Saint John ahead of me. During my time in Ottawa, I quickly realized that Verdon wouldn't replace Scott Paterson in my life. He was too wrapped up in Carcajou, the escalating biker war in Quebec and handling a Hells Angels informer in Montreal. Instead, my new conduit to infiltration jobs would be Verdon's good friend J.P. Lévesque. He was based in Ottawa and was the national coordinator for what's called the Criminal Intelligence Service Canada—a Mountie-run outfit that tries to get those most secretive of organizations, police forces, to share organized crime information with each other. He was as much diplomat as cop, and had endless contacts in Canada and internationally.

Whereas Scott had done little more than give me phone numbers with the message, "This person wants to talk to you," J.P. played a much larger role. He gave advice, sifted out those jobs that he felt weren't appropriate, and seemed to be actually concerned with the impact of the work in general, and of specific assignments in particular, on me, my family and my career. That's why I began to refer to him as my rabbi—law enforcement slang for a superior who watches out, formally and otherwise, for an underling. In return for the guidance and protection, rabbis tend to be rewarded with the most precious currency among police the world over: intelligence, some of which the undercover agent might not even share with his handlers, depending on his relationship with them.

The first official job I did for J.P. was a joint RCMP–Interpol operation involving a dozen police forces from half as many countries. Because of national security considerations, the details fall under the Official Secrets Act, making it a criminal offense to discuss them. Suffice it to say, the assignment took me out of Canada barely a week or two after I got to Saint John and kept me out of the country for eighteen months. My absence would have gone over worse with Natalie had she not been back near her family (although she still didn't have access to her kids; she wouldn't get that until the summer of 1998) and had she not understood that this wasn't a regular assignment. It went well beyond the scope of good guy/bad guy, catch-the-speed-dealing-biker.

I found myself back in Saint John in early 1998, and very happy to be home. Despite the long time away, the reintegration to family life was easier than it had ever been before. One reason was that the job I was coming off hadn't required me to be a completely different person; another was that I was older, more mature and more capable of keeping what I'd come to call church and state—the personal and the professional—apart.

A period of relative serenity on the home front helped also. My son was a teenager at the time, but an easy one. He had a great relationship with Natalie and an even better one with his younger half-sister. She worshipped him, all the more so because I wasn't around much in her early years, and he loved her back just as much. Natalie was also in good spirits. Shortly after her return to Saint John we'd begun legal proceedings to obtain her access to her older children again, and even if it was slow going, and even if her ex's family fought us every step of the way, by early 1998 we were clearly winning.

Needless to say, the legal action was expensive. So when J.P. Lévesque called me in March with another job, I nibbled. It led to a meeting in Kingston, Ontario, with some special squad investigators from the Ontario Provincial Police; that encounter led to me moving to Toronto on May 5. The assignment involved infiltrating the Para-Dice Riders biker club—the main gang in Toronto but by no means the only one—and gathering intelligence on, among other things, its relationship with the Quebec Hells Angels.

The biker war was still raging in that province and outlaw motorcycle gangs had come to be recognized as the most serious organized crime threat across the country as a whole. The buffer treaty I'd witnessed being negotiated in Sturgis more than a decade earlier had led to a global shakeout of the biker world during the 1980s and 1990s. There had been a huge expansion in the number of members and chapters of the Hells Angels and Bandidos; meanwhile, independents had gone extinct by the dozen. Toronto, however, resisted the trend, and remained misleadingly calm. Its biker scene was still diverse and dynamic, with a handful of independent gangs—the Para-Dice Riders (known as the PDR), the Loners, Satan's Choice, the Vagabonds, the Last Chance—all coexisting more or less happily. It was a rich market, and the bikers seemed to recognize that the pie was big enough for all of them.

The police knew that this could change very quickly. The HA were increasingly putting pressure—with both carrot and stick—on the PDR and the other gangs active in what's known as the Golden Horseshoe, an economically thriving area that begins east of Toronto and wraps westward around the tip of Lake Ontario toward the U.S. border at Niagara Falls. In addition to developing an accurate picture of the interaction between the PDR, the other Ontario gangs and the expansion-minded Quebec Hells, I was to collect any evidence I could of drug, gun and explosives trafficking between the provinces and among members.

To gain an in with the gang, I decided to use the concert-promoter background I had established in Ottawa-Hull a couple of years earlier. It worked like a charm. I'd perused the PDR's website to get a feel for my new target and noted that they were suing police for illegal harassment on their way to and from club events. The case had been going on for a while, with the PDR usually losing and always appealing when they did. To pay their legal bills, the gang was soliciting for donations. All bikers know that their mystique can charm the stupid and that sometimes the stupid have money to throw away. But the gang didn't really need the cash; rather, they needed a way to legitimize some of the cash they already had. With police specialized in tracking and identifying proceeds of crime keeping a vigilant eye on them, the PDR regarded donations as a perfect vehicle to launder illegal money.

So I opened an email account with a Boston Internet service—in order to minimize the possibility of my messages being traced—and sent the following to the PDR website:

> I'm with "National Concerts" (Action West Talent Group). I
> have read with great interest about your ongoing fight for

*your rights. As you say, the cost of getting justice is very high ($300,000 by your own estimates). We are prepared to assist you throughout the summer to achieve that goal, along with maximum exposure of your cause. I will be in Toronto next week and would like the opportunity to discuss our ideas with you. If you can email me a name and number to contact I'll give you a call as soon as I'm in town.*

Within twenty-four hours I had received a terse reply: "Call Mark" along with a Toronto phone number.

My contact turned out to be Mark Staples, a patched member of the PDR who the police told me was both plugged into the music scene and a martial arts enthusiast—he even had his own club. He could be the PDR's Gunk, I surmised initially, the guy who uses his key to the club to open all its doors for me. There was a crucial difference, however, one that almost brought the operation to a premature end: Staples was extremely street-smart and suspicious, and immediately very wary of me.

Our first meeting was at a restaurant called Taro on Queen Street West, the bohemian part of Toronto. Staples came in covered in plaster dust; he'd been doing renovations on his dojo across the street. I came straight to the point: I was a Canadian promoter relocating to the Toronto area from the States and looking to get established.

"You have a cause and I want to do a show," I said. "I'll tell you right up front, I don't give a shit about this 'right to ride' stuff. I don't ride, but I will do a great show and we'll all make money."

"Money's good," he said.

"My goal is to have a few small shows over the summer and go for a big one in September," I continued.

The meeting went well. He told me about other promoters who tended to look unkindly upon upstarts—just before squashing them. We talked martial arts and he even invited me to teach a class in his studio. We blue-skied all the business we might do together and made plans to meet again soon.

But I left there a bit nervous. We had too much in common and he was clearly too smart. That made the likelihood of his figuring me out just too high. Especially since I never really planned to put on a show; I just wanted to talk about it for a while before segueing into criminal activity.

Over the next few weeks I saw Staples every couple of days, usually dropping by his club and just hanging around. I knew I was going too often, but he was pretty much all I had. In retrospect, I was probably generating activity for the file, as much to show I wasn't slacking off as anything. I tried to avoid concert talk and asked too many questions. For instance, if he told me he was going to the States for a few days, I'd ask where or whether it was business or pleasure. That probably sharpened his natural suspicion.

He'd dropped the names of a couple of his PDR brothers who might be interested in coming in on my concert plans, including one, Paul "Sunny" Braybrook, who ran an annual bike show in the Toronto area: custom bike contests, live music, wet T-shirt contests, the works. I'd spoken with Sunny, but hardly in circumstances that would allow me to broach illegal activities—he was doing a short stretch in Mimico Correctional Center on a coke charge. As for giving me the phone numbers or an intro to any other members, Staples was clearly in no rush.

One afternoon in late June, I had a meeting set up with Staples at his studio. When I showed up at the appointed hour, however, an underling told me he wasn't there. I left, got back in the Intrepid the police had provided me with and used my cellphone to call my handler, Detective Constable George Cousens, who was in position and probably had a visual on me at that very moment.

George told me where to meet. But, being directionally dysfunctional, I soon got confused, pulled over and got out of the car. Before too long, George and his partner, who were following me at a distance, joined me. After being shown which way to go on a map, I got back into my Intrepid and we duly met at the safe location, which that day was the public parking lot in High Park. No big deal, I thought.

Two days later, however, after I'd taught a class at his studio, Staples came up to me and got straight to the point.

"Who were those guys you were talking to Tuesday?" he demanded.

"Where?" I asked, genuinely confused.

"Down on King. You had pulled over on the side of the road and were talking to two guys in a beige car. They looked like cops. Standing there stoic like cops. One had brown hair and mustache."

It all became clear in an instant: Staples had set me up. Called me to a meeting, had his grunt tell me he wasn't there and then followed me when I left. Well, time to get my back up, I decided. After all, as I knew from past experience, the best defense is a good offense.

"What are you saying here?" I asked, staring hard at him.

"I'm saying that I don't really know you and then I see you talking to those guys, it gets me thinking."

"Are you saying I'm a cop?"

Staples backed off a bit, but not much. "I'm not accusing you of anything, but something was going down."

"Maybe I had a deal going down? Anyway, who I was talking to is really none of your business."

"It's my business if you're coming in and out of here."

"Rest assured they're not cops," I said. "In fact, they're about as opposite of that as you can get."

"Either scenario is not good for me," Staples said. "If it's cops, I don't want you around, and if it's the other, then I don't need the heat. There is some of my brothers that I've asked not to come here 'cause of the things they're involved in. I was planning to introduce you to my other brother who wants to get into shows, but now I have to be careful—I don't want to be doing the wrong thing. I'm going to have to check you out a lot more now."

"You should have done that from jump, man. I'm easy to check up on. And look, if you feel uncomfortable, I can get in my car, forget this place exists and just be out of your life. Just say the word, right now, and I'm gone. How's that?"

That backed him off some more. "No, that's not it. I just don't want any heat on this place. If you're doing stuff, that's your business. But keep it away from here."

I'd dodged that bullet—but just barely. And it didn't bode well. Staples would be watching me extra-closely now and, as he'd said, wouldn't be introducing me to any other PDR.

After that incident, I saw a lot less of Staples. I would have cut him off completely, but it would have looked too suspicious. Instead, I focused my attention on Braybrook and, since contact with him was limited, his wife, Alana. I'd met her a couple of times prior to meeting Sunny in jail and it had been immediately apparent she had seen better days. She was in her mid-forties with dyed black hair and had that hard look of someone who's been struggling for way too long and doing too much coke to cope with it all. With Sunny in jail, she was left way out of her depth trying to get the bike show together. To boot, she was obviously broke, or as good as. That was clear not just from the chaotic state of her home, her wreck of a car, her swarming brood of kids and their clothes, but from the almost endearingly small-time maneuvers she used to get me to foot some of her bills.

On my way to talk to her about Sunny one day at her house in Barrie, fifty miles north of the city, I phoned to say I'd be there in an hour.

"Well, if you're going to be here that soon, can you pick up something for me on the way?" she asked. Sure, I said, and she proceeded to give me a long grocery list. Needless to say, she neglected to reimburse me.

Another time, her son wanted a dollar to buy something from the corner store.

"Do you have change for a five?" she asked me. I did and gave her a handful of dollar coins. She gave one to her son, put the remaining four in her pocket and left it at that.

It was one of Alana's less modest requests that finally got me an in with an influential (and not very cautious) member of the gang. By then I'd visited Sunny a couple of times in jail and become pretty tight with him—as much by convincing him we'd once run into each other during one of his many stretches in prison as by the fact that I wanted to do business with him. He also appreciated that I was helping out Alana and their kids, or at least that I had no problem with her hitting me up for cash on occasion.

One day Alana phoned me in a state from a clothes store at Danforth and Victoria Park in Toronto's east end. "I owe someone fifteen hundred bucks and only have thirteen hundred. Can you please, please help me out?" she begged.

"I'll see what I can do," I answered. "Phone me back in half an hour or so."

I immediately called George, my handler, and asked his opinion on bailing out Alana. I gave him all the details I had—that Alana was at a place called the Jeans Store with a woman called Brenda—and he said he'd have to consult his own bosses. But he wasn't optimistic. "She's just trying to rip us off. Take you for as much as she can."

"Of course she is," I said. "But it might just pay off."

He said he doubted it and promised to call me back in the next few minutes, after going upstairs.

As soon as I hung up, the phone rang. I expected it to be Alana again. It wasn't. It was Sunny from jail.

"Listen, you help my old lady out now and I'll make it up to you as soon as I'm out," he said. Hearing a biker ass-licking rather than ass-kicking was novel, and further convinced me that bailing out Alana was a smart move. Still, I didn't commit myself.

"I'll go over there and check it out," I said. "Do what I can."

After getting off the line with Sunny, I phoned George back. He made it sound as if the issue was already resolved—that I wasn't going to give Alana the two hundred dollars. I told him about Sunny's call. "That's what bad guys do—they help out the families of their friends who are in prison," I said. "This could score us some serious points. It's not easy for him to ask me, you know. And it's only two hundred fucking dollars."

"It's not a question of two hundred dollars," George said. "It's a question of him leeching on you. You give it to him now, he'll keep coming."

"Well, I don't really care. He comes to me again, I'll just say no. So today, I'm going to go and give her the money—even if it comes out of my own pocket."

George, who would turn out to be the best handler I ever had, was smart enough to recognize that I wasn't going to be swayed, and he relented. He didn't promise to reimburse me, but he and the team would cover me when I went to meet Alana.

"Just to give you a heads-up," he added, "Brenda is a friend of Brett Toms and he's a real target of ours."

If I'd heard his name earlier in the investigation, I'd forgotten it. But Toms, it seems, was a high-ranking member of the PDR. He was sergeant-at-arms and considered by the police to be one of the smarter and more dangerous members. One member of the police team had been trying to nail Toms for more than a decade, to no avail. If a measly two hundred bucks could perhaps buy me an audience with him, it was all the more worth it, I thought.

I took all the cash I had available—about two thousand dollars—made a roll so I'd look like a crook of substance, and headed over to the Jeans Store. There, I peeled off the two hundred and put it on the counter in front of Alana. She pushed it over to Brenda, who folded and pocketed it. Alana was groveling in her thankfulness and promised to pay me back.

"Don't worry about it," I said. "I'll deal with Sunny for it."

I had no doubt that I was paying off a drug bill for Alana; she had cokehead written all over her, and the $1,500 she'd owed suggested she'd bought an ounce. She soon left the store and I hung out for a while, chatting with Brenda. Brenda was a whole lot smarter than Alana—she ran the Jeans Store and clearly had a mind for business—but she wasn't nearly as smart as she thought she was. Brenda was so intent on making money, and therefore so focused on how she might make money off of me, that she was oblivious to any danger I might have represented. I told her about my concert plans—which she had already heard about from Alana—while admiring the clothes she was selling. All of the clothing, it turned out, had come from stolen shipments.

"You should meet my friend Brett," she said as I was finally preparing to leave.

"I'd like to very much," I replied.

"Well, come on by tomorrow and we'll grab a beer next door."

Brett didn't show the next day, but we met soon enough at a steakhouse in Scarborough. He was a tallish, heavyset man of about forty with what people call hockey hair: business on top, party at the back. To draw more attention to it, the business part was bleached blond. He opened up immediately, telling me he owned through a proxy the shop Brenda sold the hot clothes from and that he worked for the city driving a snowplow in winter and other vehicles the rest of the year. At our first meeting I ordered from Brett a bunch of T-shirts with *SECURITY* written on them in big letters. He had a contact from the Last Chance motorcycle gang who had a silkscreening shop, and I told him I needed the shirts for the concert I was putting on.

Later I got the green light to buy $10,000 worth of stolen clothes from him on the pretext that I wanted to open my own clothes store in Niagara Falls, Ontario, as a front business. By then I'd hinted to both Sunny and Brett that one of my criminal activities was smuggling, so Niagara Falls, right on the U.S.–Canada border, was a logical place for me to set up.

However, once I told Brett that I was in for $10,000 in clothes, the OPP brass informed me that I only had $5,000 to spend. I revised the order, saying I didn't want to tie up too much cash in something that wouldn't bring much, if any, profit. Brett wasn't thrilled, but he was cool with it. Then, when I was meeting George minutes before I was to connect with Brett at his house to inspect the clothes, he told me they only had $500 for me. I lost it.

"You're fucking me up totally," I said, adding a few more choice words for the police bureaucrats and bean counters. This was our first buy of any kind in the case and for a while I thought it would be the last. I was convinced that that would be it for my relationship with Brett—anyone who does business with bikers and doesn't make good on his word can expect to be cut off, perhaps even cut up. And after the close call with Staples, I figured we might as well fold up the investigation then and there.

"Just work your magic," George said, as if nothing was the matter. With no real options, all I could do was cool down and continue over to Brett's place.

In their basement I started picking through the clothes thoroughly. I'd looked them over briefly before, but this time I played the discriminating customer and after a while started shaking my head. Inside, however, I was smiling: the clothes were obviously second-rate and that might save the day.

"I have to be honest with you, man," I finally said. "This is not the type of clothes I want to have in the store. I was hoping for something more in boutique style. This is too Kmart."

Luckily for me, Brett knew I was right and showed a reasonable side. "Ah, well. I'll line up better stuff for you."

"I feel bad, so I'll tell you what," I went on, trying to make it easier for both of us. "I can use a few sweaters, so I'll give you five bills for these."

I grabbed a handful of clothes, he took the five hundred dollars, and everybody left happy.

A couple of weeks later, Brett accompanied me down to Niagara Falls to introduce me to another PDR member who lived down there. I had mistakenly thought that the orbit of the gang didn't extend so far from Toronto, and had chosen the Falls as the location for my store expecting that the distance would spare me a certain scrutiny. But as soon as I'd mentioned setting up there, Brett had said I'd have to meet "Hollywood"—Jason Bedborough—who was the PDR delegate in the diverse and active criminal community in Niagara Falls. So much for my staying under the radar.

By then I was fairly tight with Brett and Sunny, as well as Psycho Dave, a tattoo artist, his business partner Dirtbag and a couple of other members. I was gathering relatively good intelligence on the gang's relationship with *les Hells* and other criminal groups, but hadn't got anywhere in our secondary goal: making drug buys. The PDR were well aware that the cops were on their case. The Quebec biker war had opened the taps across the country for the funding of police operations targeting bikers, and the PDR knew it. They also knew that police expected Ontario—in particular Toronto—to be the next battleground, and so were watching bikers there very closely.

Still, I expected to be able to make a drug buy soon enough. After all, it was late October by now and I had been consorting with these guys for almost six months.

Hollywood certainly seemed like the guy to know in Niagara Falls. Tall and tattooed and in his late twenties, with long black hair rather than the blond mane his name might suggest, he ran a bunch of clubs in town. He didn't own them, but he controlled what bands played where and, of course, the drugs sales therein.

"I know a guy with a building downtown that has a storefront we can get for next to nothing," Hollywood said after Brett and I told him of my plans. His use of "we" confused me at first, but that was cleared up quickly. "You sell your clothes out the front, I can run my bands from the office. And whatever else either of us wants to move through the back door, well, that's what it's there for."

Brett had been very open and lacking in the usual criminal caution when it came to new faces, but Hollywood was completely off the charts. Sure, I came to him with the blessing of Brett; still, he seemed too forward, too fast—if I'd been a woman I figured he'd already have asked me to marry him. And his recklessness went even further: when we went down to the basement of his home, there was a bag with what I calculated to be about an ounce of coke lying on a table. Hollywood just idly cleared it away, not making any effort to shield it from me.

Perhaps encouraged by Hollywood's openness, on our drive back to Toronto I pulled a small glass coke vial from my pocket and gave Brett an interrogative look. Brett simply nodded and said, "Because of the heat on me and the guys I may have to go outside the club for it."

"I don't care if you go to Nebraska for it. It's just between me and you."

He asked me how much I wanted. I said I wanted to stay small to see how the thing worked out—a quarter or half a pound, see how it goes. I asked him how he wanted to play it.

"Straight across," he said, meaning it would be simple: I'd give him the money, he'd give me the coke. There would be no half up front or running around picking up keys to bus station lockers. His terms sent the message that he had no doubts about me.

Some of that was probably thanks to Sunny, who by that time was telling anyone who cared to listen that he knew me from way back, that we'd served time together, and that I was connected to the "Red and White," the Hells Angels.

A week or so later, in the middle of the day, I got the call from Brett. "You have one hour to get here."

A little late but not much—and all wired up and with a full undercover backup nearby—I knocked on his door. After a bit of small talk, Brett said, "I got what you wanted."

"How many?"

"Four."

"How much?"

"Fifty-eight should do it."

I counted out fifty-eight $100 bills onto a coffee table while he got up from the couch, went to the sideboard and took down a small brown paper bag. He handed the bag to me when he came back to sit down. Inside was a zip-lock-type bag with what appeared to be four ounces of cocaine.

"Great," I said. "You've saved me a trip to Montreal."

"No problem," said Brett. "Now that we got this out of the way, the next time we can do a bigger deal."

"No doubt." I got up to leave.

"Don't you want to test it?" asked Brett.

"Why?" I asked in return. "Is there something wrong with it?"

"No. It's great!"

"That's good enough for me. Anyway, I know where you live." I smiled with this last sentence, but it wasn't entirely a joke.

"That's true," said Brett.

We shook hands and he walked me out. I got into my car and went directly to the Howard Johnson's on Keele Street, where the police were set up in room 909. Following OPP protocol, I was strip-searched by my handlers. It allowed the police to be absolutely certain that I wasn't holding back a gram or an ounce. It also infuriated me big time—even in prison I'd never been strip-searched. And this was by my colleagues, who had neglected to tell me that I should expect such treatment.

I went home fuming. We had to meet the next day at the same hotel. I had calmed down considerably by then, but was still upset. My anger dissipated immediately, however, when I walked into room 909 again. All the guys were in their underwear. George was sitting at the desk writing in his Fruit of the Looms. Craig Pulfrey, a top-notch undercover agent who would become my Niagara Falls sidekick, was standing in the middle of the room reading a paper as good as naked. It made it all all right again.

I arranged a secondary buy from Brett a couple of weeks later—one that made him look especially bad in court. It was for a slightly larger amount—half a pound—and lining up the deal took a few days, during which time his dad had a series of heart attacks. That made Brett cancel a weekend of partying with Hollywood down in Niagara Falls; it didn't, however, change his business plans. Even after his dad died on the Sunday evening, Brett said that doing the deal on Monday wouldn't be a problem. "Everything's still a go," he told me. The only difference was that since his mother was at his house, we had to do the transaction in his pickup truck.

The buys multiplied once the ice had been broken. Hollywood was next, just two days later. I met up with him at a peeler bar, Features, in Toronto's west end after he'd called to get together to discuss our business in the Falls. The place was a PDR haunt and, looking around, I recognized some members, including Psycho Dave. Hollywood introduced me to others, referring to me as his partner.

"So what's up?" he asked me when we were alone. Earlier, on the phone, I'd told him I was in a bind and I now gave him the details: I'd bought eleven thousand dollars' worth of coke for some clients in Montreal and the stuff had turned out to be crap. Now I needed to buy some better-quality coke to kick up the purity or else I'd have trouble, I said.

At first Hollywood wanted to go get the guy who had sold me the weak coke, but I discouraged him. "It's not that he ripped me off, it's just that the stuff is not good enough to do anything with."

I added that I liked the guy and that was another reason I didn't want to make a big deal out of it. That led him to ask who had sold me the lame product. I told him I wasn't one to name names, but I let him jump to his own conclusions.

"How close is this guy to us?" he asked.

"Real close."

"That what I thought. Anyway, I'll take care of you. I'll give you a couple of o-z's for fourteen each and that'll take care of me too. This stuff will be so clean, you'll be able to cut it fifty percent and it'll still go. We'll do it Monday. After that, if you need more, you'll know who to come and see first."

His only problem was the small amount. "I'll have to tell the people I get my shit from that you just want a sample. They're big-time. I'm not kidding you, man, fifty pounds is nothing to them."

All investigations, and especially longer ones, take on a life of their own. Invariably, new avenues of pursuit will open up thanks to an introduction to a previously unknown bad guy or an unexpected tidbit of intelligence. Sometimes the whole probe will veer off into a completely new direction; usually the new information just adds value.

In the case of the PDR investigation, the openness of Hollywood—combined with Mark Staples's suspiciousness and the fact I had no plans to actually put on the show that had got me in with him and Sunny Braybrook—meant that shifting our focus to Niagara Falls would probably produce more results. The gang was moving into the area, laying the way for their increasingly close allies the Hells Angels, so I could monitor that activity. And Niagara Falls was just over an hour from Toronto, and all the town's hoods tended to go back and forth regularly; keeping track of Angels activity in the big city—the main goal of the investigation—would thus be no problem from the Falls.

So, after three weeks back in Saint John for the Christmas holidays, I moved from the house I'd rented in Richmond Hill, north of Toronto, to a small apartment building near Niagara Falls' downtown.

Shortly after settling in, I fell in with an older biker type by the name of Joe Toth. He was a mechanic in the orbit of the Outlaws, but had never been a member of the gang or of any other major club. Still, he was very well plugged in to the town's criminal community, to the point that every week during the summer he held a barbecue at his house that amounted really to a networking event for the town's crooks.

I met him well before I attended one of these, however. One day I had planned to meet Hollywood at our shop and, as always, he was late. As I waited outside, two men pulled up in a van. One was Toth. He quickly proved to be as open and forthcoming as Hollywood: he told me readily that he was there to deliver 3,800 Percodans, prescription painkillers popular on the street. We had a pleasant chat that only ended when Hollywood arrived, handed Toth a pile of bills and was given a paper bag in return.

I barely recognized Toth the next time I ran into him, a couple of months later. One of the principal hangouts for hoods in Niagara Falls wasn't too subtle in its choice of name: Goodfellows. I went in there one evening and as I was talking with the bartender a guy beside me said, "Hey, how's it going?" It was Toth, looking much the worse for wear. It turned out that shortly after our first meeting he had been jumped in another bar, beaten to within an inch of his life and left for dead beside a Dumpster. He'd spent weeks in hospital but now was back in business.

"Next time you get some Percodans, put some aside for me," I said after we'd talked for a while, and I gave him two hundred dollars as a deposit.

I saw Toth regularly after that and, once the weather got warm, started going to his weekly barbecues. It was at one of these that Freddie Campisano, an Italian mobster I knew from Goodfellows, offered to sell me four hundred pounds of plastic explosives. After getting the green light from my handlers, I told him I was interested. By then, however, only 330 pounds remained.

"Who took the other seventy pounds?" I asked.

"Some crazy fuckers from Quebec," Freddie answered.

"Hey, that's where my buyers are from," I told him. "But they're not so much crazy fuckers as dangerous fuckers."

A couple of days later we did the deal for $30,000—$26,000 for the explosives, $2,000 each in middleman fees for both Freddie and me, all very up front. I'd already introduced Craig Pulfrey—whose happy disposition prompted his colleagues to nickname him Barney, after the cartoon dinosaur—as my runner, and the buyers' rep was an OPP sergeant named Randy Kreiger, an explosives expert who, with his long hair, well-worn Hells Angels support shirt and beat-up pickup truck, played the biker role to a T. It was an act he had to reprise a month later when Freddie came through with another five hundred pounds for $45,000.

The barbecues and the people I met at them also led to a flurry of drug deals, almost exclusively coke, during the summer of 1999.

Craig and I bought from at least a dozen different people, most of them bikers, and from a variety of gangs: Outlaws, Vagabonds, even old members of a defunct gang called the Breed, as well as the PDR, of course. Sometimes it was just an ounce, sometimes as much as five pounds. But quantity wasn't a big consideration; the brass actually preferred a small or mid-sized buy to a large one. It cost them less.

Even so, the investigation was memorable as much for its missed opportunities as for its successes. In June, an Italian mobster I'd initially met through Sunny in Toronto and then bumped into at the barbecue told me he had two million dollars in counterfeit twenty-dollar bills. The quality of the funny money was excellent, but there was one problem: there were only eleven serial numbers. So a condition of the sale would be that any buyer agreed to only start passing the money on the July 1 to 4 weekend. That would ensure the longest possible time before banks on either side of the border would be open and possibly notice the phony money and raise the alarm.

The mobster offered me $500,000 in the counterfeit bills for forty-five cents on the dollar to distribute through Niagara Falls. The rest of the load would hit the streets through Toronto and other cities. George, my handler, took the idea of buying the counterfeit cash to his bosses, but it was just "nice to know" information to them. They had no appetite for dropping $225,000 in real money on a bunch of fancy paper.

At another barbecue, this one at Freddie's in a nice suburb on the south side of Niagara Falls, our host showed us boxes and boxes of traveler's checks. They were from partially used packs—ones that had been sold to people and then returned to the bank. Protocol required that the checks be shipped back to a depository to be destroyed. Somewhere along the line, however, a bunch had been waylaid. Again, however, there was no interest from above in moving to acquire the checks or to prevent their circulation.

It's easy enough to speculate on the OPP's priorities in light of these decisions. They wanted to prevent violence, so they didn't hesitate in pulling out the checkbook to buy the explosives. When it came to the counterfeit twenties and the stolen traveler's checks, the only real damage would be to the bank accounts of the unlucky stiffs, most of them merchants, who accepted the worthless paper. I think, however, that there was probably another agenda at play. Moving on the counterfeit cash and the traveler's checks would have instantly brought in the RCMP. That wasn't something anyone in OPP biker squad was particularly interested in.

The bosses also seemed less than interested in having me pursue a contract to kill an informant that was indirectly offered to me by a mobster. At least a decade earlier, the informant had ratted out the mobster and some of his friends, who had an interest in a chain of restaurants, East Side Mario's, out of which they moved drugs. A handful of the men had ended up in prison; the informant was given a new identity and relocated to British Columbia. Now the mobsters were out and the informant had been tracked down—a task that was made easier by the fact that he apparently had a head that was much, much too large for his body, earning him the nickname Melonhead.

Considering that the scheme indicated a breach in the witness protection program, I naturally assumed the bosses would be interested. They weren't. They didn't even ask me to meet the mobster to discuss the job, as he was requesting. If I had, I could have worn a wire; we could at least have got the guy on conspiracy. Again, I think the provincial police weren't interested because it would have brought in the Mounties.

The OPP did move, and fast, when Moby, another mob acquaintance from the barbecues, announced that his wife had been accepted into the OPP. Even if she wasn't due to begin training until November 1999, he and the rest of his crew were already gloating in July over the fact that they would soon have "our own undercover agent," as Freddie put it.

"But we'll have to be patient until she moves into an area that concerns us," cautioned Moby. "Like drugs."

Drugs certainly concerned Moby—both Pulfrey and I had bought from him. In fact, I'd scored my biggest buy of the case, five pounds of coke, from Moby.

"Still, she'll be able to run people through the system for us before then," Moby added.

"And she knows this plan, or will she need convincing?" I asked him.

"Know about it?! She's looking forward to it."

After the bust—and after Moby was charged—the woman was promptly told thanks but no thanks by the OPP. But that wasn't the end of the story, according to George and Barney. They told me she sued and ended up eventually being given a post with the force—after she divorced Moby. And it was nowhere near Niagara Falls—somewhere up in northern Ontario, I understand, in what's called a "non-sensitive" position.

Speaking of the bust, it came a whole lot sooner than it should have as far as I was concerned. Not that I particularly enjoyed living in Niagara Falls or spending all my time with hoods, my family almost a thousand miles away. But Barney and I had got in very tight with the entire criminal elite of the Falls, and it was a highly criminalized town.

That, in fact, is one reason I think the brass decided to call for the takedown: they were shocked at just how much we were digging up. Sometimes police would rather not be told about crimes they feel they can't do anything about. Still, I was quite convinced that we could have made a clean sweep of the criminal element in the Falls. We were in with and accepted by everybody.

It was a very different story with the PDR in Toronto. We had drifted away from them—the initial targets of the investigation—and were continuing to drift ever further. Most of the people I was doing deals with in Niagara Falls were more Mafia than biker, though a few crossed over quite happily between the two. At the same time, relations with my PDR pals had deteriorated. Mark Staples, whom I hadn't seen in months, had never got over his suspicions of me. That didn't affect the investigation until Mark started telling his PDR brothers about the time he saw me talking to a couple of guys who looked like cops.

He mentioned it to Brett that summer, and suddenly Brett stopped returning my calls or talking to me. When I finally went by his house, Brett assured me he didn't believe I was working for the cops. Nevertheless, he ran his hand down my chest as if searching for a wire. He narrowly missed the one I was wearing.

"Still, I'm fucking pissed off that I only hear this story after I do deals with you," Brett fumed. "And I'm also fucking pissed off that Hollywood has been greedy and started selling to you. He's a fucking jerk-off for doing that to me."

Needless to say, I didn't point out the contradiction to Brett. Instead, I reassured him I wasn't a cop and told him about the counterfeit twenties deal, which distracted him.

Hollywood had also heard from Staples about the incident on King Street. He had even got his own glimpse of me with the biker squad one day as he drove along an overpass and looked down to see us all meeting behind an industrial building. Bizarrely, it didn't seem to faze him. He told people about seeing me with the cops—one of whom, Reg Smith, he actually recognized—but at the same time didn't seem to believe it was possible I might be working for them. So he simply chose not to believe what he had seen. He was far more concerned that I wasn't doing much business with him anymore and had, in some ways, usurped him in the Niagara Falls criminal community. After all, he'd never been invited to Joe Toth's barbecues.

Even Sunny Braybrook, who was about as low on the PDR totem pole as you could get (a fact suggested by his club nickname, Zero), and certainly no great confidant of Staples, had heard the story of me talking to the cops the summer before.

"Of course, I don't believe a fucking word of it," he said one day when we were in a cafeteria at the Canadian National Exhibition fairgrounds in Toronto. "All the same, I don't want to do any more deals with you. Just to be on the safe side."

I wasn't doing any deals with Sunny anyway in those days, but had kept seeing him on occasion. I could always count on him to run off at the mouth if he knew anything worth talking about. First Brett and now Sunny—my credibility with the PDR was definitely at an all-time low.

"Well, go fuck yourself then," I said to Sunny, and got up and left. I wasn't in the mood to be told by a guy called Zero that I was above suspicion in one breath but then questionable in the next.

All that being said, the real catalyst for the bust wasn't a deliberate, rational analysis of the state of the investigation and a cost-benefit

evaluation of continuing it or not. Instead, it was a showdown between me and a staff sergeant in the OPP, Steve Rooke, a man I knew
as Mouse even if he was George's boss's boss.

The PDR owned a nice piece of property near the town of Caesarea on Lake Scugog, barely an hour northeast of Toronto, on which
they would hold a big weekend party every August. It was a mandatory run for all the members of the PDR and also drew a good crowd
from other gangs, including all the Last Chance, a few Vagabonds and
Loners, and, of most interest to us, a good sample of Quebec Hells
Angels, including Walter Stadnick, who was in charge of the Angels'
expansion into Ontario and elsewhere in Canada.

The year before, in the summer of 1998, I had been invited to attend by Staples and Psycho Dave. Even so, I'd had to go through three
lines of biker security just to get in. It might have been worth it had
there been some payoff, but there wasn't. All I really did was spend an
afternoon sitting around being ignored. It was like going to a picnic
for a company I didn't work for.

In the summer of 1999, I wasn't invited. Whatever the reason for
not being on the guest list—my relocation to Niagara Falls, my dicey
relations with various members of the club, simple oversight—I was
perfectly happy being snubbed. I'd been getting signals from various
members in the days previous that I was on the outs, not least an instruction from Sunny not to talk to any other club members except in
his presence.

Mouse, however, was intent that I go to the Caesarea party, as
much, I think, to show his own bosses that we were still in tight with
the PDR as for any intelligence purposes. After I'd told George I
wasn't going to the gathering that year, Mouse appeared at one of our
regular meetings at the Keele Street HoJo.

"What's this about you not wanting to go to Caesarea?" he asked
me straight out.

"Well, first of all I wasn't invited, and second of all I don't think
it's secure," I told him.

"You went last year and there were no problems. I'm sure if you
just show up, they'll let you in. Or call up one of the guys and get
yourself invited."

I didn't much like the direction this was going but still tried to be reasonable. "There aren't very many left who are talking to me right now. Anyway, we've moved on since then—getting into the Falls and so forth. It's a step backward, I think. Circumstances just aren't the same."

Mouse didn't like that at all. I suppose he felt that I was trying to tell him what direction the investigation should be going, so he decided to get alpha male on me.

"Well, make the circumstances the same," he ordered. "I want you there, so you're going."

"No, I'm not," I insisted, getting alpha right back at him. "I don't think it's safe, so I'm not going."

That brought out the trained interrogator in him. There was the textbook transition pause—no less than ten seconds, no more than fifteen. Then the sigh. Then the calm voice and the false paternalism.

"Listen, I'll tell you what. If it's a security concern, there's nothing to worry about. The guys will be out there covering you. It'll be safe."

"It's not safe," I said, seeing right through his technique. "There are three checkpoints and they're setting off fireworks in there all the time. How you going to tell a gunshot from all those? How you even going to get the boys in there in a hurry? I tell you, I'm not going."

That set him off again—he wasn't backing down. "Sounds to me like you're just scared to go," he sneered.

"Yeah, I am—and that's not necessarily a bad thing," I shouted.

"You either go or I pull this investigation."

"Then pull it."

"Okay, then, that's it," he said, and left.

And that was it. Two days later we were all summoned to a meeting to plan the takedown. Lining up all the affidavits and warrants would take time, as would mobilizing the tactical squads, so brass chose September 9 for the bust. Ten a.m., to be precise.

In the meantime I didn't have a great deal to do, other than putting in orders to buy as much product as possible that day—after all, it would all be free. I sent out some feelers, sounding out various bad guys on buying drugs, guns, even grenades. Then I went home to visit the family in New Brunswick for a week or so while the OPP got ready.

Back in Niagara Falls in the last week of August and first week of September, things didn't fall into place as we'd hoped. It might have been expected, I suppose—all of a sudden we were asking that everyone be ready to deal at a precise time on a precise date. The deals for the guns and grenades fell apart in the days before the takedown. We had taken too long. Someone got to the Uzi and other handguns ahead of us; the grenades never seemed to materialize.

But we did have two firm orders for five kilos of coke from two different sources. Neither source, however, understood our timetable or felt particularly obliged to play by it. So to get them onside we decided to flash some cash, showing them each the $225,000 we had for the purchase (we'd also agreed to pay top dollar, $45,000 per kilo).

That seemed to do the trick. Then, on September 7 or 8, a classic police blunder screwed up one of the deals. The Niagara Regional Police were doing backup for the operation but were still using open radio channels—frequencies that could be picked up on a simple scanner. One of their jobs was to follow Freddie, our source for one of the buys. The problem was that he didn't yet have the drugs—and his own source had a scanner. The source heard the chatter from the police tail on Freddie as Freddie approached the bar where the drugs were stored, and greeted him at the door saying the deal was off.

The other deal vaporized because of the OPP brass's, or perhaps just Mouse's, fixation on everyone—*everyone*—kicking in the doors at precisely 10:00 a.m. on September 9. That was also the time Barney and I had arranged to buy five kilos from Moby and an associate of his. We were to do the deal at Joe Toth's place on Taylor Street, and we arrived there around quarter to ten. We'd already phoned to say we were on the way, had the money and that everything was cool. Joe relayed the message to Moby and he got his people and the drugs moving. But not fast enough. Joe had encouraged us to come inside, but Barney and I told him we wanted to wait in my car in the driveway. As the seconds and minutes ticked down, there was no sign of Moby et al., although they were probably only a few streets away.

We were under strict orders to get out of there at 10:00 a.m.

sharp—even if we were in the middle of doing the deal. So when the clock struck (we'd gone so far as to synchronize watches earlier), we started the car and pulled out.

"Where you going?" shouted Toth, sticking his head out the screen door. "They're on their way!"

"Just going to Tim Hortons," I said from my red Sebring convertible. "We'll be back."

Of course, I was really just giving up my parking space to the tac squad. Moby arrived in the midst of it all and was arrested on the spot. His associate, however, had the drugs and got away.

So, because of police obsession with punctuality (something I usually share) and a radio scanner, we didn't get the ten kilos of free coke and a few bad guys we might otherwise have busted slipped away. Still, the investigation landed more than a dozen PDR and other mobsters in prison.

The court proceedings that resulted from the PDR investigation dragged on for twice as long as the operation itself—thirty-two months. The reason was simple: all the accused pleaded not guilty, at least to begin with. For me it meant regular trips to Toronto, where I was greeted at the airport by a tactical team, hustled off to a secure hotel room and kept there until it was time to testify. Then I was bundled into one of three black SUVs with tinted windows and driven to court, sometimes in Toronto, sometimes in Welland, a small town nearer to Niagara Falls. I'd be on the stand for a day or two, maybe even a week, and then I'd be sped back to the airport again, having seen nothing much beyond the inside of the hotel room, the SUV and the courthouse. It wasn't much fun, but there was a definite financial upside: I received $4,400 per month for as long as the cases dragged on, plus any expenses incurred on those days when I was actually in court (which maybe totaled a month to six weeks).

There was also a certain satisfaction in seeing all the bad guys sent off to prison, even if the stretches most pulled weren't very long. Hollywood was one of three or four who changed their plea to guilty after being shown all the evidence against them in the preliminary hearings. He got eighteen months or so for selling me cocaine. Not long after he was released, he headed out west to try his luck as a B.C. biker. He didn't find much: someone put two bullets in his head, killing him.

Sunny also ended up pleading guilty, getting a short sentence and having things end badly. While he was in jail, his son was killed in a traffic accident. A year to the day afterward, Sunny, by then released, was riding his Harley near Alliston, Ontario, when a pickup truck ran a stop sign and hit him broadside. That was it for him.

Death also got in the way of Freddie Campisano, who might have expected the stiffest sentence for his role in selling me the explosives. I testified against him and he was found guilty, but, with money to spare, he'd managed to get out on bail while awaiting sentencing. During that time, he got sick—with what I'm not sure—and underwent surgery. Within days of his release from hospital, however, he was finding convalescence a bore, so he went downtown and started partying with some friends. A bit too heavily, it seems. After a lot of booze and coke, he collapsed from a heart attack. This time he left the hospital via the morgue.

Joe Toth was the one bad guy from the operation whom I felt kind of sorry about putting away. He was a very pleasant and friendly fellow, but he just couldn't *not* be a crook. Not violent, not nasty—just a guy who wanted to make it in his ill-chosen field. He got provincial time, so not more than a couple of years.

Brett Toms got the longest sentence—three years—but beat it on appeal. The judge, it was decided, had erred in his instruction to the jury. By the time the appeal court ruling came in, Brett's time was as good as served, so the prosecution didn't challenge it. The net difference was that he didn't have the conviction in his record and was allowed to own a gun again.

When, in December 2000, the inevitable occurred and the PDR patched over to the Hells Angels—along with the Satan's Choice, the Last Chance, the Annihilators, some Loners and a couple of Outlaws, somewhere in the neighborhood of two hundred Ontario bikers in total—Brett was among them. He remains a member in good standing.

Mark Staples and Psycho Dave, neither of whom were charged as a result of the investigation I took part in, also became full-patch

Hells Angels when the PDR finally succumbed to the bigger club's wooing.

In that respect, if part of my assignment was to prevent the Hells from moving into Ontario, I suppose our investigation was a spectacular failure. But I never heard it described that way. By 1998 everyone already considered the Hells' conquest of Ontario a foregone conclusion; the police just wanted intelligence on how it was proceeding and whether it was likely to be bloody. I was really just supposed to be a bystander, reporting back on the Hells Angels action, and of course the PDR reaction.

The next job would be very different. It involved going into the belly of the beast.

My father (left) and Uncle Alfred (or *mon onc'* Fred, as I used to call him). They fought together in the Canadian navy during WWII, including the D-Day invasion of Juno Beach.

The Hong Kong police had no shortage of extra bodies on hand during our joint operation, including this unlikely looking guy in the hat.

Rocky was planning to get the heroin to Canada using these Vietnamese boat people as mules. Fortunately, thanks to a successful operation, the drugs never got out of Hong Kong.

Me on my first bike, an old Norton 900 the cops found so I could fit in with the Blaine Bandidos. A Harley Davidson would have been more than a beginner like me could have handled, though I did get one eventually—a small one.

This was more like it. A bike a patched Bandido could be proud of, with room for a girlfriend or two on the back.

Left: My DEA handler Andy Smith in Blaine, Washington. He got promoted to Washington D.C. after the case wrapped up with a slew of arrests. Right: Having a job in a medical laboratory and being reasonably intelligent can get a guy a lot of prestige in the biker world. Though Dr. Jack, plenty tough, was never afraid to earn respect the old-fashioned way, too.

PETE AND GEORGE

Bellingham Bandidos vice-president George Wegers and Mongo (Pete Price). Unlike some other members, Mongo treated his bike gang like an old-school brotherhood, not an entree into organized crime. A few decades later, George is now world president of the Bandidos.

Four hundred Bandidos and girlfriends on our way to Sturgis, South Dakota, the biggest biker party of the year. With all the partying along the way, it took us five days just to get there.

Karate Bob didn't like my attempts to get into the martial-arts business with him. He was a purist. He disappeared one day without a trace—left behind his wife, his bike and his colors. I can only imagine what, or who, happened to him.

Here I am, really looking the part, on Bandidos business in Texas. My guide and I stopped for this memento while visiting a contact at the local county fair.

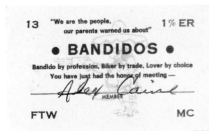

My Bandidos membership card. They made me a patched member in record time.

It was one thing for the Bandidos to accept that I didn't drink. But if I didn't get a girlfriend at some point I knew they'd really start to find me suspicious. Vicki (left, with Terri and another girlfriend) was a coveted cutie who worked at our favorite bar. She was good company; too bad I was married and working for the cops.

BLAINEDIDOS
DEA F F DEA

Andy Smith looking pretty nasty at the head of the DEA's Christmas gang. It's a hard life if you don't have a sense of humor.

Left: That's Brandon Kent (smiling, second from the left), along with a friend, a prospect and Christian Tate (second from the right), whose funeral ride would later save my bacon on the day this case ended.

Right: That's Chris Devon showing off his ink with a couple of prospects. It wasn't easy being a little guy in company like this.

Here's Chris Devon coming to church. A little flattery went a long way with this guy. When he learned I was a photographer he couldn't get enough of posing for me.

The Dago Hells Angels posing for me outside their El Cajon clubhouse. You can see the special Quebec rocker low on Brandon Kent's cut (second kneeling from the left). Also, that's Bobby Perez on the far right, holding his colors up for the camera.

Left: Ramona Pete's bar in El Cajon, the real home of the Dago Hells Angels. Tearing out of this parking lot in my little pickup was the last I ever saw of them.
Right: After Brandon Kent, Taz, who used to be an extra on the TV series *Oz*, proved to be my in with the San Diego Hells Angels.

Ramona Pete poses in typical bike porn, which the gang loved me to shoot—their colors, their ride and their preferred accessory, a girl.

The bigger they are. . . . Dago chapter president, Guy Castiglione. He's now serving life for murder.

Yes, that's me and the one and only Sonny Barger, legendary world president of the Hells Angels. Try to name anyone else who has gotten tight with George Wegers, president of the Bandidos, and Barger too. Bet you can't.

# CHAPTER NINE

# Dago Hells Angels and the Russians

—

Back in New Brunswick after the PDR case, I went into what I called 'borg mode—doing very little but sitting on the couch waiting to be activated again. The family was doing well. My son was sailing through high school; my elder daughter had moved east from Vancouver and enrolled in the University of New Brunswick; the baby wasn't such a baby anymore. Natalie had access to her older kids and was running a little hobby business, fixing up and reupholstering old furniture.

Everything was cool, but still, none of it really interested me. I was completely back in the game. Not in the same way I'd been with the Bandidos—I'd simply rediscovered my taste for the thrill, the excitement and the adventure of the work. The white-hat aspect of the job played a role in my reborn enthusiasm—being on the side of the good guys makes sleeping easy—but it shouldn't be exaggerated. The work was noble, sure, but it was also fun.

I remained in close contact with the boys from Ontario, but the province, especially the Toronto and Niagara regions, would be a no-go zone for me for a long while. Instead, I was waiting for the call from my rabbi, J.P. Lévesque. I knew he wouldn't call with just any old gig; he'd say no to jobs he thought weren't right without even running them by me. So I wasn't necessarily holding my breath.

He finally called in late January 2000. J.P. had met a DEA analyst by the name of Bob McGuigan and the two had become friends. At some point, McGuigan told J.P. about a French Canadian whom the DEA suspected of running cocaine from Colombia up the Pacific coast of Mexico in his yacht. The guy and his family lived on his boat and harbored just south of San Diego in a Mexican enclave for rich Americans. There, the DEA figured, he unloaded the drugs, which were then smuggled across the border by—or at least for—the San Diego Hells Angels.

The French Canadian had proven very slippery; his boat had been searched on several occasions and nothing found. Still, the DEA was convinced he was moving major volume. To begin with, they knew he had close ties with the bikers through a member, Brandon Kent. In turn, Kent was known to be well connected to Quebec's Hells. Not too long before, he'd been in a house in Montreal when the police raided the property and found a large quantity of coke. (Kent wasn't charged, just told to go home.) Kent was also the only international Angel known to sport a side patch that said *Quebec,* which suggested he was some sort of honorary member.

So there was an intriguing association that led to a great deal of speculation by police. One popular theory: Kent moved the coke north to Quebec and exchanged it for Canadian pot, the quality and exports of which were exploding in the 1990s. This, of course, was all conjecture or intel from less than perfect sources. McGuigan and the DEA were eager to nail something down.

"I've got the perfect agent for you if you want someone to get inside and help you build a case against this guy," J.P. said to McGuigan, obviously thinking that my speaking French would be a big asset. The idea appealed to McGuigan, and by early 2000 he had approval from the DEA bigwigs. That's when I got the call from J.P.

I phoned McGuigan and we spoke at length a few times. As I look back on it now, his plan seems clumsy. He wanted to set me up in my own yacht in a neighboring slot at the marina, have me establish a rapport with the guy—"You're from Quebec too!? *C'est incroyable!*"— and take it from there. But at the time it sounded fine. I'd been idle for four months, winters are long in New Brunswick, and this was a yacht and sunny southern California beckoning. I was down there by the end of February.

The operation never got off the ground. The French Canadian and his family disappeared the day before my arrival; they and the boat were suddenly nowhere to be found. Needless to say, it struck me as odd not only that he would vanish just when the investigation was about to begin but also that no one could figure out where he'd gone.

That was the first of many times over the next couple of years that the Angels seemed to have extraordinary luck—or advance information. I was also surprised by the DEA's lack of surprise at this turn of events. Nobody appeared to think it remarkable, McGuigan included. So much for my yacht. I expected to be back in Saint John for the next snowstorm.

Then Bob McGuigan suggested I attend a barbecue the next evening hosted by the Hells Angels at the main location of San Diego Harley-Davidson, on Kearny Mesa Road. Anyone could attend—it was one of those public relations stunts that Hells Angels chapters undertook occasionally to show neighbors that they were nice, misunderstood guys. McGuigan thought it was worth a shot going there and trying to find out where the French-Canadian guy went. He figured if I connected with Brandon Kent, I could say, "Hey, I'm down here from Quebec to meet up with my buddy, but now he's gone. You know where he went by any chance?"

I never got the opportunity. It was southern California, but still the cops hadn't bothered to provide me with a car, so I was left taxiing it. And either the taxi driver or I had the address screwed up. I eventually got out of the cab in an industrial area thinking that the shop was nearby and tried to find it on foot. Maybe it *was* nearby—again, my sense of direction is about as reliable as a compass in an iron mine—but I certainly didn't find it. Pissed off, I just said "Fuck it" and took another taxi back to my motel in San Diego's old-town area.

Bob McGuigan said not to worry when I phoned him—there were barbecues at San Diego Harley every week, and since three or four patched Hells Angels worked there I'd get another chance to make contact over a burger. The next morning, however, Bob and his DEA sidekick Hunter Davis seemed to have reconsidered.

"How do you get lost in a taxi?" they asked.

"You don't know me—I can," was all I could say.

That didn't impress them much. Bob told me that I would be leaving for home the next day. "Fine," I said.

The next day, however, came and went with no talk of my leaving. Instead, Bob had another plan up his sleeve; it was slowly becoming apparent that he was desperate to get an investigation going one way or another into the San Diego—or Dago—Hells Angels. He now wanted me to rent a storefront with, ideally, a back room to live in, and to set up a cover business that, somehow or other, would allow me to consort with the bikers. It wasn't a yacht, but the idea sounded fine to me and I said I'd look around.

A couple of days later, I'd found a store that fit the bill on Turquoise Street in Pacific Beach, a touristy area right next to La Jolla. The place was in a four-store strip mall fronting a two-story apartment building only half a block from the ocean, boardwalk and beach. Still, it was reasonably priced. I'd also figured out a good cover business, one that would require minimal capital investment, not necessitate any inventory and, most importantly, provide me with an excuse to introduce myself to Brandon Kent and the boys: I'd become a photographer, specializing in custom posters and specialty shots of bikes and babes.

Bob liked the idea, and within a week he secured funds to buy me a computer, a very expensive Olympus SLR digital camera and a commercial printer. I went to a store, picked up a bunch of classic posters of rock stars and the like, and plastered my shop walls with them. I even got a couple of easels and used them to display some mounted posters. All I needed now was a name. Bob came to the rescue there: Posterplus. I blacked out the windows and painted *Posterplus. By appointment only.* In the workspace/office at the back of the shop, I set up a bedroom for myself. I'd survive without a kitchen, but happily there was a bathroom with a shower.

Second time was lucky for finding the barbecue the following weekend. It wasn't a full-on Hells Angels event this time, but since a few members, including Brandon Kent, worked at the shop, there was a presence—Kent included.

He was sitting behind a glass counter at the parts department shooting the shit with some friends. Milling in front of the counter, I noticed, taped inside, an eight-by-ten photo of him riding his bike on a racing track. I knew Kent raced motorcycles for the HA's official team and so I used this to break the ice with him. I asked him if he would let me make a 24-by-30-inch poster of the picture to put up in my store; in return I would give him a free copy to put on display in the Harley shop. He went for it.

I left soon afterward, taking the picture with me, and the next day went to a reproduction shop downtown, ordered the enlargements and had them laminated. The next week I brought his poster to the barbecue and Kent was impressed big time, for which I took full credit.

While I had his attention, I told him a bit about my business. I liked shooting runs, custom bikes and dogs, I said, and also went to parties and made photo albums of the event. Media kits for strippers was something I was into as well, I added; did he happen to know anyone who might be interested?

Sure, he said, and gave me the name of a guy called Taz who ran a mob-owned strip joint called Cheetah's. I was off and running—or at least moving forward in familiar territory.

I dropped by Cheetah's several days later and was greeted by a large doorman. He was covered in tattoos, including a large swastika on his shaved head. He looked like an extra on the TV show Oz— something I later learned he actually was. I asked if Taz was in.

"I don't know no Taz," the doorman replied.

"Can I leave a message for him?"

"What's it about?"

"Brandon from the bike shop gave me his name. Said he might be able to help me."

"Brandon Kent?"

"Yeah."

"I'm Taz," the guy said, "but hang on a minute."

He picked up a phone and dialed someone I assumed to be Brandon. He talked for a couple of minutes then hung up. "Okay," he said to me finally. "What can I do for you?"

I explained my photo business and said I had a shop in Pacific Beach. It turned out Taz lived only a few blocks away. He was busy, so we decided he would drop by the shop sometime later that week to talk. I gave him my card with the address and split.

Taz was one of those people who was warm and welcoming to

people he considered to be on the inside and a real asshole to everyone else. Since I came on the say-so of Brandon Kent, I was okay. When he came by a few days later, he brought along a tall, muscle-bound friend—who just happened to be wearing the cut of a full-patch Hells Angel. It was a completely unexpected bonus.

The biker's name was Chris Devon. I initially let him be and talked only to Taz, but in a way that made me intriguing to Devon and gave him ample opportunity to join the conversation. Then, at a given point, when discussing my photo projects, I turned it on with a big ego stroke.

"I want to do a poster of the quintessential tough guy," I told Taz. "Someone who just radiates power. Someone like him." And I pointed at Devon.

Devon didn't just bite, he swallowed the entire hook. Then and there, I did a shoot, and before long he was back to see the poster I had produced. He loved the idea of me displaying it prominently in the store.

During those first weeks I would slip away as often as possible for photography lessons from a sheriff's department cop who took pictures of murder victims and crime scenes. The man was an exceptional photographer but entirely without a sense of humor. I tried constantly to make him laugh, asking him if he was concerned about stiff competition, or saying that people were dying to be in his pictures. He'd just give me a confused look. After a month or so he had turned me into a passable photographer—certainly up to the standards of the Hells Angels, strippers and other less than demanding subjects.

When I was not taking lessons, I'd hang around my store and Chris would drop by occasionally, almost always with company. Sometimes he'd bring girls—strippers—interested in having me shoot their portrait. Other times he came by with Taz or another friend of theirs, a guy who called himself the Indian, who was a weapons specialist on a navy battle cruiser. There's a huge military presence in San Diego, which the Angels understood was both a hungry market for drugs and girls and a superb potential source of weapons. The gang members didn't have much time or respect for the Indian—he was too eager to be liked. As Dago chapter president Guy Castiglione later told me dismissively, "He calls himself the Indian, but he's really just a nigger"—a supreme insult in their world. Still, the Indian was an entree into the big military market and one the Angels were exploiting eagerly.

Ever hungry for friendship, the Indian cultivated me as well. I hinted to him—and to Taz, Chris and whoever else happened into the store—that the photo shop was really just a cover, that my true business was crime. But we never discussed any specifics, at least in those early weeks and months.

I would also see Chris, along with Brandon, at the weekly Harley-Davidson barbecues, which I attended scrupulously. I'd always bring my camera and take pictures of bikes, which provided a good pretext for chitchat. Often the bikes' owners—patched Hells Angels or not—were only too happy to have their pictures taken as well.

My next contact in the club didn't come from the barbecue, however. One day I was telling Chris that I wanted to get some other merchandise in the store. "I want something—postcards, whatever—that will make it look like I'm doing some business. The last thing I need is for cops to come sniffing around because there's no activity."

I was letting him understand that I was a career criminal, of course, without going into specifics. Chris took it a step further.

"Then why don't you sell some support stuff?" he said, referring to the T-shirts, sweatshirts, hoodies and ball caps that the Hells Angels sell to make a little money and improve their public image.

"That's a great idea. Who would I call?"

And just like that, I had the number of and an intro to Ramona Pete (Pete Eunice), the Dago member who ran the club's bar in El Cajon, the town twenty miles to the east that, more than San Diego itself, was the home of the San Diego chapter.

Pete came to the shop and liked the support merchandise idea. Soon I was running out to El Cajon—by then the DEA had bought me an old white Chevy van—to pick up supplies and hang out a bit at the bar, which was named Dumont's after Pete's business partner. In many ways the Dago Hells Angels were more approachable than the Bandidos or the PDR had been. It was easier to get a nod, a sign of recognition and a bit of small talk from members. Even so, it was superficial recognition, like you might get from professional athletes or celebrities conscious of their public image but really not interested in having anything to do with you. Getting any more out of the Angels was much more difficult. Even if I played the crook—and I did—no one proposed any criminal activity to me, and I wasn't about to propose any to them. That, I got the impression, would have been a guaranteed ticket for a quick and rough ride out Dumont's door.

Even if I hadn't yet penetrated the inner sanctum of the Hells Angels and wasn't doing drug deals with them, I was making reasonable progress. Bob McGuigan and his team seemed perfectly satisfied with the way the investigation was developing. After all, I'd only been there three or four months. And Bob's superiors didn't seem unhappy. If anything, they were indifferent to the criminal information I was bringing him—Taz controlled most of the drugs in Pacific Beach and lots of the girls—and the Indian's military connection hadn't got their radar buzzing either. Try as they might, Bob and his counterpart in the San Diego Sheriff's Department, Billy Guinn, couldn't get their bosses motivated. In fact, they still couldn't obtain funding for a full investigation. I didn't yet have a firm contract and was only getting paid sporadically with money my handlers could scrounge out of various budgets—two thousand dollars this week, then nothing for a couple of weeks, then nine hundred, and so on.

My rabbi, J.P., whom I was speaking with a couple of times a week, apologized about the situation he had got me into and initially urged me to just pack it in. George Cousens, whom I was seeing fairly regularly on my trips back to Toronto to testify against the PDR and my friends from Niagara Falls, was giving much the same advice. I felt loyalty to Bob, however, and I liked Billy a lot, and I saw that they were doing their best. So I stuck with them, justifying the project to myself and to J.P. as good groundwork. If nothing developed in San Diego, I reasoned, I could at least establish some good HA contacts and use them for an investigation into the club elsewhere. J.P. liked the idea.

Then along came the Russians.

My little shop on Turquoise Street was at the ocean end of the small strip mall. At the opposite end, on the other side of a Latino hair salon, was a very expensive furniture store. Since I lived at my shop, I would often sit out front and relax, and after a while I noticed that the furniture store did even less business than I did. Its owner was a big and burly Czech called Henry, and he was always walking past my shop on his way to visit some guys who ran a used car lot on the ocean side of my store. Eventually Henry and I got to talking, and before long he was matter-of-factly admitting to some pretty serious criminal activity.

Until a year or so earlier, he'd been dealing heroin in volume in Los Angeles on behalf of some Russian mobsters. Then he made a very big mistake and started using his own product—perhaps because of all the sadness and stress associated with his young daughter being born with a crippling genetic disease. Whatever the case, before long he was spending day after day barely moving from his rocking chair except to shoot up. That, of course, had got him in trouble with his boss, who, he said, only spared his life because they'd served in the Russian military together. Henry's partner, who hadn't shared a history with the boss, hadn't got off so lucky. Even though Henry had been allowed to live, no one in L.A.'s Russian mob would have anything to do with him—he had been effectively exiled from the city.

Now he was in San Diego trying to get back on his criminal feet. He'd been importing furniture with hollowed-out legs filled with smack, but there wasn't much money in it. The drugs weren't his; he was really just a glorified mule. So he was spending a lot of time on the phone with his connections in Russia, where his reputation hadn't been so tarnished by his drug habit, trying to put more profitable deals together.

Like any self-respecting criminal, Henry was wary of wiretaps. So, before long, he was asking to make and receive phone calls at my store. No problem, I said. After all, I wasn't paying the bill, and getting in good with Henry couldn't hurt.

Of course, I kept Bob McGuigan up to speed on what was going on, and the DEA ran the numbers Henry was calling and being called from. That's when the bells went off. The numbers were linked to a handful of criminals some federal agencies were already after, a few of them former KGB agents who'd turned to crime.

Soon I was called to a meeting at the ATF's San Diego offices. There were maybe a dozen suits and agents in a big conference room. I only knew two of them: Bob from the DEA and Brooks Jacobson, the ATF agent assigned to work alongside Bob in our investigation of the Hells Angels.

We started off discussing progress on the biker investigation, which Bob played up as being pretty significant, all things considered. Some of the guys around the table were barely listening, however. Something else was obviously in the works. Sure enough, one of them soon cut Bob off.

"Well, all that's on the shelf for now," said a casually dressed man with hair past his shoulders, who nonetheless exuded authority. "We're now going to focus on Henry and his friends."

At that point one of the suits chimed in, asking me, "What do you know about stolen art and art in general?"

"Stolen art is art that has been stolen," I joked.

That got me a withering look.

"Basically nothing," I added.

It seems some of Henry's Russian connections had been involved about a year earlier in hijacking a vanload of art being loaned from one museum to another. That interested the agencies represented around the table—but there was more. Basically, the Russians were into anything—drugs, guns, stolen vehicles and other goods, girls—and the feds were into everything the Russians were into.

The suit made some notes on a pad and conferred with some of the brass at the other end of the table. Meanwhile, Mr. Authority, who was sitting a seat away from me, announced in his arrogant, damn-the-torpedoes manner, "From now on you'll be reporting to me and me alone. Can you keep good notes?"

"I can keep great notes. I was trained by the Mounties."

"Okay, I want you to write down every meeting, every name mentioned, everything said, everything you do with these guys."

By this time Bob, who was also sitting near me, was looking very uncomfortable. He clearly didn't like Mr. Authority but felt compelled to defer to him.

"Would you like the notes he's kept up to now?" he asked the man, who would only ever be introduced to me as Joe.

"I don't give a fuck about what he's been doing up until now," said Joe, not even bothering to look at Bob.

That was it for Bob. His voice got louder and higher, and he started going on about how the work we'd accomplished so far would be wasted and how the operation was being shortchanged.

Joe listened for a while and then said, "That's the way you feel, but this is the way it's going to be. If you don't like it, you can leave this meeting right now."

Defeated, Bob began gathering his papers. But before he left, Joe, just to prove he carried the weight, swung his satchel onto the table, opened it and took out a large bundle of cash.

"Here's your first payment. For four months. If there are any additional expenses, just let me know."

The bundle contained US$20,000. The message was clear: after all the scrimping, begging and financial sleight of hand Bob had had to do to keep our biker investigation going, he was being big-footed by someone with real influence and easy access to cash.

Soon enough, Joe ordered me to not even talk to Bob.

Of all the handlers I ever had, Joe was easily the most mysterious. At first I heard he was DEA, but someone else told me he was ATF. I suspect he was something else altogether. He also didn't seem to have any bosses; everyone deferred to him. And I never learned his last name. Those, however, were the least of his mysteries. He also happened to be both handler and fellow undercover. In fact, I was now to introduce him to Henry, who in turn, we hoped, would connect us to his contacts, most of whom were across the Atlantic.

Fortuitously, Henry was hoping to exploit us in a similar way. In his efforts to impress his contacts in Russia and elsewhere, he was bragging about his new American friends. We were big-time, he said. No matter how mean and nasty the Russians were, they still seemed to suffer from something of an inferiority complex. American crooks, I suppose, were the stuff of Hollywood, and thus the real deal in the Russians' eyes. (The fact that I was actually Canadian was a mere technicality for Henry.)

One reason Henry believed I was a hardcase criminal was an ugly encounter he'd had with Chris Devon in my store a week or two before the big meeting at the ATF offices. Chris had come by with one of his girls to set up a shoot for her and had just parked wherever. But wherever just happened to be one of Henry's parking spots. A few minutes after Chris showed up, Henry stormed into my store.

"Who's za fock-ing ass-hole in my parking?" he shouted. Clearly, he wasn't having a good day, but that didn't mean Chris was going to coddle him.

"Who wants to fucking know, jerk-off?" Chris shouted right back.

Immediately they were nose to nose, and it looked like it would get physical very quickly. Henry, however, pre-empted that by pulling out his Glock and sticking it in Chris's face. Chris simply responded likewise, pulling out *his* Glock and pointing it at Henry's abundant gut.

That was my cue. "Not in my goddamn shop," I yelled, getting in between them as best I could. "You guys want to fucking kill each other, go out into the alley. But don't disrespect me by wasting each other here."

It took another minute or two—a very long minute or two—but Chris and Henry eventually backed off, snarling all the way.

"Give him a few minutes," I said to Henry as I pushed him gently out of the shop. "He's here talking business. We'll be done soon and he'll leave."

I never spoke with Chris about the altercation, but there was no doubt he took note of the fact that I had some other brave and/or reckless acquaintances, likely criminal. Similarly, Henry was impressed by the fact that I had HA connections. Next time he came into the shop, he was eager to talk about Chris and what had happened, but I shut him down.

"Forget it," I said. "It's over. I don't want to talk about it."

By the time of the ATF meeting, Henry and I had agreed to do business, even if we hadn't got too precise about it. In his eyes, I was like him and his associates—into whatever might make a buck. He had, however, given me a price on one specific business opportunity: ecstasy, one dollar a hit, minimum purchase 200,000 hits.

Still, even the episode with Chris didn't stop Henry from being skeptical of Joe when I introduced them at my shop about a week later. I had described Joe as one of my money men—a financial backer for my criminal ventures—and told Henry that Joe wanted to meet the supplier he was going to be dealing with. Joe played the part of the wheeler-dealer well, but Henry wasn't convinced.

"I don't feel all good about him," said Henry, who, like almost all criminals, operated on instinct. "I don't want to insult you—he's your friend. But he's always in a hurry. That makes me feel strange."

Henry had a point. Joe wasn't around much and whenever he was, he was always rushing away. I'd see him every week or two, give him my notes, and then he would disappear to wherever he disappeared to. Joe's absences, and Henry's wariness toward him, meant progress was slow.

But there were other reasons the operation took a while to get going. International cooperation is hard to come by in most fields, and law enforcement is no exception. If anything it's worse, thanks to the jealous manner in which most forces guard their turf. Furthermore, I was frequently absent too, since I was regularly going back to Ontario to testify in the PDR and Niagara mob cases, then often taking a few extra days to visit the family in Saint John.

Despite all of these factors, things did advance and we eventually firmed up an order for 200,000 hits of E and a pound of heroin. I'd also indicated an interest in whatever else—guns and art in particular—his contacts might provide. I was hoping Henry would nibble and in some way acknowledge the art theft. I wasn't disappointed. He didn't say anything, but he returned from a trip to the Czech Republic sometime in early 2001 with a present.

I picked him up from LAX, and when we got back to my Turquoise Street shop he said, "I have a gift for you." Then he opened his suitcase. But rather than rummaging around in its contents, he gently tore the lining away. There was the painting—a smallish portrait of a wrinkled old man smoking a pipe—as well as a sample of the drugs we were going to buy: a few grams of heroin and twenty or so hits of ecstasy, with several different logos stamped on the pills.

In my campaign to penetrate all fingers of "the hand"—the Russian organized crime network Henry was involved with—I had also told Henry that I could be more than a customer, I could be a source of supply too. In particular, of stolen luxury cars. Henry introduced me to the owner of the car lot on the ocean side of my store. Like Henry, he was a Czech, with a Russian partner, and the pair were friendly enough, but discouraging when it came to me getting involved in their business. Besides, thanks to the Latino gangs in the area, he had all the cars he needed to smuggle overseas.

The one business the hand was involved in that didn't interest me at all was girls. Not because I didn't have the opportunity and not because it wasn't serious; on the contrary. Rather, it was a slave trade, the girls working sometimes as strippers but usually in "massage parlors" and other fronts for prostitution, and it would have been impossible to get involved without taking part in the crime. The women were kept under strict surveillance at all times and were regularly moved from city to city, never staying more than a few months in one place, so as to keep them from developing contacts and perhaps making friends who would help them flee.

At last, in the summer of 2001, almost a year after I began working with Joe, it was time for us to make a trip to Europe to meet with Henry's contacts. I knew one of them already from phone conversations when he'd called my shop looking for Henry. His name was Mirek and he was the brother-in-law of Henry's wife, Gabrielle. Mirek was Henry's protector and patron, and eager to help him get some business going. It's hard to know who's who among Russian mobsters; contrary to American crooks, they always downplay their seniority. Mirek, however, clearly had influence—that much was obvious from his relationship with Henry. Not as much, however, as one of the other men Joe and I were on our way to meet with. Jivco was a former major in the KGB—and there was no doubt he was a heavyweight due to his political and military connections.

After flying into Amsterdam and then driving to Nancy in

France, we finally met Mirek and Jivco in Ditzingen, a small town near Stuttgart. Two others accompanied them: a chemist who was introduced only as the Doc and a hit man called Bouy. We weren't there to negotiate a buy, deliver cash or discuss the logistics of a delivery, just to meet face to face. The Russians had wanted to get a personal feeling for us, and Joe and I had told them we felt likewise. Coming this far to meet also gave them proof of our seriousness. If we were willing to fly from California to Europe just to sit down in a café for a couple of hours, then we certainly didn't lack for cash or determination to do business. Still, I found it strange that Joe and whoever was telling him what to do didn't have more of a plan.

Back in San Diego the following week, it was full speed ahead for the heroin and ecstasy deal, at least from Mirek and Jivco. They were phoning at least once a day and had Henry coming by regularly to ask how we were progressing.

Every time I phoned Joe, however, he stalled me. "I'm still working on the international connections," he'd say. Or, "I'm trying to get things organized." Or, "You can't do this kind of thing overnight." He'd gone from being a cop who could move mountains to an ineffective bureaucrat.

Finally, perhaps a week after returning, I called up Bob, whom I'd stayed in contact with despite Joe's orders, and vented. "This is bullshit. I'm getting it from all sides to do a deal but can't get any commitment from the cops. I'm just fending people off and twiddling my fingers. And then I have orders not to do any work on the Angels. I might as well be at home."

Later that day or first thing the next morning, Joe called. "I agree with your plan," he said.

"My plan?" I asked. "What plan?"

"To go home and lay low."

"Okayyyyy," I answered.

I couldn't figure out what was going on. Were they firing me? At that point I didn't care. I could handle not knowing what exactly the criminals were up to. But the cops? Whom I'm supposed to be working for? That was too much. Two days later, I was on my way back to Canada.

Somewhere en route a light went on. I realized that I was being cut out of the deal. Joe was simply acting like a real crook. I also began suspecting that maybe the cops had turned Henry. He was the ideal candidate, vulnerable in all sorts of ways: his daughter's crippling illness and the medical bills that came with it; the fact that Gabrielle, his wife, had no papers. And of course, he was a junkie, reformed or not.

I didn't give a damn about being cut out, but I did care that they didn't tell me. They were playing me like a chump. Or, worse, acting as if I were a crook who couldn't be trusted, rather than a colleague. Coming off the PDR case, where we'd been a real team, made this treatment all the worse.

Back in Saint John, I called up J.P. and told him that I was home, perhaps for good, and didn't know what the hell had happened to the San Diego Russian investigation. And, I added, if the Mounties wanted to make their own bust on the back of the work I'd done with Henry, well, I'd help them.

I'd already got an inkling the RCMP were open to such a deal. Months earlier, in California, they'd arranged for two new passports for me—one of which they'd kindly hidden, along with five thousand dollars cash, in a safety deposit box in Amsterdam in case I got in trouble. During the dealings involved in obtaining the passports, Joe had told his Canadian security contacts the basics of the case. The RCMP in turn told me that Canada, in particular Toronto, had its own problem with Russian mobsters; anything I could do to help them on that front would be appreciated.

So, a year or so later, here I was ready and willing—and willing, I suppose, to go behind Joe's back just as he'd gone behind mine.

The Mounties didn't hesitate. They asked me if I would set up a deal with Jivco that would have drugs delivered to the Toronto area. That would allow them to find out who his Canadian contacts were and bust them. I said sure. A day or two later, I was on the phone to Jivco.

"I'm going to be in Amsterdam later this week and I'm ready to do business," I said. "Can you get someone there?"

"I'll go myself. Call me when you're there."

A day or two later I flew to Amsterdam, where I was picked up by two Dutch cops. They took me to the Renaissance, the same hotel I'd stayed at with Joe a few weeks earlier. I checked in and met a man named Loderus, another Dutch investigator, as well as an official tied to the Canadian embassy—basically a spy. I was also introduced to a younger Dutch undercover cop who was supposed to play my man in Europe. I'd introduce him to Jivco and his people and then back off, leaving the details to be sorted through by my young Dutch sidekick.

I phoned Jivco's land line phone, which was a Hungarian number. He wasn't there, but the guy who answered was expecting my call. I gave him the name of the hotel and my room number, and within a couple of hours Jivco called. He was already in Amsterdam.

"Where do you want to meet?" he said.

"How about Brasserie Noblesse?" I answered. It was right next door and Loderus had suggested it for reasons unknown to me.

Two hours later—it was suppertime by now—the young undercover and I were waiting for Jivco when he walked in with two gorillas. The bodyguards sat at an adjacent table while Jivco sat across from us. He wasn't the small-talk type, so I made a little conversation. I told him I'd been in Canada for a bit and hadn't seen Henry for a week or so.

"Never mind about Henry," said Jivco. "He's a junkie."

"No he's not!" I said. "He might have been, but he isn't now. I live right next door to him."

"Once a junkie, always a junkie," he shot back.

"Whatever," I said. "I'm here to do business, so let's get it done."

"How much you want?"

"The minimum on both." We both knew that meant 200,000 hits of E and a pound of heroin.

"What logo and shade do you want?" he asked, referring to the ecstasy.

"Jaguar head logo and off-blue."

"All of them?" Jivco told me it was better business to buy an assortment of colors and logos. Even if it was all the same stuff, some clients would be convinced that, for example, the pink was better than the blue, or the white stronger than the yellow. I followed his advice. Then he asked, "Do you want to pick it up here or have it delivered?"

"Delivered."

"It's going to cost you more, of course."

"Of course. How much are we looking at?"

"Twenty thousand dollars."

"Fine. My associate here will take care of it."

That cued the young Dutch undercover to pipe up—something that always scares me. In this case, however, he came up with the perfect question. "Which account should we use?" he asked.

At that point I knew he could be relied upon. I'd never told Jivco I wanted the drugs in Toronto. I left that to the undercover to do later, along with paying the $20,000 down payment and delivery fee.

The next day I flew home and never saw Jivco or any of the Russians again. A week later the RCMP surprised me by paying me twenty-five thousand dollars for my middleman services. It ended up being worth it, I suppose, because a few weeks after that they arrested two Russians in Richmond Hill, a Toronto suburb, with the 200,000 hits of ecstasy and a pound of smack.

# CHAPTER TEN

# At War in Laughlin

―――

I hadn't heard from Joe or anyone else since leaving San Diego and didn't figure I would. That was fine with me. Back in Saint John, it was summertime, the sun was warm and we had more than enough money, especially since Joe was still paying me and I was still getting money for the PDR case.

Then one day Bob McGuigan called. His voice was so uncharacteristically cheerful that it took me a minute to recognize him.

"How's your holiday?" he asked.

"Great," I answered. "Wish you were here."

"Ready to come back to work soon?"

"Sure, I guess," I said, surprised.

"Well, we've got you a nice place in El Cajon and we're getting it ready for you. So when you get back here, we can finally get back to doing what we were supposed to be doing in the first place."

No wonder Bob was happy—we now seemed to have the green light to be going after the Hells Angels. I didn't ask what happened with Henry and the Russians; I figured I'd learn soon enough, and still just assumed I'd been cut out.

"But this time we'll have to play it right, no more fucking around," I added before signing off, and gave Bob a short list of demands. On the material side of the ledger, I wanted the same money as I'd been getting for the Russians, plus all expenses, a vehicle other than the big van and, most important, a bike. If I was to go into El Cajon, also known as Hell Cajon, I was going onto their turf, and I wanted all the tools. On the operational side, I just told him that I wanted to make sure there wouldn't be any of the vagueness that had characterized my first few months infiltrating the Dago Hells Angels.

Bob agreed to everything and met me at the San Diego airport when I arrived two Fridays later, the keys to a rented pickup in his hand. After a bit of chitchat he handed over the keys and said, "Follow me."

Half an hour later we were standing in front of a large single-story industrial building on Cuyamaca Street. The DEA had rented almost all of it for me, about 2,500 square feet. Its only other occupant was a small takeout sandwich shop that operated out of the street side of the building. The plan was to move my Posterplus business to El Cajon. Space wouldn't be a problem: there was ample room for a studio, an office, living quarters and even a small police listening post right in the building itself. In fact, the whole place had already been wired up with cameras and microphones. Clearly, the money had come through.

They'd even got a task force together for the investigation. It would be called Operation Five Star because of the five police forces involved: the DEA, the ATF, the San Diego Sheriff's Department, the San Diego Police and the El Cajon Police.

I spent the first night in a motel and returned to my place on Turquoise Street to pack things up the next day, a Saturday afternoon. That's when the Russian mystery deepened. There was no sign of Henry—his storefront was empty, all the furniture gone. Likewise the car lot on the other side of me: all the vehicles had disappeared, even the trailer at the back of the lot that had served as an office. The only store left in the strip mall was the Latino hair stylist. I went in to talk to one of the girls.

"You know where Henry is?" I asked.

"He's gone," she said simply.

"Well, what about the car lot owner?"

"He's gone too," she said. She drew a finger across her throat.

I didn't inquire further.

While working the Russians, I had seen virtually nothing of the biker contacts I had made during my first months in San Diego. Taz and the Indian had come by a couple of times and I'd run into them by chance around the neighborhood on occasion, since they both lived there. Chris Devon had come by maybe once, but then found better things to do. Brandon Kent I hadn't seen at all. That I'd stopped going to the Harley-Davidson barbecues made as much difference as anything, I suppose. What I didn't expect was that my extended absence would turn out to be a great boon to my credibility with the Hells Angels. If I'd been a cop, they figured, there was no way I would have just lain low like that for a year or so; I would have kept coming at them.

That first Saturday night I was back in San Diego, I dropped by Dumont's and told a few people that I was moving my shop to Cuyamaca Street, slipping it casually into the conversation as the opportunity arose. I didn't overplay it, though I did take pains to mention the news to Purple Sue, Dumont's veteran barmaid, whom I knew to be the bar's main purveyor of gossip and intelligence. The next afternoon I went to the weekly barbecue and did the same.

The first weeks were relatively slow. I wasn't about to suddenly get in the Angels' faces. But I did gradually become a regular at Dumont's, spending more and more time chatting with the owner, Ramona Pete, and Bobby Perez, the tough-as-nails member whose job it was to patrol the surrounding block or so of El Cajon Boulevard that might as well have been declared an independent republic of the Hells Angels. It was home to the gang's clubhouse and Stett's Iron Horse Ranch, a bike shop owned by a former member who had quit the club in good standing and did all the customizing anyone needed. Nothing happened on that block without the say-so and knowledge of the Angels. Even the cops kept a low profile there.

Despite having formed a task force and obtaining funding for the investigation—and despite Bob's assurances otherwise—the police had no real plan of action. They had no fixed list of particular individuals for me to pursue. They didn't instruct me to focus on drugs or guns or prostitution or any other criminal activity. Rather, they seemed happy for me simply to be rubbing shoulders with different members, taking vanity photos of as many of them as possible and collecting idle intel.

The vague parameters of the investigation were fine by me, at least to begin with. I could hang with the members who seemed receptive and steer clear of those who were more wary—really, just approach the bikers as a regular criminal joe might.

My first real breakthrough came after about a month in El Cajon, in late September 2001. I hadn't been around too much. In fact, I'd spent most of a week or so in Toronto, initially testifying at a PDR trial and then grounded when the skies over all of North America turned into a no-fly zone after 9/11. But I'd been around enough that I was clearly on the Hells Angels' radar.

That was made abundantly clear to me early one Thursday evening when I was at Dumont's. I'd taken to eating there—there was a microwave and they sold things like corn dogs, which make for a satisfying supper in my books. I'd just finished when an Angels prospect came into the bar and beelined it straight to me.

"The Boss wants to see you," he said. "At the clubhouse."

"Okaaaaay," I answered. The Boss was Dago chapter president Guy Castiglione, a cold-blooded killer who also happened to be intelligent, soft-spoken and usually quite reasonable. I didn't bother searching the prospect's face for any indication that this was good news or bad; I knew he wouldn't know.

Despite a moment of anxiety, a couple of factors suggested I had nothing to fear. I doubted that anything nasty would happen to me in the clubhouse—too incriminating. Anyway, if it was a thrashing I was in for, they would have just done it out back of the bar. Also, it was the Dago chapter's church night, the one night of the week when there was consistently a police presence—both undercover and uniform—on that strip. The bikers knew it and I knew it. So I was more curious than concerned as I followed the prospect the fifty yards or so down the street and into the clubhouse.

Castiglione was sitting on a stool behind the bar. A bunch of other members were sitting at tables or playing pool in back, but the Boss was alone. I sat down on a stool across the bar from him and, like a well-bred boy, waited for him to address me.

"I hear you're a good photographer," he said.

"I do what I can," I said, relieved.

"How much would you charge for a charter poster?"

I didn't know what he was talking about exactly, but I did know this was a chance to win him over by showing some respect for the club. "What? Money?"

"Yeah. Every five years we have to take a chapter picture and send it to all the chapters worldwide. It's time, and I want to know how much it'll cost."

"Listen," I said. "You guys let me operate in your town. Some of your guys have helped me out. I conduct my shit, my business here. This is your town, these are your streets. So because of that, I would do it out of respect."

It was definitely the right answer. He puffed up. Not smiling, but certainly not frowning.

"That's good," he said.

"When do you want to do it?"

A week later, on the afternoon before the next church, I was standing on El Cajon Boulevard taking shots of the Boss and seventeen other Dago Hells Angels in front of their clubhouse. Any who didn't know me before sure knew me now.

And just in time. Shortly after the chapter photo shoot, Chris Devon—my first good contact in the gang—was arrested and imprisoned on a murder charge. It didn't end up hurting the infiltration assignment at all. In fact, an incident that flowed out of Chris's incarceration ended up scoring me more points with the chapter—even if it damaged relations with the DEA.

It began with a phone call from one of Chris's girlfriends a week or two after his arrest. "Chris wants you to take some photos of me to send to him in jail," she said.

I'd never met the woman, and if she was talking about the kind of photos I thought she was, I wasn't going to do the shoot without talking to Chris first. It's a fundamental rule of crooks the world over: you steer well clear of women of guys who are in jail.

"When are you next going to be speaking to him?" I asked her.

"He's phoning me tonight."

"Okay, well, I want to be there and to hear it from him."

I was over at her house that evening and spoke to Chris. He appreciated my initiative and told me how risqué he wanted the photos: not very, because the San Diego jailers were very strict with personal photos.

A day or two later, Chris's girlfriend phoned me to book the shoot and presented another issue. Chris wanted the photos as soon as possible, but the only time she was available was the next night after ten.

Even if I had the green light from Chris, I wasn't going to put myself in her house late in the evening taking revealing photos—it was a recipe for trouble. All I needed was for another member to drive by, see my vehicle in the driveway, come inside and jump to all the wrong conclusions.

So I talked things over with Bob and we agreed that the best strategy was for me to take along my own "girlfriend"—an undercover cop. It's not something I really should have brought up with Bob. He was an analyst, and so my dealings with him should have been limited to providing intel to incorporate into the endless flow charts he drew up with photos of the members I talked to and where they fit in the scheme of things.

Instead, I should have gone to Pat Ryan, the DEA handler in charge of operations who had come onto the case with the move to El Cajon. So far, however, Ryan and I hadn't clicked. Anything but. The problems had started with his bad reaction to the standard spiel I'd give to investigators when they or their bosses hired me for the first time, a spiel I'd delivered to him soon after settling into Cuyamaca Street.

"I don't want to be treated special, but I don't want to be treated like an asshole either—I am not one of them," I would say, knowing that many police assumed that because I was good at pretending to be a bad guy, I really was one. I'd remind my new handlers that I was a professional and finish off with a not very original but nonetheless honest line: "I'm not here to make friends. I'm here to do a job."

Most cops didn't mind the spiel. Some even liked the fact that I immediately established the boundaries and ground rules of our relationship. Ryan, however, didn't think it was the place of a contracted agent to give such a talk. And he seemed personally insulted by the fact that I wasn't interested in forming deep and lasting bonds with my handlers. As Ryan left the meeting, he'd told Brooks Jacobson, my ATF handler, "If he doesn't want to be friends, then fuck him."

Things hadn't improved when, not long after, I flatly refused to take on an undercover cop as my sidekick. It wasn't that I had a problem with the idea of an undercover sidekick. Rather, it was the cop he tried to foist on me. Skinny, red-haired, freckled: the guy might have been useful in an undercover operation at Microsoft or an Orange County high school—although even then he would probably have suffered daily wedgies—but the Angels would have eaten him alive.

From that day on, Ryan and I got along about as much as we looked alike. I hadn't grown—I was still five-six, 130 pounds on a big day. Ryan, meanwhile, is six-four if he's an inch and at least 240 pounds, none of them fat. Our relationship wasn't all bad. Ryan could surprise me with acts of generosity. On Thanksgiving, I found a full turkey dinner waiting for me at my door. I suspected it was from one of my other police contacts but later discovered it was Ryan who had prepared and delivered it. On another occasion, he picked me up on the pretext of our having an important meeting to attend, only to take me out to a surprise meal with other agents involved in the investigation. Again, it had been Ryan's idea. But the day after each friendly gesture, he would act like nothing had ever happened, and our icy relations returned.

When I made my request for a girlfriend, Bob passed it along to Ryan. He brought a suitable and almost-pretty candidate dressed in standard San Diego attire (jeans, T-shirt, sandals) to our planning meeting an hour or so before I was to do the shoot—and proceeded to give her all sorts of absurd instructions.

"Anybody comes in, you leave. Anyone there besides the girl when you arrive, you leave. If you get up from the couch, it's because you're leaving. You don't go to the bathroom, the kitchen or anywhere. Don't make conversation or talk to the girl any more than you have to." He had no shortage of ridiculous, patronizing orders. Finally, I couldn't take it anymore.

"Is she a cop or what?" I asked Ryan.

"Of course she is," he said, giving me a severe look.

"Well then, let's treat her like one. Give her a bit of credit."

That got me an even dirtier look.

When we left the meeting, the policewoman climbed into my

truck. She had been silent in front of Ryan, looking resigned. In the truck, however, she immediately started going on about her treatment.

"They're always like that with me," she said. "They feel like they have to hold my hand and protect me all the time."

After hearing her out, I set about contradicting all the orders that Ryan had just given her. I told her to simply follow my lead, not do anything stupid, and said that if it was time for her to leave I would tell her.

My phone rang. It was Ryan, as I expected; my truck was completely wired and they had been listening to our conversation.

"Stop with your bullshit," he shouted. "It's got to be done my way. There's a protocol and we have to follow it. You tell her to follow my instructions."

I didn't bother trying to convince him otherwise. All I said was, "We're the ones who are going to be in there. We're the ones risking anything. So we're going to do it my way." Then I hung up.

The photo shoot went well, and a couple of days later I dropped a bunch of prints by the downtown San Diego jail, depositing a hundred dollars in Chris's canteen account for good measure. It wasn't that I was all that intent on currying his favor—he was out of the game, after all. But I knew that the biker telegraph would quickly get word back to all his HA brothers and my reputation as a stand-up guy would be enhanced.

I wasn't wrong. A day or two later, Ramona Pete and a member known as Hatchet Dave dropped by the studio to get a photo enlarged of the original Hells Angels—a squadron of WWII fighter pilots.

"I hear you deposited a hundred bucks in Chris's account," said Pete. "That was a good thing to do."

"Hey man, I was there anyway bringing him the pictures," I replied.

"Yeah, I heard about the pictures," said Dave. "Smart thing for you to take your girlfriend over there."

The bikers got the point, but the cops didn't. I mentioned the hundred dollars I put in Chris's account and there was no offer to reimburse me.

"Fuck him," Brooks Jacobson said about Chris Devon, resolutely failing to see the brownie points the small gesture won me. "Let him rot in there."

Even if I was getting in tight with the Dago Angels, the cops still weren't directing me to do deals with any of the members. On the contrary, the instruction I most frequently heard from my handlers, almost from day one in El Cajon, was to slow down.

"Give us some time to catch up on our notes," Brooks and Ryan would say.

I'd tell them that actually I was going slow, but it didn't seem to make any difference—they still always acted swamped.

In the meantime, not initiating any deals was solidifying my standing in the gang's eyes. The longer I didn't pursue any criminal activity with them, the less likely it seemed that I could be a police agent. And the California Hells Angels tended to presume that pretty much everyone was out to bust them.

Not doing deals with the Angels, however, didn't mean I wasn't doing any deals at all. A bunch literally came knocking at my door, most thanks to a connection I had made back on Turquoise Street with the most motivated of young hoods.

His name was Bobby and he was the nephew of the Indian, who had brought him to me a year or so earlier. The Indian hoped I would give Bobby some sort of criminal apprenticeship. We got along very well and hung out some but hadn't done much in the way of business; I was too absorbed with the Russians. When I moved to El Cajon, however, that changed. Bobby lived just up Cuyamaca Street in the neighboring town of Santee, and that meant I saw a lot more of him. And seeing more of him led to more deals.

Bobby worked as a journeyman plumber on housing developments, but all of his creative energies—and he had energy in spades—were spent middling deals. He was invariably bright, cheery and enthusiastic, and had absolutely no qualms whatsoever about engaging in whatever non-violent criminal activity presented itself. He would middle guns, drugs, stolen vehicles, even illegal immigrants over the Mexican border, always with a smile.

One of the first deals Bobby brought me was a pound of crystal meth—crank—from a co-worker of his whose uncle was a major Mexican gangster in San Diego. The pound was called a football because of the way it was bundled in duct tape and car grease to kill the smell and make it easy to hide in a car's spare tire or engine block when crossing the border.

That deal led to three more buys, each for a football of crank, from the same colleague of Bobby's. Normally we wouldn't have bothered to do more than two buys, but the co-worker kept coming over to do the deals with different buddies, so we ended up nailing nine guys for the price of one.

Bobby and his buddy also led me to Smokey, a Mexican gangbanger who was one of the most absurd and dangerous people I met in San Diego—and that's saying something. Smokey had recently finished a stretch in Pelican Bay State Prison, a facility designed for the baddest of the bad, and was looking to make up for lost time. He was short and fat, and the basics of his costume never changed: a wifebeater undershirt and a fedora. He drove a Delta 88 that was both pimped out and rusted out, with multicolored dingle-balls trim inside the windows and windshields. The car was never without a good handful of homeboys hanging out the windows, and the stereo was always cranked to the max. To be heard above the din you had to shout, and Smokey was always shouting. Everything he said, or shouted, was complemented by macho hip-hop gestures. He was perhaps the most abrasive person I'd ever met.

Still, I liked him, perhaps because he was such a walking caricature. I made very sure, however, that he never realized I was laughing at him rather than with him; because he thought he was dangerous, he was, and would probably have killed me, or anyone else, at the drop of a fedora if he thought any fun was being had at his expense.

Smokey sold whatever could make him a bit of money. We began with a few handguns, moved on to modified shotguns (with the barrels sawed off and a folding stock) and then got into drugs, in his case Mexican heroin. The first time he offered me smack, Ryan told me to pass on the purchase—Mexican heroin dealers weren't our assignment. I did and it hit the streets through other middlemen. The second time I approached Ryan, I suggested to him that I might make some noise if he refused me again, so I got the green light for a thousand dollars' worth.

Just as Bobby had led me to Smokey, Smokey led me to a truck driver called Robert whose specialty was smuggling people and anything else across the Mexican border. Robert was in a bit of a bind. He'd been working for a network of coyotes—people smugglers—who had brought in a bunch of Middle Eastern types just days before 9/11 and who, after the Twin Towers fell, disbanded in a panic. So Robert was unemployed and was offering his services to me.

I told him that I was interested but said any border running I'd be doing would be into Canada and that he'd need phony papers. These I offered to provide him with—and used the opportunity to take his picture and one of his truck.

I took what I had to Brooks and Bob and suggested Robert be used to get to his former employers. I expected it would be a no-brainer; this, after all, was mere weeks after 9/11 and border security was the hottest of issues. But within hours they came back to me and said forget it. The rationale: it would bring in the Secret Service. "They'll definitely take the case away, the biker investigation will fall apart and you could find yourself back in Canada," said Bob. It had happened with the Russians, and the Hells Angels investigation had been sidetracked for a year. They weren't going to get big-footed again.

My first deal with the Hells Angels wasn't hand-to-hand. Rather, it happened through a dealer who sold coke and crank on behalf of Mark Toycen, the Dago chapter's sergeant-at-arms, and as such one of its most feared and fierce members.

The dealer was a very overweight woman in her fifties called JoAnn who spent her days and nights making drug deliveries all around the San Diego region. She was pretty small-time, eight balls and quarter ounces, and would regularly come into Dumont's, where Toycen often left her supply, to stock up. I was at the bar shooting the breeze with Pete one day when she dropped by. Purple Sue the barmaid introduced us and JoAnn and I got to talking. A few days later she stopped by the shop, saying she just happened to be in the neighborhood. Soon she was a regular visitor, sometimes alone, sometimes with Sue, sometimes with other people.

JoAnn was a real chatterbox and—given that she'd been consorting with the Dago Hells Angels for years—a fount of intelligence. But it was almost all just nice-to-know information. Her insignificant status—and probably her big mouth—meant that she wasn't privy to much that was actionable.

Like Sue's husband, JoAnn's son was in prison for murder, and she complained that she wasn't allowed to visit him for some reason. I assumed that her dealing for Toycen meant that her son received protection inside from the gang.

On her second or third visit she offered to sell to me. "If you're ever looking for something, you can come to me," JoAnn said. I took the bait.

"Sure. It might be good to have a bit, a quarter or something, for when people drop by."

I did a couple of small purchases, figuring that down the road, if need be, the cops could pick her up and likely turn her without much effort.

By this time I'd bought myself a bike, a souped-up 1999 Harley Sportster 1200, and started going on rides with individual members and associates. Sometimes we'd go out after the weekly barbecue; often we went into the desert. On the weekend of December 8/9—I remember because it was my fifty-third birthday—I went to one of the California Hells Angels' big promotional events, the Toys for Tots run. It was the Berdoo (or San Bernardino) chapter's turn to host the event and Brandon had asked me to produce a poster for it.

I rode to San Bernardino on my bike, followed by a full detail of cops: Ryan, Brooks, Billy from the sheriff's department—a half-dozen or so in total, spread over three vehicles. Angels were coming from across the entire state, and all of Dago was going to attend, so it was a choice surveillance opportunity, with or without criminal activity. The Angels were holding the run at a country lodge–like establishment owned by two of the Berdoo members, and gullible members of the public were encouraged to drop by with "new or gently used" toys. The gang would then pass the toys on to charity organizations, which distributed them to needy kids in time for Christmas. If I remember correctly, they amassed something like four eighteen-wheelers full of goodies over the weekend.

I spent much of the weekend taking photos of the assembled, always asking permission beforehand, of course. A few times it was denied. Still, despite my deference, around eight o'clock on Saturday evening, about when the public was sent on its way, I felt a large hand on my shoulder. I turned and it was the president of the Berdoo chapter.

"Who are you and why are you taking all these pictures?" he asked politely, but nonetheless menacingly.

"I'm with the Dago chapter and they asked me to come up and shoot some pictures for them," I said hopefully.

Brandon Kent shouted from about twenty feet away, where he was leaning against a wall. "Hey, it's okay! He's with us." I was happy to hear his voice and even happier to hear what he said after he walked over. "He takes all our charter pictures. Don't worry, he's cool."

The Berdoo president then gave me his stamp of approval. "You have any problems, tell them to come to me."

An hour or so later, when the party had become an exclusive Angels event, I realized how much weight Brandon's word carried. The only other photographer had been shooting for *Easyriders,* a tits-and-choppers magazine dedicated to the hagiography of the Hells Angels and their ilk. He was told that his presence was no longer required. I, on the other hand, was allowed to stick around as long as I liked. I did so for most of Saturday night.

The next day, I returned to the party to hang out some more. Toward the end of the afternoon, after many of the Dago members had left, Cisco, a member of the Oakland chapter, was looking for someone going back to San Diego and someone pointed me out to him.

"Bring these down to the Dago chapter," he instructed, handing me three advance copies of the next Hells Angels calendar. "One's for Mark," he said, meaning Toycen, "one's for the Boss and one's for the clubhouse."

Obediently, I took the calendars.

On the way back to San Diego I rendezvoused with the team at a rest stop on a highway east of San Bernardino, a different road than any HA would be riding. Except for a brief phone call, I hadn't been in contact with my handlers since arriving the day before, and they were eager to know what I had to report. I gave a summary debriefing and told them about the calendars, which were individually vacuum sealed in plastic. Ryan took them and looked them over.

"I guess I'll be taking these," he said. "You'll have your hands full printing up your photos."

"I need those things," I protested.

"Well, then you better hurry up and get those pictures to me," Ryan said, turning and starting to walk to his DEA-supplied SUV.

I lost it. "You're a fucking asshole," I screamed, adding a long list of expletives. I suppose I was a bit ragged from having spent two days alone with two hundred Hells Angels, not having had much sleep, and having a two-hour drive through the cold, high desert ahead of me. Still, I knew Ryan was just provoking me and getting a kick out of it. He knew perfectly well that any credibility I had with the gang could easily be shot if I failed to deliver the calendars promptly. I swore some more at him. "Come back here, you fucking jerk! I've had it with you! Let's do it! Now!"

He turned, handing the calendars to Bob or Billy, and started to come at me. But the rest of the team was on its toes and jumped in the middle to keep us apart. All we could do was yell at each other some more. Eventually, Ryan was corralled back to his truck and I got on my bike again. Whoever had the calendars gave them back to me.

That was it for Ryan and me. News of our roadside standoff reached the bosses and they ordered Ryan to step back and not have any direct contact with me. They didn't pull him from the case, though, and before long I realized that Ryan was letting himself into the listening post next to my shop in the evenings and monitoring my activities. It was creepy and unnerving, but there wasn't anything I could do about it. Bob, always playing the mediator, told me that Ryan was really only coming by the listening post for refuge; apparently things were even worse for him at home than they were with me. I hoped that was the reason for his off-hour visits. The circumstances of the investigation also meant that eventually he and I had to converse, and it wasn't more than a few weeks before he was phoning me with instructions and orders—one of which, in my opinion, would bring the whole case down.

I went back to New Brunswick for a couple of weeks over Christmas and New Year's and wasn't especially eager to return to San Diego in January, even if it meant trading snow and cold for sun. The investigation didn't seem to be going anywhere. The cops were content just to let it meander along, I felt. So, once back in El Cajon, I decided to set my own targets and get things moving.

Bobby Perez had offered to sell me drugs at least once, but we'd been at the bar at the time and I was without backup, so I had refused. The offer would come again, I knew, and likely when we were in the comfort of my shop, where the surveillance would pick everything up. He was always dropping by, and at all hours; as far as Bobby was concerned, if he was awake, you should be too. Sure enough, one night at about three a.m., he came by eager to sell.

"I've got some great crank—you interested in buying some?" he said.

I went for it this time, telling him I had a courier coming down soon who would probably be interested. I ended up with a couple of ounces of crystal meth. Not long afterward I did a second buy from him.

My next target was a Hells Angels prospect whom I'd got to know at the toy run. His name was Zach Carpenter and he worked at a tattoo parlor across from Dumont's. He'd done a cover-up tattoo for me before Christmas and at that time I'd sounded him out about scoring some drugs.

"I don't have anything now but will soon," he'd said.

We saw each other at church night in mid-January and I mentioned it again.

"I'll come by your place tomorrow," he said, and did. I bought an ounce of meth from him.

My handlers didn't try to stop me from making the buys, but they weren't excited about them or even the least bit encouraging. It struck me as somewhat odd.

Their lack of enthusiasm, however, was easier to handle than some other shit they pulled. One time Purple Sue dropped by for a visit and before leaving asked, "Is it okay if I do a line before I leave?"

"Sure," I answered, though the question was more rhetorical than anything. Sue was already pulling out her little bag of crank, and had drawn out a line and snorted it within seconds. Then she got on her purple Harley and sped off.

Later that day, the phone rang. It was Ryan, who wasn't even supposed to be calling me.

"We could arrest you for that," he announced.

"For what?" I answered, honestly mystified. I'd forgotten about Sue's line, and even if I'd recalled it I wouldn't have thought it cause for anyone, even Ryan, to come down on me.

"For letting someone do drugs on your premises," he said.

"What?!" I answered.

"For letting someone do drugs on your premises."

There was a pause. Finally I had to ask him, "Are you on drugs now?"

They didn't let it go at that. A couple of weeks later I was asked by a gang member if I could use my photo and computer skills to concoct some fake ID for a Dago Angel who was being sought by police. I said sure and scheduled a shoot for the following afternoon, duly informing my handlers.

As the fugitive and a buddy of his pulled into the parking, the phone rang. It was Ryan, who was monitoring the cameras from the listening post, telling me the guys had arrived. "And don't let them do drugs in your place and thereby contribute in the distribution of narcotics yourself," he said.

Again it seemed like nothing more than an effort to provoke me.

Eventually, I began to think that the DEA or someone within it had a hidden agenda, perhaps to derail the whole case. It was an idea that seemed more and more plausible after a phone call I received later in January. It was from an FBI agent in the force's San Francisco office. He asked if I could come up and meet him. "We'd like to talk to you about a few things," he explained.

A few days later I met with the G-man, who was a Hells Angels specialist, and a colleague of his at a restaurant in San Mateo or San Carlos—one of San Fran's southern suburbs. He seemed to know all about the case even if the Feebs were conspicuous by their absence from Operation Five Star. Then he got to the point of the meeting, which may have explained that absence. The FBI, it seemed, had very deep misgivings about the San Diego DEA office.

"We think there might be a leak there and we'd like you to help us figure it out," he said.

It didn't take me long to say no. My life would have just got too complicated, too messy, if I'd agreed to help investigate the lead agency employing me to investigate the Angels. I needed someone I could be straight with, someone I wouldn't have to watch my back around—even if they weren't necessarily being straight with me.

Just as would have been the case if I'd been dealing with criminals, refusing the offer meant that I couldn't know anything more about it. So I didn't ask, nor did I share with him my own misgivings about Ryan and some of my other handlers. I just didn't know the G-man well enough, and suspected that saying something could come around and bite me in the ass later.

"You will let us know if you notice anything out of the ordinary or illegal, won't you?" he asked before I left.

"Of course," I said, and headed back to El Cajon.

The notion that my handlers had a hidden agenda of some sort—whether it was torpedoing the investigation, edging me out of it or something else altogether—was buttressed a week or two after my return from San Francisco when they told me to introduce two undercover ATF agents into the case as my "associates." As had been the case months earlier, I didn't have a problem with this plan in theory. In fact, I thought it could actually help. Associates could show that I had a life beyond El Cajon and the Hells Angels; I could pretend that the two were part of my crew from a past criminal life; and, of course, they would serve as backup for me against both the Hells Angels and the Mongols, who had recently been flexing their muscles in the San Diego area.

The San Diego Mongols chapter was small and low-key, maybe a half-dozen members, but that hadn't stopped them from causing trouble. In January, the Hells Angels had planned a barbecue in a downtown parking lot. That same day, coincidentally, about four hundred Mongols passed through San Diego on a run from L.A. to Mexico and decided to drop in. Needless to say, the Angels lay low. The Mongols later retired to Cheetah's, the strip bar Taz managed—a fact that had made Taz *persona non grata* among the Angels. According to Angels protocol, he should have refused them entry and taken the inevitable beating.

The Mongols had also made a much more subtle show of force in Hell Cajon. Monk, the San Diego chapter president of the Mongols, had quietly walked into Dumont's alone and wearing his colors one weekday afternoon, sat down at the bar and ordered a pitcher of beer.

The barmaid, whom I always knew as the Wiener Girl for the tricks she would perform with a hot dog, didn't know what to do, so she phoned Ramona Pete at home. He told her to serve the guy, and sent Bobby Perez and another member over to keep an eye on him. But Monk was making a statement, not trouble. He just drank his pitcher and left.

The Mongols' actions had put the Hells Angels on edge—and me by extension, since I was by that time what the police would describe as a known associate. So I thought having a backup or two might be a good thing. But the way Ryan and Brooks insisted on me bringing the two ATF undercovers into the Angels fold struck me as not just ridiculous but dangerous. They demanded complete and immediate immersion; they wanted the two agents to be with me at all times. I was suddenly to go from being a lone-wolf operator to a guy who didn't travel anywhere without a couple of shadows. It made absolutely no sense, even after Ryan and Brooks argued that the two could corroborate drug purchases and eventually testify in court if need be. That could have been done by one agent who was with me occasionally, or simply by the video and audio tape. Being accompanied by both agents, at all times, would just have been a red flag and, in its own way, a provocation.

Making matters worse, the two undercover ATFs seemed to have both studied Badass Bikers 101 and were happy to play the part without any originality. I knew them as Rocky and Highway Mike.

Rocky had a black ponytail most of the way down his back and mus-cled, tattooed arms. Highway Mike was a bit older, a bit balder and, at five-eleven, several inches shorter than Rocky. He wasn't quite as muscular or tattooed, but he made up for it with his aggressive, in-your-face attitude. Their style ran counter to what I had built my whole career as an infiltrator on—being small and easy to get along with, not a walking, talking cliché. In other words, a convincing hu-man being and a pleasant respite for bad guys in a testosterone-charged world.

My handlers turned a deaf ear to my protests, and as of mid-February Rocky and Highway Mike were my constant companions. Immediately, my relations with the Angels deteriorated.

"Who are those fucking guys?" was a regular refrain the first time I dared bring the pair to Dumont's, one evening when there was a party and most everyone was welcome. And once the two became fixtures at my shop, I suddenly saw a lot less walk-in traffic. Gang members just stopped dropping by or would call beforehand. "Make sure you get rid of those guys before we get there," they would usually insist before coming over.

That was easier said than done. The two agents had orders to stick with me as much as possible, and often wouldn't leave even when the bikers demanded that I receive them alone. "They have to meet us sometime," Rocky and Highway Mike would say.

On one occasion when Zach Carpenter and another member in-structed me to be alone but my shadows wouldn't leave, the bikers turned on their heels and left as soon as they saw Rocky and Highway Mike. It wasn't that the gang members suspected the pair were cops. Rather, their first concern was that they were bikers with loyalties to another club. Given the recent tension with the Mongols, that was even worse.

Regularly I'd plead with my handlers, especially Brooks from the ATF, to pull Rocky and Mike, or at least one of them, from the op-eration, but I was always stonewalled.

"Do the best you can," they'd say. "They're not going anywhere."

The investigation effectively ground to a halt. It was worse than before Christmas. Even if I hadn't had any direction then, the Angels had at least seen me as an ally. Now they regarded me much more cagily.

I was thoroughly discouraged, especially because I felt that I had finally been getting somewhere. I wondered if I was introducing the two agents so I could be yanked, and I contemplated bailing on the whole investigation. I began to wait for the inevitable, really just putting in time.

Then, about a month after Rocky and Highway Mike had landed on me, Pat Ryan came into my store on Cuyamaca Street and told me to set up a major coke purchase. There was no exchange of pleasantries. "This is what I want you to do," he said, his usual opener. No consultation, no "Do you think it might be a good idea if . . ." Just a direct command: "I want you to get a hold of Bobby and make an order he can't fill himself, an order he'll have to go to his SOS for," Ryan said, using police shorthand for "source of supply."

"Fine. How much are we talking about?"

It sounded like standard procedure, a move that might let us begin climbing the ladder to the bigger players. Since most of my previous deals had been for four ounces, the biggest a pound, I thought Ryan would want three or four pounds, five maximum.

"About a hundred pounds," he replied.

"Okay," I said, keeping my surprise to myself. This was it, I immediately assumed, the takedown deal. If I'd been speaking with Brooks or any other cop in the operation, I would have simply asked. Or more likely they would have just told me. With Ryan, however, things were so strained that had I put the question to him directly, he would have refused to answer just to spite me.

Like that, the meeting was over.

Later that day, I phoned Bobby Perez. As much as anybody, Bobby was at the top of the police's wish list of gang members they wanted arrested—another fact that made me think this was the takedown buy. They weren't after him for his contacts, influence or big-league criminal activities, as they were with Brandon Kent; they wanted Bobby off the street because of his raw viciousness. A street-educated dealer and club enforcer, his only loyalty was to the gang, his only concern the protection and promotion of its interests. Bobby hadn't had any time for me when I began to show my face around El Cajon, but he had warmed to me after his girlfriend started a fight at Bonita's, a Mexican bar next door to Dumont's. Bobby had found himself facing down an angry horde with no one but me backing him up. The incident ended when everyone went their own way after an angry staredown. Bobby, however, didn't forget who had stood by him.

He'd later volunteered to back me up on a crystal meth deal I'd done with Smokey. He didn't have much to do—he just sat there in a corner of my office wearing his colors and looking bad, his hand inside his vest and obviously very close to a piece, as I bought a football of meth. The deal went as smoothly as it could, the Mexicans evidently impressed by Bobby's scowling silence.

Since then I'd bought from Bobby himself, so he'd never become as wary of Rocky and Highway Mike as other Dago Angels. And besides, the big buy was too tempting to resist; Bobby was chronically broke and this promised a major payday.

Nothing incriminating was ever explicitly mentioned over the phone with the Angels, of course, so when I called Bobby after receiving my orders from Ryan, our conversation was brief.

"I want to talk to you," I said. "Can you drop by?"

"Okay," he answered, and that was it—as long as most phone conversations with Bobby.

The next day, he came by the store. Happily, he dropped in on one of the rare occasions when Rocky and Highway Mike weren't around, and he was open and relaxed. Beyond selling me drugs, Bobby had another good reason to visit. His house had been raided around Christmas, and police had found a substantial arsenal inside—sawed-off shotguns, a couple of machine guns and half a crack of hand grenades, six or so. The house wasn't rented in Bobby's name and he wasn't there at the time; still, police charged him with possession of illegal weapons. A condition of his bail prohibited him from leaving the state unless it was work-related. So he needed a job—that's where I came in. That day he was picking up a letter confirming he was an employee of Posterplus. He was supposedly going to attend motorcycle runs across the Southwest on my behalf, and hand out pamphlets promoting our services. But we also talked about what I'd asked him there for.

"I finally landed this big customer I've been chasing for over a year," I told him. "These guys are cool. They buy once, maybe twice in a given year. Minimal risk, you know. That's why they want serious volume."

"That's the way to do business," Bobby said.

"Problem is, where am I going to find one hundred pounds?"

"I might be able to help you," he said—exactly what I'd wanted him to say.

Nothing was mentioned of the big coke buy for at least a week, which hardly surprised me. The police and I had expected it would take perhaps a couple of months, maybe more, to put together. Bobby was also not someone you expected regular progress reports from. Then, perhaps ten days later, Bobby came up to me at Dumont's and told me that he'd be over to see me at my office later. If the subject was too delicate to talk about even at a friendly bar like Dumont's, he must have news about our coke deal, I figured.

I made my way back to the office, on the way phoning Ryan's partner to tell him to make sure he got the meeting on tape. There had been no one in the police listening post adjacent to Posterplus to press the record button during the first meeting, and I didn't want that to happen again.

Within ten minutes of my return, Bobby walked in, and not alone. To my surprise, he was with Mark Toycen, Dago's hard-ass sergeant-at-arms. A sergeant-at-arms's job was to enforce club discipline and ensure the club's security. For the Dago chapter, this meant being particularly paranoid about any new faces—that's why I was so surprised to see him in my office. His presence could only mean one of two things: either he was directly, personally involved in the procurement of the coke or it was going to be a deal that involved the whole chapter and he was there as its representative. If he simply wanted to check me out, he would never have shown up to a meeting where a major drug sale was going to be discussed—that would have been just plain stupid.

Bobby got straight to the point. "We have a hundred kilos going through the River Run."

That was more than twice as much as the hundred pounds I'd ordered, but I figured if this was to be the takedown deal, then the bigger the bust the better.

"Great," I said. "I'll call my contact. We might be able to take all of it, but I have to check first."

I asked Bobby about delivery—whether the cocaine would be brought to me in El Cajon or whether I would have to pick it up myself in Laughlin, Nevada, the tiny casino town in the southern tip of the state, on the Arizona border, that hosted the big biker gathering known as the River Run every April.

"You got to take it from there," Bobby said.

We didn't talk about price—it was understood it would be less than ten thousand dollars per pound—and I didn't want to commit myself to a set quantity too quickly. Ideally, things would be left as loose as possible and final details would only be nailed down at the River Run. Then, as negotiations proceeded, I would perhaps have the opportunity to meet Bobby's partners in the deal—or at least find out who they were. Bobby didn't want to push too hard either. However nasty he was and however long he'd been a Hells Angel, it was by far the biggest deal he'd ever put together, and it offered the promise of a major payday. He didn't want to say or do anything that might mess it up.

So we left things like that. Toycen hadn't said a word the entire meeting and kept it that way as he and Bobby walked out barely twenty minutes after they'd entered.

As soon as they were gone, I got a call from Ryan in the listening post saying he and the others wouldn't require a debrief. They'd heard everything and got it on tape.

Two days after my big meeting with Bobby and Toycen, Rocky came by my store.

"Let's go for a ride," he said, and we got on our government-supplied Harley-Davidsons and headed over to El Cajon Boulevard.

There we went to what we called a "civilian bar"—one not frequented by the gang. He ordered a beer and I got a Pepsi. Then he told me something that left me not knowing what to think—though the cowboy in me kind of liked the craziness of the idea.

The police couldn't afford to buy over two hundred pounds of coke, he explained, but there was no way they were going to let all or even any of it hit the street. And it wasn't yet time for the takedown.

"So we've decided to steal the coke," he said.

I was speechless. For a moment. Then I saw the flaw in the plan.

"Bobby will know I'm involved," I said.

"Not if we're wearing Mongol patches," he said flatly.

As it turned out, about a year earlier the DEA and ATF had come down hard on the Mongols in California, Arizona, New Mexico and Nevada, arresting dozens on drug and gun offenses and seizing all sorts of evidence, including more than fifty club patches. These had been moldering in some police storage room ever since. Now, Rocky said, they would be pressed into service.

I was shocked, but also intrigued and excited. The plan had an audaciousness that I found appealing. At the same time, the term "rogue cops" came into my head and wouldn't leave. Especially after Rocky's parting instructions: "Never discuss this inside the studio because it might end up on tape and we'd have to explain it later."

I stayed at the table in the bar for a while after Rocky left, nursing my Pepsi and thinking. The police were looking for plausible deniability, I figured. They wanted to be able to deny the operation ever existed and to be able to cover their asses if the operation blew up. I didn't want to be the only one without a chair if the music stopped. But how I might accomplish that, I had no idea.

The River Run wasn't more than a week or two away, and the following days were filled with planning the trip and the logistics of the deal with Bobby. I presumed that the cops were themselves busy orchestrating the burn, but I was entirely out of the loop on that. In other operations I had been treated as a full member of the team, kept up to speed on any developments in the case, my advice and expertise solicited, appreciated and often acted upon. In this investigation, however, I had got used to being treated as an outsider. My debriefings were more like interrogations and I was never given enough information to form a complete picture of where the operation was going. I didn't know when I had surveillance with me; I didn't know when the tape was rolling. The police, I had the impression, considered me suspect simply because I didn't have a badge.

I wasn't just being sensitive. One day that week I left my computer webcam turned on in my studio, but turned off the monitor so it looked as if the computer was shut down. When I later reviewed the video, I saw Ryan and his partner Hunter carefully sifting through my things, in particular my papers.

The only direction I got from the police regarding the burn at the River Run was to tell Bobby to deliver the goods to a house in the north end of Bullhead City, Laughlin's much larger sister town on the Arizona side of the Colorado River. The house was rented by an undercover ATF agent known as Jaybird (Jay Dobyns), who by then had been infiltrating the Arizona Hells Angels for about two years. His cover was a loansharking and collections operation—*Imperial Financial Corporation, Investment and Recovery Guidance,* his business card read—and he was well inserted into the gang.

Jaybird, I told Bobby, was a criminal associate of mine and I would be staying at his house for the duration of the run. There was room for him and his girlfriend, too, I told Bobby, and initially he was going to take me up on the offer. Then he had to head to Laughlin a couple of days earlier than planned and took a room at the Gretchen Motor Inn in Bullhead, the headquarters of the Hells Angels rank-and-file for the run. (Most of the gang's bigwigs stayed at two large casino hotels on the strip in Laughlin itself, the Riverside and the Flamingo. Many police were also staying at the Flamingo.)

Even if Bobby wasn't going to stay at Jaybird's, he had no problem with my request that any negotiations regarding the cocaine transaction take place there. It was all academic, as they say—or at least supposed to be. Through an informant close to Bobby, the police not only had learned that he was not to be part of the smuggling run but also had a good idea of the route the coke would be taking up from the Mexican border. They planned to have the drugs stolen before any negotiating took place. Still, they wanted to cover all the bases, and be sure there would be no last-minute surprises.

I made the drive from El Cajon to Laughlin, via Berdoo and Barstow, on Tuesday, April 23. With stops, it took the better part of the day, and I didn't regret taking my Nissan pickup instead of my Harley. Originally, Rocky and Highway Mike were supposed to travel with me, but then Bobby had expressed interest in scoring a ride. So my ATF shadows made other plans, which suited me just fine, only to have Bobby go on ahead a couple of days early to organize the coke deal, I presumed. That was also just fine. Even if the truck was old and beginning to fall apart, it at least had air conditioning.

It also allowed me to take along a dog that, despite my best intentions, had become my near-constant companion over the preceding few months. Soon after I arrived in El Cajon, I'd run into a speed freak named Daryl trying to pawn the pooch outside Dumont's. The dog was a Bichon Frise, but the tweaker had shaved him—or half of him—like a poodle in hopes the animal would fetch a better price, at least enough for his next high. I made a deal with Daryl: he'd give me the dog for free and I wouldn't make him regret mistreating the poor thing. A DEA agent with a sense of humor got him a tag with the name Q-Dog—I was known to the bikers as Q-Bob, a nickname that had been given to me by Taz soon after my arrival when I'd mentioned I was from Quebec—but I never called him anything but Dog. It wasn't that I lacked imagination. Rather, I'd planned to find him a new home as soon as possible. But after a month or so I'd grown attached to Dog, and he would come almost everywhere with me. He was a regular at Dumont's, where Ramona Pete routinely gave him a little bowl of beer and let him drink it off the bar. And he never got in the way of my meeting people—just the opposite.

Dog was well received when we got to Jaybird's in Bullhead as well. Without Bobby there, the house that week became a crash pad and hangout for undercover agents who were infiltrating biker gangs across the U.S. I'd never seen anything like it. There were agents inside the Pagans in the Northeast, the Outlaws in Florida, the Mongols in

California, as well as several, like myself, infiltrating the Hells Angels in various parts of the country. The only major biker gang not at the River Run—and thus without a representative agent at Jaybird's—was the Bandidos, my old friends. In the two decades the run had existed, the Bandidos had never shown up, just as the Hells Angels had never gone to the Four Corners Run, the other big biker get-together in the Southwest, where the Bandidos held court.

The parade of agents gave Jaybird's place the feel of a small convention—a relaxed one since there were no handlers or suits to monitor the goings-on. It was fascinating and fun, but it also struck me as a crazy security risk. Pretty much all of law enforcement's undercover biker eggs were together in one basket. Bobby knew exactly where I was staying, and had he dropped by he could easily have come across an agent affiliated with one of the Hells Angels' rivals sitting on the couch having a beer. That might have got him asking some very awkward questions. And had one of us been targeted for any reason, a single bomb would have torpedoed any number of operations.

None of the other agents, however, seemed particularly bothered by the risks they were running. It took them no time at all to get into the spirit of the run and treat the week as a party. Beyond going down to the strip on rare occasions to hang with the clubs they were infiltrating, none of them were doing much work. Most of their time was spent sprawled on Jaybird's couches or sitting around his dining room table drinking beer and telling stories.

Some of these agents seemed to have been playing their roles too long for their own good. Jaybird, for example, had gone so far as to get his biker name—Jaybird—tattooed across the top of his back in the shape of a top rocker. Worse, according to what I heard from the ATF handlers, he never reported or called in unless pressured to. His wife had thrown him out, and he didn't seem to care. He referred to her as "the bitch," without fail, as a biker would.

Then there was Bubba. He had been under in the Los Angeles area for about five years and knew absolutely everyone. He was an exceptional case—he hadn't created an entirely new identity for his undercover work; rather, he continued to live with his real wife and kids, who became part of the act. Whether it was because they kept him grounded or the fact that he was only intel and not operational, Bubba didn't seem as subsumed by his character as someone like Jaybird. He'd managed to keep a solid fix on who he was, to remember that he was a cop.

Some agents at Jaybird's went beyond drinking and telling stories in their bid to have a good time. As a late arrival at the run, I got stuck sleeping on the living room couch. It wasn't a big deal; I'd bedded down on much worse. The second night I was there, I fell asleep around midnight and then woke up about four-thirty. The house was dark and quiet. All I could hear was my rumbling stomach. I turned on the kitchen light and checked out the fridge. As I started to make myself a sandwich, one of the bedroom doors opened and a female ATF agent I knew as Barbie came out, also heading to the fridge. She seemed embarrassed, and I assumed it was because she was wearing only a T-shirt and underwear. Then Highway Mike stuck his head out of the room and asked her if she had found any beer. I looked at him, then at her.

She looked at the floor and mumbled something like "How you doing?" before grabbing two beers and heading back to the bedroom.

I sat down and clicked on the tube. Out comes Rocky with a woman.

"Could you tell Mike I just went to drive my lady friend home?" Rocky said to me. The girl was obviously a stripper, but I had to make sure.

"And you are?" I asked.

"Oh, hi, my name is Candy and I'm a dancer. I met Rocky last night at the club."

I couldn't believe it: this was supposed to be a safe house for undercover agents! And Rocky brings over a woman who, if she was like most of her colleagues, partied regularly with bikers and provided them with some of their most valuable intel. I should have gone home right then.

Instead, an hour or two later I put Dog in my truck and headed toward town. There was a pancake joint right across from the Gretchen Motor Inn and the parking lot was filled with dozens of bikes and men and women having breakfast beers and hanging out.

After my recent experience with the agents, I found the scene strangely comforting. Instead of going in for my own breakfast, I got a Pepsi from a machine and sat on the tailgate of the truck, idly chatting with whoever went by and just blending in.

I had been there a good half-hour when my cellphone rang. It was Rocky, telling me to get back to the house immediately. No reason provided.

When I got there, he met me at the door. "We're out of here," he said and, pointing at a pickup with huge tires, a rebel flag in the back window and a vanity license plate that read *Cowboy,* added, "Follow that truck." Again he gave no explanation.

When we got to the first major intersection, I expected to turn right, back toward the Gretchen, the bridge crossing to Laughlin and the River Run action. Instead, we turned left and headed south on Highway 95. Soon we were rolling through the desert, and I realized we weren't going on a short drive. I turned on the AC, mostly for Dog, who was panting.

After about twenty miles, Cowboy pulled into a Tempo gas station in Needles, on the California–Arizona border. I drew in beside the pickup, and Cowboy himself—who looked more biker than cop (in fact he didn't look at all cop)—came over and, without saying a word, pushed a leather vest with the Mongols colors through my lowered window.

I pulled off my Hells Angels support T-shirt—*When in doubt, knock 'em out,* it read—and put on the vest. It was several sizes too big for me, but I had a feeling style wasn't going to be an issue wherever we were headed. I wore it inside when I paid for my gas and stocked up on supplies—several bottles of water for me and the dog, chips and other snacks. We were clearly heading to the burn, and I didn't want to be stuck hungry and thirsty in the desert. Cowboy either already had his own supplies or didn't share my concerns. I didn't ask.

Once I was back in my truck, we headed south on 95 again. We hadn't traveled more than a dozen miles when we turned right onto a gravel road and then quickly turned left again onto a dirt track running parallel to the highway. We drove along it a short distance, up a rise to a point where we were perhaps thirty yards above the highway,

at the top of a steep slope. The area was treeless and exposed, but sufficiently elevated from the roadbed that we and our vehicles couldn't
be seen by anyone traveling either direction along the highway. I
found myself a spot among about a dozen pickups parked crookedly
and just out of sight of the highway. Before I got out of the truck,
Rocky came over.

"Leave the keys in the ignition in case someone has to move it,"
he said.

I did as I was told, rolled down the windows to keep the truck
from becoming an oven and stepped out, Dog scampering along at
my heels. Then we followed the track a bit farther up the rise into a
bizarre and busy scene. Fifteen or twenty men—some of whom I
knew, including Highway Mike, others I recognized from Jaybird's,
still others I'd never seen before—all wearing Mongols colors, were
digging shallow trenches to lie in, taping ammo clips together to allow
for quicker reloading, inspecting their guns. Some of the agents had
MP5s, others MAC-11s. One was carrying an AR-15. I began to feel
uncomfortably under-armed. My only hardware was the KA-BAR
knife that had been issued to me twenty-two years earlier on my way
in-country in Vietnam—a place this scene in the desert was beginning to take me back to.

An agent I remembered from Jaybird's house threw one of the
small folding shovels my way and told me to find a spot. I found a
place on the high edge of the bluff, as far from the trucks and up the
track as almost anyone else. We were all spaced anywhere from one to
five yards apart and there were only two agents to my right. In
retrospect, it wasn't the best spot. It gave me an excellent view of the
road, but I was very exposed from behind.

As I prepared my hole, Dog ran around, greeting those agents he
knew, making friends with new ones and earning himself at least one
enemy.

"The dog shit in my hole!" one guy down the line shouted all of
a sudden. A chorus of guffawing went up.

"Better you than me," another agent answered.

"Can't think of a better place," said another.

I kept quiet. No one had really spoken to me yet and there didn't seem to be a great deal to talk about. Whatever was going on, I figured we'd be there for a while, more than enough time for chat and to get somebody to share some information with me. Then someone's radio crackled. A second later the guy yelled, "They're coming down the road now!"

Everyone hit his hole and looked down 95. So much for finding out what was going on, or for eating any of those chips I'd brought with me. Either our intelligence on this operation was more precise than usual or the bad guys had watches. After a couple of minutes I could see a small convoy of SUVs coming down the road to my right. I looked to my left, back up the highway in the direction we'd come from, expecting to see interceptor vehicles ready to block off their escape, but the road was clear. Maybe they were just well hidden, I thought.

Within moments, the first of the four SUVs was directly below us. I was still wondering how they planned to stop the vehicles when the agents all around me opened fire. In seconds, the SUV was ventilated by bullet holes, screeching and swerving to a stop. The four doors opened and men piled out. The driver, clearly a Latino, came out shooting, but not for long. He hadn't taken more than a step or two before he was shot in the head and it literally exploded. He'd either been hit by an armor-piercing round or by two bullets simultaneously. The guy behind him never even got his second foot on the ground before he was hit several times. The two on the passenger side fared better. They were shielded by their SUV and were able to get into a crouch before they ran toward the other three vehicles arriving behind them. Swirling dust and dirt kicked up by the trucks and the bullets helped their cover. Still, their chances of making it would have been slim to non-existent had the police operation not gone south at that particular moment.

With all the automatic gunfire, no one noticed the roar of the approaching bikes until they were almost right behind us. When the sound finally got my attention, I looked toward it, behind me and to my right. About twenty yards away, roaring up the track we had followed ourselves, was the vanguard of a staggered line of at least a dozen Harleys, most of them with passengers on the back. They had come out of nowhere and weren't happy to see us: the passengers on the back were shooting at me and the line of agents, all of us exposed from behind. Mercifully, the firepower they were packing was a lot less impressive than our side's. Most of them only had semi-automatic handguns.

But all it takes is one bullet, as the agent a yard or so to my left found out. I glanced over at him and he was lying on his stomach half out of his hole. He wasn't the only victim on our side. After the SUVs on the highway came to a stop, several agents had recklessly gone over the top and run down toward them. But after starting down the hill, they were distracted by the shooting and shouting behind them. In their confusion, at least three hesitated and stood up from their crouches— then promptly went down after taking bullets from men in the SUVs. The drivers of the vehicles seized the moment and got the hell out of there—apparently only the lead truck had been crippled. They hit the gas and tore off around the far side of the stalled SUV, using it for a moment's cover.

Behind us, the bikes roared past, going as fast as was possible on a bumpy dirt track. Only two went down, hit by agents' bullets. A cloud of dust rose behind the others as they turned off the track and raced north on 95.

By this time I had grabbed the nine-millimeter semi of the dead agent beside me—he was one of the less well armed—and pointed it at the fast-disappearing line of bikes. I fired off a round and then another and another. I didn't come close to hitting anyone, but the act of shooting gave me a sense of relief. When the magazine was empty, I threw the gun back toward its owner. The firefight, which had lasted only a matter of seconds even if it seemed an eternity, was over.

Dust filled the air and an eerie silence descended, broken only by the groaning, coughing and wheezing of injured men. For a moment everyone seemed to keep to themselves, catching their breath, checking to see if they had indeed made it through unscathed, and trying to figure out what the hell had just happened. Then, just as the uninjured agents began to tend to the injured and inspect the dead, Cowboy grabbed me.

"We gotta get outta here," he said, pulling me to my feet by my vest.

That was when I noticed for the first time the large tattoo on the inside of his forearm: *MFFM* in two-inch-high letters. Mongols Forever, Forever Mongols. It was another mystery on a day full of them. But I couldn't afford it much thought. I hurried to keep up with him as he strode back to the truck. On the way, I had to step around a downed Harley with a dead Hells Angel next to it—his patch said *Arizona*. I glanced down the slope to the highway. There I counted three bodies around the abandoned, bullet-riddled SUV, and one more farther back. Turning toward our trucks, my eyes met those of a DEA colleague of Ryan's. He didn't acknowledge us or say anything; he just stood there, staring.

When I got to my pickup, it was already running. I opened the door and Dog, who had run around in a panic through most of the shootout until he found me again, jumped in. He scuttled into the rear of the cab and hid, shaking, as rattled as I was. When Cowboy's truck pulled out, I was right behind it, and we were soon hauling ass back toward Laughlin and Bullhead.

On the way, question after question rushed into my head—none of them with any answers. Why hadn't whoever was at the other end of the radio warned us about the outriders? How could the motorcycles have avoided detection? Why hadn't there been any interceptor vehicles? Had police *wanted* some of the Hells Angels to escape? Why had the agents gone over the top like a bunch of kamikazes—just so their Mongols colors would be seen? It had been reckless to the point of suicidal. And what was with the MFFM tattoo on the muscled arm of the man driving the pickup I was racing to keep up with? I had never run into another agent or infiltrator who went so far as to get a gang tattoo. Who was this guy?

I wasn't about to ask him, however, as he pulled back into the Tempo station in Needles and took my Mongols vest back. As he leaned into my window, he asked, "Can you make your way back alone from here?"

As directionally dysfunctional as I am, I wasn't about to become a problem. I wanted to get as far away as possible, as quickly as possible, from the scene of the ambush and anyone involved in it.

"Yeah," I answered as I put my Hells Angels support T-shirt back on.

That was the last I ever saw of Cowboy.

I pulled up to Jaybird's confused and not knowing what to do next. I didn't have much time to dwell on it, however. My cellphone rang. It was Brooks, my ATF handler.

"I want you to come over to the hotel," he said. "We're in room 303."

I pulled a U-turn and headed toward the bridge to Laughlin. It was mid-afternoon by now and the River Run party was getting under way. Traffic was bumper to bumper, festive and boisterous. It all struck me as surreal. Didn't these people know what had just happened?

I fought to get a grip on myself. Of course they didn't. Still, I knew that important meetings were happening somewhere and instructions would soon be coming my way. By the time I reached the Flamingo Hotel, I felt better, in control of myself, if not of the day's events.

I took the elevator up to 303 and found one of my handlers alone in the room. Brooks was nowhere to be seen. He was a talkative man, but today he offered only perfunctory chitchat. "How you holding up?" he asked. I just shrugged.

Then he got straight to the point. The ambush that day was not to be discussed with anyone, period—not my handlers, not his superiors, not anyone who might come sniffing around. If anyone, cop or otherwise, brought the subject up, I was to tell him right away. As far as everyone was concerned, he said, it never happened.

"You got that?" he stressed, looking me deep in the eyes. "It never happened."

The other orders he gave me were delivered almost as an after-thought. I was to hang around town and wait for further instructions from Bobby Perez as to the completion of our drug deal; disappearing from town at this point would look suspicious.

The meeting lasted no more than fifteen minutes. No one else had come into the room, and I didn't run into any other cops I knew at the Flamingo or outside. I got into my truck and headed to Jaybird's once again. I was dirty and tired and needed to just sit for a while.

I had a lot to figure out. Strange as it may seem, one of my main concerns was how I would ever write notes of the day's events. On all jobs, since my first operation in Hong Kong more than two decades earlier, I had been contractually required to keep accurate notes. But that didn't seem to be the way they did business in southern California. I had done so anyway, as much from force of habit as anything else. Today, however, there were just too many question marks, starting with a verified body count. I had seen a lot of people get hit, but I had no idea how many died. Except, that is, for the Mexican, the agent next to me and the Hells Angel from Arizona—there was no way any of them survived.

I could be reasonably sure of one thing: the drugs and most of the Hells Angels had got away. Unless, of course, the cops nabbed them farther down the road, but I doubted that. To arrest them at that point would have risked exposing the whole operation, which surely wasn't in the plans, judging by my conversation at the Flamingo.

I had other unanswered questions. As far as I knew, I was the only non-cop to have taken part in the ambush or to have any knowledge of it. That made me a loose cannon in the eyes of my law enforcement employers, one they might want to tie up in any number of ways, some of which were highly unpleasant to contemplate. I had been asking myself all afternoon why they had even brought me to the ambush or let me know about it. Everyone involved had to be considered a security risk in this kind of black op; as the only non-agent, non-American, I had to be seen as far and away the biggest such risk. I wondered if their original plan in taking me out to the desert with them was to kill me or let me be killed. If so, why hadn't they done it? Why had Cowboy pulled me out of there in such a hurry? Surely my death would have been even easier to cover up in the chaos of the outriders' counterattack.

Of course, in retrospect, a lot of my thinking was paranoid confusion. Nothing made any sense to me. Except one thing: it was time to get the hell out. As soon as I got back to El Cajon, I would gather my shit together, throw it in the truck and head home to Canada.

I spent that night hanging out on the strip and the next day took it easy at Jaybird's. The mood at the house had changed after the ambush. The subject everyone wanted to talk about—at least those who were aware of it—was off limits. So, more often than not, an uneasy silence filled the place. I didn't mind—all the storytelling and bragging had worn thin on me, and the quiet gave me the chance to catch up on some sleep.

That's what I was doing the next day when Jaybird came over to the couch and shook me awake. "We all have to go into town and hang out for a while," he said.

It was Friday night, and Laughlin's Casino Drive, which hugs the Colorado River as it flows south past the town, was rocking. The Flamingo was at the top end of the strip and that's where I headed once again. The hotel was home to many top Angels as well as cops that week, and it had been reckless for my handlers to call me to a meeting there the previous day. I had taken it as an indication of their disorganization in the aftermath of the botched ambush. My cover, however, seemed to be still intact and when I arrived that evening I found Ramona Pete, the owner of Dumont's, hanging around the front of the hotel. I chatted with him for a bit and then wandered about, making my way casually down the strip.

As I walked, I saw small groups of Hells Angels talking in a serious, conspiratorial manner at odds with the backslapping bonhomie that otherwise pervaded the run. In front of the Colorado Belle, I noticed Brooks. Since he was new to the ATF, not well known to the bikers and dressed like any other tourist, I judged it safe to chat with him briefly, making it look like a casual conversation between strangers.

"Something's going on," I said.

"I know," he answered. "I can feel it too."

He also relayed to me some intel that he'd just been given: about eighty Mongols had recently arrived and were taking over the south end of the strip. I was wearing another of my Hells Angels support

T-shirts and a vest with a patch that read *Red & White supporter,* so Brooks offered a bit of advice: "Stay out of the area."

I didn't disobey him, at least not immediately. Instead, I wandered across the street from the Belle to the Ramada, where a group of Iron Horsemen I knew from San Diego and El Cajon were standing around shooting the breeze. Along with the Red Devils, the Saddle Tramps and the legendary Booze Fighters, the Horsemen were a Hells Angels puppet club in southern California. I figured that if something was about to happen, they might have been told what.

Knowing better than to pry, I just sidled up to them and listened to the conversation. Before I heard anything interesting, however, I noticed groups of Hells Angels, including Ramona Pete, briskly heading down the strip in twos and threes. That's when I disregarded my handler's advice. It was about 1:45 a.m. and all hell was about to break loose.

When I arrived outside Harrah's, I came across Pete and a small group of Hells Angels and supporters waiting for reinforcements. I joined them and within five minutes there were about twenty of us—enough, it was determined by some fool, to make a respectable fighting force. We headed through the automatic sliding doors. I stuck close to Pete. He was as influential as Hells Angels got in El Cajon, and even if I had resolved to cash things in as far as the investigation was concerned, I still reflexively wanted to impress the right bikers. If he saw me, a short, slight, aging supporter, standing tall beside him and the rest of the gang, it could only pay off in the long run.

The Mongols were clustered around a bar in the middle of the casino. The men around me headed straight for it. There was no question what was about to happen. There were a few words, but not many. The fists and feet—and any object at hand that might be used as a club—started flying almost immediately. I landed one blow—a high side kick—on a Mongol who was going after Pete. But it was soon every man for himself, and Pete and I were separated. A herd of stampeding seniors and other gamblers—screaming and clutching their change buckets—made the confusion that much worse.

It didn't take long before knives were drawn. That—along with the fact that we were seriously outnumbered—was my cue to get out of there, and quick. When I reached the doors, I heard shots ring out. That only made me move faster.

I hightailed it back to my truck and headed for Bullhead City. I felt like a fish swimming upriver. All the traffic, pedestrian and motorized, was moving toward Harrah's. News of the confrontation had evidently spread quickly. I made it across the bridge to Bullhead just in time: state troopers closed it almost as soon as they got news of the battle, and many of the rank-and-file Hells Angels, staying at the Gretchen, were stuck on the Arizona side of the Colorado River. But that didn't stop them trying to get to the action. As I passed the hotel, I noticed activity along the shoreline. People were getting into boats. I tried to call my handlers and warn them, but the cellphone system had collapsed under a surge of activity.

When I got to Jaybird's, he was there with two or three other agents. I filled them in on what had happened and told them about the bikers trying to cross the river by boat. Jaybird then used his radio to pass the information on to the troopers, and several boatloads of Hells Angels were subsequently stopped. Not long afterward, I was fast asleep on Jaybird's couch again, for the last time, thankfully.

The next morning, Jaybird's house was abuzz with chatter about the shootout at Harrah's. Finally, some action they could talk about, and they did so eagerly, to the exclusion of doing anything useful. By noon I had had my fill and headed out, under orders from my handlers not to stray far.

I went to the Gretchen, where the Hells Angels were on a war footing. They'd learned that three of their brothers had been killed in the fight with the Mongols the night before, and they were feeling both under assault and intent on revenge. They had forced all the other patrons to find other accommodation and posted members of the Red Devils and Iron Horsemen around the hotel as security. I parked on a side street near the river and walked around to the front, where two rows of cars formed a makeshift barricade by the entrance. When I was twenty or thirty feet from the front door, a shotgun-packing Hells Angel asked me what my business was.

"I'm here to see Bobby Perez, HA Dago," I answered. "My name is Q-Bob."

The biker radioed in and after a few minutes a Hells Angels sergeant-at-arms came to check me out. I explained that Bobby was on probation and wasn't even supposed to be out of California. "I'm his emergency ride out," I explained. "I'm here to see if he needs me."

Another call was made on the radio, this one by the sergeant-at-arms, and Zach Carpenter appeared. He gave the okay and accompanied me into the main reception area. Given the mood, I got the impression the gang was expecting an all-out attack on the hotel. There were patches everywhere, all armed and very serious. Zach handed me over to yet another Hells Angel, who led me to the hotel office. There was no manager in sight; the gang had turned it into their war room. I was patted down and vetted once more before another sergeant-at-arms accompanied me down the hall to Bobby's ground-level room. He was with his girlfriend and another couple. Seeing me, he beckoned me outside and back to the lobby area, where we talked.

After a bit of small talk I told him I was hoping to leave that day because of all the heat resulting from the shootout. "But I don't want to abandon you here if you guys need a ride back to El Cajon."

"None of us can go anywhere without the say-so from above," Bobby said. "But thanks for coming and asking."

It was as warm and effusive an expression of thanks as I'd ever heard Bobby make. When he then grabbed my hand and hugged me to emphasize his point, I had to wonder if I was talking to the same Bobby Perez.

"If you want me to stay and help out in any way, I'll hole out somewhere," I said, caught up in the warmth of the moment.

Bobby thought for a second. "Well, you can help by taking a couple things back for me."

"Sure," I answered. "Whatever you want."

With that, he instructed me to wait there while he went back to his room. A few minutes later he returned and handed me his Fender Stratocaster guitar and a .380 semi-automatic wrapped in a nylon stocking.

"Thanks again, man," he said after he'd accompanied me to the Gretchen's back gate, where my truck was parked.

He hadn't mentioned the coke deal. Bobby and the rest of the gang were obviously too preoccupied with the events of the night before—and the botched ambush—to think of much more than circling the wagons. And considering that I didn't have a couple million or so in cash handy to hold up my end of the bargain, I certainly wasn't going to bring the matter up.

I returned to Jaybird's house and filled my handlers in. Just being seen in the Hells Angels compound under such circumstances was a major coup for my street cred with the gang members. Being asked to help out an influential member was an even greater sign of trust. Even if I had decided to pack my bags as soon as I got back to El Cajon, the gang's confidence made me proud of my work. Perhaps, I began to think, there might be a way for me to stick with the investigation.

My enthusiasm didn't last long.

Brooks asked me for the .380. I thought the agents would just want to take a ballistic match and register the serial number before I took it back to El Cajon, but Brooks told me it wasn't going to work that way.

"It might be evidence," he said. "You can't have it back."

I was dumbfounded. "What do you mean I can't have it back?"

"Well, he's a convicted felon."

"So?"

"We just can't release a gun back to him under these circumstances."

I told him that not giving Bobby the gun back was going to destroy any credibility I had built up with the gang and, in particular, with one of its most influential and dangerous members in southern California. But Brooks wouldn't listen.

"All you have to tell him is that there was a roadblock and you threw it out the window," he said.

It was clear that arguing my case was as futile as it had been when I pleaded with my handlers to give me some breathing room from Rocky and Highway Mike. Still, I was so beside myself that I phoned my rabbi in Ottawa.

"This is totally nuts," J.P. said, promising to phone up Bob McGuigan immediately to plead my case.

When I phoned J.P. back an hour later, he told me Bob had shut him down just as Brooks had done to me. "I can't help you," he said, and after railing against the tactics of his American counterparts, he gave me a simple piece of advice: *"Décrisse de là,"* he said. "Get the hell out of there."

I had heard stories about contracted agents being cut loose by their handlers and left to drift and, ultimately, hit the ground hard, like a kite without a string. It looked like it was about to happen to me.

I drove back to El Cajon that night, too beat to think, too overwhelmed by the events of recent days to process everything that had happened. Upon arriving back at the studio in the wee hours of the morning, I crashed into my first good, deep sleep in what felt like months. When I awoke, my resolve to leave had softened again. I'd spent a long time working the investigation; the professional in me wanted to see it succeed, or at the very least leave it in decent shape.

At the same time, I doubted that my employers were as determined as I was to do a good job. For reasons I couldn't fathom, someone somewhere in a position of influence seemed to want the operation to fail—and me to get screwed at the same time. But maybe I was still just being paranoid.

I seesawed back and forth on the question over the next couple of days, hanging out at Dumont's, not doing much of anything, until the inevitable happened: late on the Tuesday night I got a call from Bobby.

"Meet me in fifteen minutes," he said, naming an intersection that was at least fifteen minutes from my place. Even if he hadn't mentioned it, explicitly or in code, I knew he wanted his gun back. I would have to play dumb—but not without backup.

I immediately phoned around and the only handler I could reach was Billy Guinn, from the sheriff's department. He told me to go ahead, that he would have close cover at the parking lot in a matter of minutes.

When I arrived, late in order to give my backup time to get in place, there were three carloads of Hells Angels, prospects and hangarounds in the parking lot—none of them looking the least bit happy at being kept waiting. It was clear to me they were on their way somewhere to kick some ass—or possibly a whole lot worse—a likely scenario given the events of the previous few days and the tendency, in the biker world, to exact revenge promptly and violently for even the merest of slights.

Bobby was standing alongside one of the cars. As I rode up, he extended his hand, but not in greeting.

"You bring the piece?" he asked.

"Oh! No . . . you never said you wanted me to. Besides, I'll have to dig it up from the engine where I stashed it."

Bobby wasn't the type who would have hidden his anger even if he could have, and it was obvious he was about to explode when, fortunately for me, Mark Toycen shouted from the car, "Bobby, get in, goddammit!"

So all I got was a venomous glare and an order spat at me: "Bring it tomorrow to the bar! Ten o'clock!" Bobby said, jumping in the car and slamming the door.

Shortly after I got back to my place, Billy showed up for a debrief. It didn't take long for me to tell him what Bobby had told me. Then I asked him how much cover I had had for what had been a potentially ugly encounter—after all, it had been a dark and desolate parking lot and there had been three carloads of California's nastiest, one of whom was seriously pissed at me.

"There was me and Barbie," he said, referring to the agent whom I'd seen blushing in her panties at Jaybird's house.

"You and Barbie—what could you have done?" I asked, incredulous.

The plan, Billy explained, was that at the first sign of anything unpleasant happening to me, Barbie would have jumped out of the car and started screaming to create a diversion.

"If they were going to kill me, they would have just done her as well," I said.

"Well, I was there with my shotgun," Billy answered defensively.

I felt completely hung out to dry. Billy should have phoned and told me not to go to the meeting if he couldn't round up adequate support. Still, something kept me from packing my bags then and there.

The next morning, a memorial ride was planned for Christian Tate, a Hells Angel from the Dago chapter who had been gunned down on Route 40 heading out of Laughlin back to El Cajon less than an hour before the fun and games broke out in Harrah's. His killing was a mystery. There was speculation in the media that it had provoked the attack on the Mongols in the casino, but I doubted it. I didn't see how the news of his killing could have spread so quickly when he had died alone more than a hundred miles away in the Mojave Desert minutes earlier. I also wondered what Tate had been doing leaving the River Run just when the real party was getting started. My gut feeling was that he had been in one of the SUVs or on one of the bikes that had escaped the ambush the day before. I suspected that either he had been slightly hurt and was heading out of town for medical treatment or he was taking the news of the Mongols burn back to California. And needless to say, I was willing to bet that the attack on the Mongols was prompted by that same event.

It all meant that I was curious to see what the mood at the memorial ride was going to be—and what kind of scuttlebutt was being whispered. There wouldn't be any danger, I was certain—few gatherings anywhere attract such police scrutiny as biker funerals or rides. Along with dozens of uniformed officers, there were usually dozens of plainclothes cops not even bothering to make a serious effort at blending in with the gawking onlookers.

There was a hitch, however. The ten a.m. meeting Bobby had ordered me to attend coincided with the gathering of the Hells Angels, their friends and associates at the gang's clubhouse before the ride. Since Dumont's was just a few storefronts away from the clubhouse, I would almost certainly have to deal with Bobby if I wanted to join the gathering. My only hard and fast rule, I decided, would be a simple one: stay in the open.

I did stay in the open—for the minute or so during which I was in the company of the Hells Angels that morning. When Bobby ordered me to accompany him to the back of the bar, any illusions I had that I might finesse the situation were shattered. So I jumped in the

Nissan and burned rubber the hell out of there. The case was over for me before I'd even wheeled around the corner.

Back at the studio, Brooks, Hunter and a couple of other cops helped me pack my things. What I couldn't carry in the box of the pickup, my handlers said they would ship to me.

They seemed to understand my need to get out, and to agree that the investigation, or at least my part in it, was finally, completely done. There was no saving it, no going back. Nevertheless, they wanted me to hang around one last night, to toast our successes and commiserate together over our failures. But once I got back in my truck and started driving east, I wasn't about to stop. I just kept going, heading home.

# EPILOGUE

———

Home safe in Canada, I wanted nothing more than some downtime. Time to think about what next—retiring, maybe another career. And, sometime, telling my story as had been suggested by so many of my handlers: George Cousens and Barney, Bob McGuigan and Billy Guinn, the Rabbi, the Blainedidos (as my handlers back in Washington had called themselves).

It was not to be. After my return to New Brunswick, things quickly fell apart at home. Once again, I had been too gone for too long. There wasn't any warmth left between me and Natalie. We weren't fighting or angry—there was just nothing there except a cold silence. My inability to open up precluded any real relationship. My disdain for her family, to whom she had become very close again since moving back to Saint John, didn't help. Even if Natalie could forgive them, I couldn't get over the way they had sold her out when she had fled Bashir a decade earlier. I was also hugely irritated by their constant romanticizing of life in Lebanon and their habit of disparaging Canada at every opportunity.

I blamed it all on Natalie. She made no effort to understand what I had been through, I thought at the time. In fact, I was burned out physically and emotionally and not really fit for small-town society. After about a month in Saint John, instead of staying and working on my marriage, I got back in my Nissan pickup and headed west again. Ostensibly I was visiting my son, who had a summer job in Ottawa, but really I was doing what I always did, fleeing from the clouds of discord at home.

Shortly after my arrival, I began to renew old contacts in the Ottawa-Hull region. Some were family, whom I got in touch with because I felt I should; some were criminal, whom the Rabbi had suggested I look up in anticipation of possible future assignments. The two didn't present as much of a conflict as they might have. After all, since my relatives still had no idea what I did for a living, they figured I was a big-time crook who dropped in and out of their lives, usually loaded down with cash and tales of faraway places.

That didn't mean family and crooks necessarily intersected—until they did, in a collision that really messed up my life and that of my son.

A few years earlier, my sisters Louise and Pauline had left their subsidized apartments overlooking the ocean in Vancouver to return to what the tourism people now call the National Capital Region, Ottawa in particular. The reason Louise came back east was, I always presumed, to live closer to her grown children. It was a mistake as far as I was concerned: her daughter was a drug-addicted screw-up; her son, Danny, a hateful neo-Nazi skinhead who had long been considered the scourge of the family.

I knew Danny's father, Johnny, well. He had been part of the old gang all his life, and in his younger days had been an armed robber of some repute. But his luck ran out when he and four other guys relieved a bank courier of sixteen thousand dollars at gunpoint. They were all soon arrested and Johnny was sentenced to five years in the pen. He had been going with my sister Louise at the time and she decided to wait for him. But he wasn't so loyal once he was out and they didn't last long.

Johnny was never a racist; he was just an old-fashioned crook. So even if Danny spent much of his childhood living with his dad, I don't know where the racism came from. By the time he was in his late teens, Danny's whereabouts were frequently mysterious for long periods. I heard he had lived for a time in Texas and later Toronto, so maybe that's where he picked up his hatefulness. Either way, he really despised non-whites, and back in Ottawa in the mid-1990s, where he worked as a construction laborer, he joined a hate group called the Heritage Front and became an active member.

By the time I arrived in Ottawa from Saint John in the summer of 2002, Danny was in the Ottawa–Carleton Detention Center, serving the tail end of a short prison sentence for assault. During a visit to my sisters' place, I ran into a friend of Danny's who needed help getting to the prison to visit him. At Louise's request I drove the guy, and decided to go inside and see Danny at the same time. That led to what might be called, for lack of a better term, some uncle-nephew bonding, at least from his perspective. Having grown up with hints and suspicions about my criminality—all buttressed by the occasional glimpse of me in a new car and the knowledge that I regularly bailed out his broke mother—Danny was very candid with me about his own activities.

When he was released, not long after my visit, we saw more of each other. My interest was no longer familial—I'd been in touch with J.P. In the days following his release Danny told me that he and his skinhead friends had recently sold ten pounds of explosives to the Quebec Hells Angels but were hanging on to another ninety pounds for their own use. That was cause for concern—and then some—as was information I'd learned about the friend, Paul, whom I'd driven to visit Danny in jail. He was a computer technician for a software company that, not long before, had installed security software at the RCMP headquarters. Paul had kept a copy of the program and hoped to sell it to *les Hells.*

In brief, this all led to a month-long mess of an operation that didn't result in any arrests or criminal charges but completely destroyed any relationship I had with my sisters and burned any bridge that still remained between me and my hometown. I haven't lived in or spent any time in the Ottawa-Hull region since. It also made the city unsafe for my son. When I left town, he came with me and shortly afterward moved overseas to continue his university studies. These days he only comes back to Canada for visits.

I returned to Saint John, where Natalie and I made one last effort to work things out. To no avail. When I left again after a few weeks, I knew it was for good. This time I just kept driving west, past Ottawa, eager to change my environment and, in so doing, my headspace.

Making money was suddenly a priority again. I'd left the house, our savings and pretty much whatever else there was to Natalie; all I'd taken was the Nissan pickup, my clothes and a few other personal things. Eventually I washed up in Calgary, where J.P. Lévesque had lined me up a three-month job involving a trio of dirty cops. If I'd had my wits about me and hadn't been as good as broke, I never would have accepted the assignment. Jobs like that are lose-lose situations—everyone wants to see you fail. But I was not only hard up for money, I was also confused and despondent. My second marriage was over, my son had just moved across the big water and my last two infiltration gigs had ended disastrously.

Never two without three, they say. The Calgary job wasn't the fiasco San Diego or Ottawa had been, but it wasn't a great success either. I amassed what I deemed to be the necessary proof and handed it in and that was that. As far as I know, it was handled internally from then on. Or just put in a drawer somewhere. It didn't end up in the headlines or in court. Not knowing what happened was almost as discouraging as a case ending in catastrophe.

That was it for me. After Calgary I couldn't muster any more enthusiasm for infiltration work. I drifted around. I ended up back in my second home, Vancouver, for a few months. While there, I got word from George Cousens and the Rabbi that all my work in San Diego had finally resulted in something. Seems that the boys from Operation Five Star had used the evidence I compiled to obtain warrants for dozens of wiretaps. After listening in on their conversations for the better part of a year, the cops hit the Dago Hells Angels hard, raiding the clubhouse and homes, seizing weapons and drugs, and charging most of the gang with meth dealing and conspiracy to murder Mongols, as well as RICO organized-crime offenses.

The Boss (Guy Castiglione), Mark Toycen, Ramona Pete, Zach Carpenter, Hatchet Dave and several other members all got nailed and eventually pleaded guilty. So did some twenty associates, including JoAnn. Bobby Perez also would have been arrested, I imagine, had someone not murdered him first.

The cops also finally picked up people such as Taz, the Indian, his nephew Bobby, Smokey and his homeboys, and a few other people. They'd had the goods on these guys for more than a year and could easily have arrested them without compromising the investigation into the Dago Angels. But the cops had wanted big numbers and big headlines, so they'd let these guys operate with impunity for a year while compiling a case against the Angels.

The wait may have been worth it for them in the end. Operation Five Star received an award at an international conference of biker cops and investigators not long after the bust. In his acceptance speech, Pat Ryan took pains to insist that it had all been the work of cops with badges. Sure, they'd tried to insert a contracted agent early in the game, but that had ended in failure, he stressed.

The ill will from Ryan didn't surprise me. His hostility toward me seemed clear since the belongings of mine that he was responsible for having shipped up from San Diego to Saint John a year earlier arrived severely damaged. An antique Russian table Henry had given me had been sawed in half. A couch I'd also got from Henry had its upholstery slashed. An expensive watch had been smashed, all its pieces put back in its case. Even my bike had been vandalized. On top of that, a bunch of very heavy crap had been thrown in—old steel desks and the like—just to make the load heavier. I, after all, had agreed to pay half the shipping costs.

That gesture helped to convince me that getting out of the game, one I'd been playing on and off for a quarter century, was the right idea. Infiltration is hard enough when you know who your friends are; when you don't know if the cops will stand behind you or what their real agenda is, well, there are better ways to make a living.

Adjusting to retirement isn't easy for many people. Even if there is a gold watch, a big send-off dinner, a Caribbean cruise—gifts and gestures that I, of course, never received—accepting that your services are no longer required is rarely easy.

For me, learning to say no to the infiltration assignments that came my way was hard enough, as was the fact that slowly the calls stopped coming as the Rabbi and other police I had worked with retired too. But there was a different challenge, particular to my job, that in many ways dwarfed all others: figuring out who I really am.

For a time, I imagined the real me would turn out to be distinct from all the characters I've pretended to be—something new, something different, hidden deep inside. I'd just have to dig and scrape and sweep away all the junk that had accumulated over the last twenty-five years or so.

But that's not how it works, I've learned. My mind is really a graveyard for all the people I've been. I'm not one or another of them; I'm a little of each. All the years of being someone else means, in a sense, that I can never be me. So I've quit wondering who I "really" am; it doesn't seem that important anymore. What "me" was there ever?

The few people who know of my career think of it as exciting. It certainly was at times. Mostly, however, it was just lonely. Always wearing a mask meant I could never make real friends, except perhaps with my handlers. Sure, there were bad guys whom I connected with; had the circumstances been different, there were a few I would have done most anything for. In the end, however, I put most of them in jail and then had to close the book on them as if they'd been killed. The end of a case is, in fact, the end of a life. And a man who lives many lives must endure many deaths.

My own death could arrive at any moment—that's something I've always had to accept, whether as a young hood in Hull, a soldier in Vietnam or a professional infiltrator. Just because I've retired doesn't mean that the men I was hired to befriend and then betray will have forgiven me. The risk hasn't disappeared with the paycheck. There are still contracts on my life and there is always the risk of that coincidence, that chance encounter, that unexpected meeting, which could throw my life into turmoil or end it altogether. Given that I've worked all over Canada and much of the United States, the odds aren't actually as slim as I wish they were. Maybe someday they will get me. But not today.

And today, like all the other days, I just have to take satisfaction from what I can. The good relations I have with my kids—and exes— despite my prolonged absences. (Liz is now a respected senior member of the clergy, my daughter is a teacher, and my son and his wife are planning a family. Natalie has remarried and has custody of her first daughter as well as the daughter we had together.) The bad guys I helped put in prison, many of whom the police had been after for a long time and who deserved nothing more than to be locked up in a small room for a very long time. The fact that for all the questionable and downright bad things I did—in Nam especially—I compensated by doing a little good as well.

# INDEX